Mary
Slessor of Calabar
Pioneer Missionary

by

W. P. Livingstone

Double 9
BOOKS

Mary Slessor of Calabar
Pioneer Missionary
by W. P. Livingstone

ISBN: 978-93-63052-86-4

Published by

DOUBLE 9 BOOKS

2/13-B, Ansari Road
Daryaganj, New Delhi – 110002
info@double9books.com
www.double9books.com
Tel. 011-40042856

ABOUT THE AUTHOR

W. P. Livingstone, an esteemed author and historian, has crafted a compelling masterpiece titled "Mary Slessor of Calabar: Pioneer Missionary." In this captivating biography, Livingstone delves into the remarkable life of Mary Slessor, a pioneering missionary whose unwavering dedication and courage left an indelible mark on history. Set against the backdrop of colonial Africa, Livingstone chronicles Slessor's journey from humble beginnings in Scotland to her transformative work in the heart of Calabar, Nigeria. Through meticulous research and vivid storytelling, Livingstone paints a vivid portrait of Slessor's tireless efforts to promote justice, end barbaric practices, and spread the message of Christianity. From her daring rescues of vulnerable children to her fearless confrontations with tribal chiefs, Slessor's extraordinary deeds are brought to life with poignancy and depth. With sensitivity and insight, Livingstone explores the complexities of Slessor's mission, shedding light on the cultural clashes and personal sacrifices she endured in her quest to bring hope and healing to the people of Calabar. "Mary Slessor of Calabar: Pioneer Missionary" stands as a testament to the power of faith, compassion, and perseverance in the face of adversity, inspiring readers to embrace their own callings with courage and conviction.

CONTENTS

FIRST PHASE

1848-1876. Age 1-28.

A SCOTTISH FACTORY GIRL

"It was the dream of my girlhood to be a missionary to Calabar."

CHAPTER I
SAVED BY FEAR

When the founding of the Calabar Mission on the West Coast of Africa was creating a stir throughout Scotland, there came into a lowly home in Aberdeen a life that was to be known far and wide in connection with the enterprise. On December 2, 1848, Mary Mitchell Slessor was born in Gilcomston, a suburb of the city.

Her father, Robert Slessor, belonged to Buchan, and was a shoemaker. Her mother, who came from Old Meldrum, was an only child, and had been brought up in a home of refinement and piety. She is described by those who knew her as a sweet-faced woman, patient, gentle, and retiring, with a deeply religious disposition, but without any special feature of character, such as one would have expected to find in the mother of so uncommon a daughter. It was from her, however, that Mary got her soft voice and loving heart.

Mary was the second of seven children. Of her infancy and girlhood little is known. Her own earliest recollections were associated with the name of Calabar. Mrs. Slessor was a member of Belmont Street United Presbyterian Church, and was deeply interested in the adventure going forward in that foreign field. "I had," said Mary, "my missionary enthusiasm for Calabar in particular from her—she knew from its inception all that was to be known of its history." Both she and her elder brother Robert heard much talk of it in the home, and the latter used to announce that he was going to be a missionary when he was a man. So great a career was, of course, out of the reach of girls, but he consoled Mary by promising to take her with him into the pulpit. Often Mary played at keeping school; and it is interesting to note that the imaginary scholars she taught and admonished were always black. Robert did not survive these years, and Mary became the eldest.

Dark days came. Mr. Slessor unhappily drifted into habits of intemperance and lost his situation, and when he suggested removing to Dundee, then coming to the front as an industrial town and promising opportunities for the employment of young people, his wife consented, although it was hard for her to part from old friends and associations. But she hoped that in a strange city, where the past was unknown, her husband might begin life afresh and succeed. The family went south in 1859, and entered on a period of struggle and hardship. The money realised by the sale of the furniture melted away, and the new house was bare and comfortless, Mr. Slessor continued his occupation as a shoemaker, and then became a labourer in one of the mills.

The youngest child, Janie, was born in Dundee. All the family were delicate, and it was not long before Mary was left with only two sisters and a brother—Susan, John, and Janie. Mrs. Slessor's fragility prevented her battling successfully with trial and misfortune, but no children could have been trained with more scrupulous care. "I owe a great debt of gratitude to my sainted mother," said Mary, long afterwards. Especially was she solicitous for their religious well- being. On coming to Dundee she had connected herself with Wishart Church in the east end of the Cowgate, a modest building, above a series of shops near the Port Gate from the parapets of which George Wishart preached during the plague of 1544. Here the children were sent to the regular services—with a drop of perfume on their handkerchiefs and gloves and a peppermint in their pockets for sermon-time—and also attended the Sunday School.

Mary's own recollection of herself at this period was that she was "a wild lassie." She would often go back in thought to these days, and incidents would flash into memory that half amused and half shamed her. Some of her escapades she would describe with whimsical zest, and trivial as they were they served to show that, even then, her native wit and resource were always ready to hand. But very early the Change came. An old widow, living in a room in the back lands, used to watch the children running about the doors, and in her anxiety for their welfare sought to gather some of the girls together and talk to them, young as they were, about the matters that concerned their souls. One afternoon in winter they had come out of the cold and darkness into the glow of her fire, and were sitting listening to her description of the dangers that beset all who neglected salvation.

"Do ye see that fire?" she exclaimed suddenly. "If ye were to put your hand into the lowes it would be gey sair. It would burn ye. But if ye dinna repent and believe on the Lord Jesus Christ your soul will burn in the lowin' bleezin' fire for ever and ever!"

The words went like arrows to Mary's heart; she could not get the vision of eternal torment out of her mind: it banished sleep, and she came to the conclusion that it would be best for her to make her peace with God. She "repented and believed." It was hell-fire that drove her into the Kingdom, she would sometimes say. But once there she found it to be a Kingdom of love and tenderness and mercy, and never throughout her career did she seek to bring any one into it, as she had come, by the process of shock and fear.

CHAPTER II
IN THE WEAVING-SHED

The time came when Mrs. Slessor herself was compelled to enter one of the factories in order to maintain the home, and many of the cares and worries of a household fell upon Mary. But at eleven she, too, was sent out to begin to earn a livelihood. In the textile works of Messrs. Baxter Brothers & Company she became what was known as a half-timer, one who wrought half the day and went to the school in connection with the works the other half. When she was put on full time she attended the school held at night. Shortly afterward she entered Rashiewell factory to learn weaving under the supervision of her mother. After trying the conditions in two other works she returned, about the age of fourteen, to Baxter's, where she soon became an expert and well-paid worker. Her designation was a "weaver" or "factory girl," not a "mill- girl," this term locally being restricted to spinners in the mills. When she handed her first earnings to her mother the latter wept over them, and put them away as too sacred to use. But her wage was indispensable for the support of the home, and eventually she became its chief mainstay.

Life in the great factory in which she was but a unit amongst thousands was hard and monotonous. The hours of the workers were from six A.M. to six P.M., with one hour for breakfast and one for dinner. Mary was stationed in a room or shed, which has very much the same appearance to-day. Now as then the belts are whirring, the looms are moving, the girls are handling the shuttles, and the air is filled with a din so continuous and intense that speech is well-nigh impossible. Mary had to be up every morning at five o'clock, as she helped in the work of the home before going out, while similar duties claimed her at night. Though naturally bright and refined in disposition she was at this time almost wholly uneducated. From the factory schools she had brought only a meagre knowledge of reading and arithmetic, and she had read little save the books obtained from the library of the Sunday School. But her mind was opening, she was becoming conscious of the outer world and all its interests and wonders, and she was eager to know and understand. In order to study she began to steal time from sleep. She carried a book with her to the mill, and, like David

Livingstone at Blantyre, laid it on the loom and glanced at it in her free moments. So anxious was she to learn that she read on her way to and from the factory. It was not a royal road, that thoroughfare of grim streets, but it led her into many a shining region.

Her only source of outside interest was the Church. From the Sunday School she passed into the Bible Class, where her attendance was never perfunctory, for she enjoyed the teaching and extracted all she could out of it. She would carry home the statements that arrested and puzzled her, and refer them to her mother, who, however, did not always find it easy to satisfy her. "Is baptism necessary for salvation, mother?" was one of her questions. "Well," her mother replied, "it says that he that repents and is baptized shall be saved; but it does not say that he that repents and is not baptized shall be damned." Some of her mother's sayings at this time she never forgot. "When one duty jostles another, one is not a duty," she was once told. And again, "Thank God for what you receive: thank God for what you do not receive: thank God for the sins you are delivered from; and thank God for the sins that you know nothing at all about, and are never tempted to commit."

Mary was a favourite with her classmates. There was something about her even then which drew others to her. One, the daughter of an elder, tells how, though much younger, she was attracted to her by her goodness and her kind ways, and how she would often go early to meet her in order to enjoy her company to the class.

CHAPTER III
MISERY

The explanation of much in Mary Slessor's character lies in these early years, and she cannot be fully understood unless the unhappy circumstances in her home are taken into account. She was usually reticent regarding her father, but once she wrote and published under her own name what is known to be the story of this painful period of her girlhood. There is no need to reproduce it, but some reference to the facts is necessary if only to show how bravely she battled against hardship and difficulties even then.

The weakness of Mr. Slessor was not cured by the change in his surroundings. All the endearments of his wife and daughter were powerless to save the man whose heart was tender enough when he was sober, but whose moral sensibilities continued to be sapped by his indulgence in drink. Every penny he could lay hands upon was spent in this way, and the mother was often reduced to sore straits to feed and clothe the children. Not infrequently Mary had to perform a duty repugnant to her sensitive nature. She would leave the factory after her long toil, and run home, pick up a parcel which her mother had prepared, and fly like a hunted thing along the shadiest and quietest streets, making many a turning in order to avoid her friends, to the nearest pawnbroker's. Then with sufficient money for the week's requirements she would hurry back with a thankful heart, and answer the mother's anxious, questioning eyes with a glad light in her own. A kiss would be her reward, and she would be sent out to pay the more pressing bills.

There was one night of terror in every week. On Saturday, after the other children were in bed, the mother and daughter sat sewing or knitting in silence through long hours, waiting in sickening apprehension for the sound of uncertain footsteps on the stairs. Now and again they prayed to quieten their hearts. Yet they longed for his coming. When he appeared he would throw into the fire the supper they had stinted themselves to provide for him. Sometimes Mary was forced out into the streets where she wandered in the dark, alone, sobbing out her misery.

All the efforts of wife and daughter were directed towards hiding the skeleton in the house. The fear of exposure before the neighbours, the dread lest Mary's church friends should come to know the secret, made the two sad souls pinch and struggle and suffer with endless patience. None of the other children was aware of the long vigils that were spent. The fact that the family was never disgraced in public was attributed to prayer. The mother prayed, the daughter prayed, ceaselessly, with utter simplicity of belief, and they were never once left stranded or put to shame. Their faith not only saved them from despair, it made them happy in the intervals of their distress. Few brighter or more hopeful families gathered in church from Sunday to Sunday.

Nevertheless these days left their mark upon Mary for life. She was at the plastic age, she was gentle and sensitive and loving, and what she passed through hurt and saddened her spirit. To the end it was the only memory that had power to send a shaft of bitterness across the sweetness of her nature. It added to her shyness and to her reluctance to appear in public and speak, which was afterwards so much commented upon, for always at the back of her mind was the consciousness of that dark and wretched time. The reaction on her character, however, was not all evil; suffering in the innocent has its compensations. It deepened her sympathy and pity for others. It made her the fierce champion of little children, and the refuge of the weak and oppressed. It prepared her also for the task of combating the trade in spirits on the West Coast, and for dealing with the drunken tribes amongst whom she came to dwell. Her experience then was, indeed, the beginning of her training for the work she had to accomplish in the future....

The father died, and the strain was removed, and Mary became the chief support of the home. Those who knew her then state that her life was one long act of self-denial; all her own inclinations and interests were surrendered for the sake of the family, and she was content with bare necessaries so long as they were provided for.

CHAPTER IV
TAMING THE ROUGHS

In her church work she continued to find the little distraction from toil which gave life its savour. She began to attend the Sabbath Morning Fellowship and week-night prayer meetings. She also taught a class of "lovable lassies" in the Sabbath School—"I had the impudence of ignorance then in special degree surely" was her mature comment on this—and became a distributor of the *Monthly Visitor*. Despite the weary hours in the factory, and a long walk to and from the church, she was never absent from any of the services or meetings. "We would as soon have thought of going to the moon as of being absent from a service," she wrote shortly before she died. "And we throve very well on it too. How often, when lying awake at night, my time for thinking, do I go back to those wonderful days!"

She owed much to her association with the Church, but more to her Bible. Once a girl asked her for something to read, and she handed her the Book saying, "Take that; it has made me a changed lassie." The study of it was less a duty than a joy; it was like reading a message addressed specially to herself, containing news of surpassing personal interest and import. God was very real to her. To think that behind all the strain and struggle and show of the world there was a Personality, not a thought or a dream, not something she could not tell what, in spaces she knew not where, but One who was actual and close to her, overflowing with love and compassion, and ready to listen to her, and to heal and guide and strengthen her—it was marvellous. She wished to know all He had to tell her, in order that she might rule her conduct according to His will. Most of all it was the story of Christ that she pored over and thought about. His Divine majesty, the beauty and grace of His life, the pathos of His death on the Cross, affected her inexpressibly. But it was His love, so strong, so tender, so pitiful, that won her heart and devotion and filled her with a happiness and peace that suffused her inner life like sunshine. In return she loved Him with a love so intense that it was often a pain. She felt that she could not do enough for one who had done so much for her. As the years passed she surrendered herself more and more to His influence, and was ready for any duty she was called upon to do for Him, no matter how humble or exacting it might be. It was this passion of love and gratitude, this abandonment of self, this longing for service, that carried her into her life-work.

Wishart Church stood in the midst of slums. Pends, or arched passages, led from the Cowgate into tall tenements with outside spiral stairs which opened upon a maze of landings and homes. Out of these sunless rookeries tides of young life poured by night and day, and spread over the neighbouring streets in undisciplined freedom. Mary's heart often ached for these boys and girls, whom she loved in spite of all their roughness; and when a mission was determined on, and a room was taken at 6 Queen Street—a small side thoroughfare nearly opposite Quarry Pend, one of the worst of the alleys—she volunteered as a teacher. And so began a second period of stem training which was to serve her well in the years to come. The wilder spirits made sport of the meetings and endeavoured to wreck them. "That little room," she wrote, "was full of romantic experiences." There was danger outside when the staff separated, and she recalled how several of the older men surrounded the "smaller individuals" when they faced the storm. One of these was Mr. J. H. Smith, who became her warm friend and counsellor.

As the mission developed, a shop under the church at the side of Wishart Pend was taken and the meetings transferred to it, she having charge of classes for boys and girls both on Sundays and week-nights. Open-air work was at that time dangerous, but she and a few others attempted it: they were opposed by roughs and pelted with mud. There was one gang that was resolved to break up the mission with which she had come to be identified. One night they closed in about her on the street. The leader carried a leaden weight at the end of a piece of cord, and swung it threateningly round her head. She stood her ground. Nearer and nearer the missile came. It shaved her brow. She never winced. The weight crashed to the ground. "She's game, boys," he exclaimed. To show their appreciation of her spirit they went in a body to the meeting. There her bright eyes, her sympathy, and her firmness shaped them into order and attention....

On the wall of one of her bush houses in West Africa there used to hang a photograph of a man and his wife and family. The man was the lad who had swung the lead. On attaining a good position he had sent her the photograph in grateful remembrance of what had been the turning-point in his life....

Another lad, a bully, used to stand outside the hall with a whip in hand driving the young fellows into "Mary Slessor's meeting," but refusing to go in himself. One day the girl weaver faced him. "If we changed places what would happen?" she asked, and he replied, "I would get this whip across my back." She turned her back. "I'll bear it for you if you'll go in," she said. "Would you really bear that for me?" "Yes, and far more—go on, I mean it." He threw down the whip and followed her in, and gave himself the same day to Christ. Even then she was unconventional in her methods and was criticised for it. She had a passion for the countryside, and often on Saturday afternoons she would take her class of lads away out to the green fields, regardless of social canons.

By and by a new field of work was opened up when a number of progressive minds in the city formed Victoria Street United Presbyterian congregation, not far from her familiar haunts. In connection with the movement a mission service for the young was started on Sunday mornings under the presidency of Mr. James Logic, of Tay Square Church, and to him Mary offered her services as a monitor. Mr. Logie soon noticed the capacity of the young assistant and won her confidence and regard. Like most people she was unconscious at the moment of the unseen forces moulding her life, but she came in after days to realise the wise ordering of this friendship. Mr. Logie became interested in her work and ideals, and sought to promote her interests in every way. She came to trust Mm implicitly—"He is the best earthly friend I have," she wrote-and he guided her thenceforward in all her money affairs.

She was as successful with the lads at this service as she had been elsewhere. Before the meeting she would flit through the dark passages in the tenements and knock, and rouse them up from sleep, and plead with them to turn out to it. Her influence over them was extraordinary, They adored her and gave her shy allegiance, and the result was seen in changed habits and transformed lives. It was the same in the houses she visited. She went there not as one who was superior to the inmates, but as one of themselves. In the most natural way she would sit down by the fire and nurse a child, or take a cup of tea at the table. Her sympathy, her delicate tact, her cheery counsel won many a woman's heart and braced her for higher endeavour. It was the same in the factory; her influence told on the workers about her; some she strengthened, others she won over to Christ, and these created an atmosphere which was felt throughout the building.

And yet what was she? Only a working girl, plain in appearance and in dress, diffident and self-effacing. "But," says one whom she used to take down as a boy to the mission and place beside her as she taught, "she possessed something we could not grasp, something indefinable." It was the glow of the spirit of Christ which lit up her inner life and shone in her face, and which, unknown even to herself, was then and afterwards the source of her distinction and her power.

CHAPTER V
SELF-CULTURE

For fourteen years, and these the freshest and fairest years of her life, she toiled in the factory for ten hours each full day, while she also gave faithful service in the mission. And yet she continued to find time for the sedulous culture of her mind. She was always borrowing books and extracting what was best in them. Not all were profitable. One was *The Rise and Progress of Religion in the Soul* by Philip Doddridge, a volume much pondered then in Scottish homes. A friend who noticed that she was somewhat cast down said to her, "Why, Mary, what's the matter? You look very glum." "I canna do it," she replied. "Canna do what?" "I canna meditate, and Doddridge says it is necessary for the soul. If I try to meditate my mind just goes a' roads." "Well, never mind meditation," her friend said. "Go and work, for that's what God means us to do," and she followed his advice. Of her introduction to the fields of higher literature we have one reminiscence. Her spirit was so eager, she read so much and so quickly, that a friend sought to test her by lending her *Sartor Resartus*. She carried it home, and when next he met her he asked quizzically how she had got on with Carlyle. "It is grand!" she replied. "I sat up reading it, and was so interested that I did not know what the time was, until I heard the factory bells calling me to work in the morning!"

There was no restraining her after that. She broadened and deepened in thought and outlook, and gradually acquired the art of expressing herself, both in speech and writing, in language that was deft, lucid, and vigorous, Her style was formed insensibly from her constant reading of the Bible, and had then a grave dignity and balance unlike the more picturesque, if looser, touch of later years. The papers that were read from her at the Fellowship Association were marked by a felicity of phrase as well as an insight and spiritual fervour unusual in a girl. Her alertness of intellect often astonished those who heard her engaged in argument with the agnostics and freethinkers whom she encountered in the course of her visiting. She spoke simply, but with a directness and sincerity that arrested attention. Often asked to address meetings in other parts of Dundee, she shrank from the ordeal. On one occasion a friend went with her, but she could not be persuaded to go on the platform. She sat in the middle of the hall and had a quiet talk on the words, "The common people heard Him gladly." "And," writes her friend, "the common people heard her gladly, and crowded round her and pleaded that she should come again."

CHAPTER VI
A TRAGIC LAND

There was never a time when Mary was not interested in foreign missions. The story of Calabar had impressed her imagination when a child, and all through the years her eyes had been fixed on the great struggle going on between the forces of light and darkness in the sphere of heathenism. The United Presbyterian Church in which she was brought up placed the work abroad in the forefront of its activity; it had missions in India, China, Jamaica, Calabar, and Kaffraria; and reports of the operations were given month by month in its *Missionary Record*, and read in practically all the homes of its members. It was pioneer work, and the missionaries were perpetually in the midst of adventure and peril. Their letters and narratives were eagerly looked for; they gave to people who had never travelled visions of strange lands; they brought to them the scent and colour of the Orient and the tropics; and they introduced into the quietude of orderly homes the din of the bazaar and harem and kraal. These men and women in the far outposts became heroic figures to the Church, and whenever they returned on furlough the people thronged to their meetings to see for themselves the actors in such amazing happenings, and to hear from their own lips the story of their difficulties and triumphs.

Mrs. Slessor never missed hearing those who came to Dundee, and once she was so much moved by an address from the Rev. William Anderson as to the needs of Old Calabar that she longed to dedicate her son John to the work. He was a gentle lad, much loved by Mary. Apprenticed to a blacksmith, his health began to fail, and a change of climate became imperative. He emigrated to New Zealand, but died a week after landing. His mother felt the blow to her hopes even more than his death. To Mary the event was a bitter grief, and it turned her thoughts more directly to the foreign field. Could she fill her brother's place? Would it be possible for her ever to become a missionary? The idea floated for a time through her mind, unformed and unconfessed, until it gradually resolved itself into a definite purpose. Sometimes she thought of Kaffraria, with its red-blanketed people, but it was always Calabar to which she came back: it had from the first captivated her imagination, as it for good reason captivated the imagination of the Church.

The founding of the Mission had been a romance. It was not from Scotland that the impulse came but from Jamaica in the West Indies. The slave population of that colony had been brought from the West Coast, and chiefly from the Calabar region, and although ground remorselessly in the mill of plantation life they had never forgotten their old home. When emancipation came and they settled down in freedom under the direction and care of the missionaries their thoughts went over the ocean to their fatherland, and they longed to see it also enjoy the blessings which the Gospel had brought to them. The agents of the Scottish Missionary Society and of the United Secession Church, who, together, formed the Jamaica Presbytery, talked over the matter, and resolved to take action; and eight of their number dedicated themselves for the service if called upon. A society was formed, and a fund was established to which the people contributed liberally. But the officials at home were cold; they deprecated so uncertain a venture in a pestilential climate. The Presbytery, undaunted, persevered with its preparations, and chose the Rev. Hope M. Waddell to be the first agent of the Society.

It is a far cry from Jamaica to Calabar, but a link of communication was provided in a remarkable way. Many years previously a slaver had been wrecked in the neighbourhood of Calabar. The surgeon on board was a young medical man named Ferguson, and he and the crew were treated with kindness by the natives. After a time they were able by another slaver to sail for the West Indies, whence Dr. Ferguson returned home. He became surgeon on a trader between Liverpool and Jamaica, making several voyages, and becoming well known in the colony. Settling down in Liverpool he experienced a spiritual change and became a Christian. He was interested to hear of the movement in Jamaica, and remembering with gratitude the friendliness shown him by the Calabar natives he undertook to find out whether they would accept a mission. This he did through captains of the trading vessels to whom he was hospitable. In 1848 a memorial from the local king and seven chiefs was sent to him, offering ground and a welcome to any missionaries who might care to come, This settled the matter. Mr. Waddell sailed from Jamaica for Scotland to promote and organise the undertaking.

Happily the Secession Church adopted the Calabar scheme, and after securing funds and a ship—one of the first subscriptions, it is interesting to note, was £1000 from Dr. Ferguson—Mr. Waddell, with several assistants sailed in 1846, and after many difficulties, which he conquered with indomitable spirit and patience, founded the Mission. In the following year it was taken over by the United Presbyterian Church, which had been formed by the union of the United Secession and Relief Churches.

In no part of the foreign field were conditions more formidable. Calabar exhibited the worst side of nature and of man. While much of it was beautiful, it was one of the most unhealthy spots in the world— sickness, disease, and swift death attacking the Europeans who ventured there. The natives were considered to be the most degraded of any in Africa. They were, in reality, the slum-dwellers of negro-land. From time immemorial their race had occupied the equatorial region of the continent, a people without a history, with only a past of confused movement, oppression, and terror. They seem to have been visited by adventurous navigators of galleys before the Christian era, but the world in general knew nothing of them. On the land side they were shut in without hope of expansion. When they endeavoured to move up to the drier Sahara and Soudanese regions they were met and pressed back by the outposts of the higher civilisations of Egypt and Arabia, who preyed upon them, crushed them, enslaved them in vast numbers. And just as the coloured folk of American cities are kept in the low-lying and least desirable localities, and as the humbler classes in European towns find a home in east-end tenements, so all that was weakest and poorest in the negro race gravitated to the jungle areas and the poisonous swamps of the coast, where, hemmed in by the pathless sea, they existed in unbroken isolation for ages. It was not until the fifteenth century that the explorations of the Portuguese opened up the coast. Then, to the horrors of the internal slave-trade was added the horror of the traffic for the markets of the West Indies and America. Calabar provided the slavers with their richest freight, the lands behind were decimated and desolated, and scenes of tragedy and suffering unspeakable were enacted on land and sea. Yet for 400 years Europeans never penetrated more than a few miles inland. Away in the far interior of the continent great kingdoms were known to exist, but all the vast coastal region was a mystery of rivers, swamps, and forests inhabited by savage negroes and wild beasts.

It is not surprising that when the missionaries arrived in Calabar they found the natives to have been demoralised and degraded by the long period of lawlessness and rapine through which they had passed. They characterised them in a way that was appalling: many seemed indeed to have difficulty in selecting words expressive enough for their purpose. "Bloody," "savage," "crafty," "cruel," "treacherous," "sensual," "devilish," "thievish," "cannibals," "fetish-worshippers," "murderers," were a few of the epithets applied to them by men accustomed to observe closely and to weigh their words.

Not an attractive people to work amongst. Neither must the dwellers of the earth have appeared to Christ when He looked down from heaven ere He took His place in their midst. And Mary Slessor shrank from nothing which she thought her Master would have done: she rather welcomed the hardest tasks, and considered it an honour and privilege to be given them to do. She was not blind to the conditions at home. Often when at the Mission she realised how great was the need of the slums, with their problems of poverty and irreligion and misery. But the people there were within sight of church spires and within hearing of church bells, and there were many workers as capable as she: whilst down in the slums of Africa there were millions who knew no more of the redemptive power of Christ than did the beasts of the field. She was too intelligent a student of the New Testament not to know that Christ meant His disciples to spread His Gospel throughout the world, and too honest not to realise that the command was laid upon every one who loved Him in spirit and in truth. It was therefore with a quiet and assured mind that she went forward to the realisation of the dream. She told no one: she shrank even from mentioning the matter to her mother, but patiently prepared for the coming change. In the factory she took charge of two 60-inch looms, hard work for a young woman, but she needed the money, and she never thought of toil if her object could be gained.

Early in 1874 the news of the death of Dr. Livingstone stirred the land: it was followed by a wave of missionary enthusiasm; and the call for workers for the dark continent thrilled many a heart. It thrilled Mary Slessor into action. She reviewed the situation. Her sisters were now in good situations, and she saw her way to continue her share in the support of the home. What this loyal determination implied she did not guess then, but it was to have a large share in shaping her life. Broaching the subject to her mother she obtained a glad consent. One or two of her church friends were lukewarm; others, like Mr. Logic and Mr. Smith, encouraged her. The former, who was deeply interested in foreign missions and soon afterwards became a member of the Foreign Mission Committee, promised to look after her affairs during her sojourn abroad.

In May 1875 she offered her services to the Foreign Mission Board. Her heart was set on Calabar, but so eager was she to be accepted that she said she would be willing to go to any other field. Women agents had long been engaged in Calabar. The first, Miss Miller, had gone out with Mr. Waddell in 1849-she became the "Mammy" Sutherland who did such noble service- and they were playing an ever more important part, and were stated to be both "economical and effective." Requests had just been made for additions to the staff. The application was, therefore, opportune. Her personality, and the accounts given of her character and work, made such an impression on the officials that they reported favourably to the Board, and she was accepted as a teacher for Calabar and told to continue her studies in Dundee. In December it was decided to bring her to Edinburgh, at the expense of the Board, for three months, for special preparation....

The night before she left Dundee, in March 1876, she stood, a tearful figure, at the mouth of the "close" where she lived. "Good-bye," she said to a friend, and then passionately, "Pray for me!"

CHAPTER VII
THE THREE MARYS

A stranger in Edinburgh, Mary Slessor turned instinctively to Darling's Temperance Hotel, which was then, and is still, looked upon as a home by travellers from all parts of the globe. The Darlings, who were associated with all good work, were then taking part in the revival movement of Messrs. Moody and Sankey, and the two daughters, Bella and Jane, were solo-singers at the meetings. The humble Dundee girl had heard of their powers, and she entered the hotel as if it were a shrine. Feeling very lonely and very shy, she attended the little gathering for worship which is held every evening, and was comforted and strengthened.

She found a lodging in the home of Mr. Robert Martin, a city missionary, connected with Bristo Street congregation, and formed a friendship for Ms daughter Mary. By her she was taken to visit a companion, Mary Doig, who lived in the south side. The three became intimates, and shortly afterward Miss Slessor went to live with the Doigs, and remained with them during her stay in the city. It was a happy event for her. Warm-hearted and sympathetic, they treated her as one of the family. A daughter who was married, Mrs. M'Crindle, also met her, and a lifelong affection sprang up between the two. In later days it was to Mrs. M'Crindle's house the tired missionary first came on her furloughs.

Though she attended the Normal School in the Canongate, she was not enrolled as a regular student, and her name does not appear on the books; but a memory of her presence lingers like a sweet fragrance, and she appears to have been a power for good. One who was a student with her says: "She had a most gracious and winning personality, and impressed the students by her courage in going to what was called 'the white man's grave.' Her reply to questioners was that Calabar was the post of danger, and was therefore the post of honour. Few would volunteer for service there, hence she wished to go, for it was there the Master needed her. The beauty of her character showed itself in her face, and I have rarely seen one which showed so plainly that the love of God dwelt within. It was always associated in my mind with that of Miss Angelica Fraser; a heavenly radiance seemed to emanate from both."

Her leisure hours were given up to miscellaneous mission work in the city. Mary Doig and Mary Martin were both connected with Bristo Street congregation, and worked in the mission at Cowan's Close, Crosscauseway, and they naturally took Mary Slessor with them. Another intimate friendship was formed with Miss Paxton, a worker in connection with South Gray's Close Mission in the High Street. Miss Paxton was standing at the entrance to the close one Sunday, after a meeting, when Miss Slessor passed up with a Mr. Bishop, who afterwards became the printer at Calabar. Mr. Bishop introduced her. "You want some one to help you?" he said; "you cannot do better than take Miss Slessor." The two were kindred spirits, and Mary was soon at home among Miss Paxton's classes. Her first address to the women stands out clearly in the memory of her friend, and is interesting as indicating her standpoint then and throughout her life. It was on the question, "What shall I do with Jesus?" She told them that Christ was standing before them as surely as He stood before Pilate; and very earnestly she went on, "Dear women, you must do something with Him: you must reject Him or you must accept Him. What are you going to do?" She gave them no vision of hell- fire: she spoke to their reason and judgment, putting the great issue before them as a simple proposition, clear as light, inexorable as logic, and left them to decide for themselves.

Her two companions soon came under her influence. Their culture, piety, and practical gifts seemed to mark them out for missionaries, and as a result of her persuasion they offered themselves to the Foreign Mission Committee of the Church, and were accepted for China. In July the Committee satisfied itself with regard to Miss Slessor's proficiency, and decided to send her out at once to Calabar. Her salary was fixed at £60. Before sailing for their different stations the three Marys, as they came to be known, attended many meetings together, and were a source of interest to the Church.

Miss Slessor was now twenty-eight years of age, a type of nature peculiarly characteristic of Scotland, the result of its godly motherhood, the severe discipline of its social conditions, its stern toil, its warm church life, its missionary enthusiasm. Mature in mind and body, she retained the freshness of girlhood, was vivacious and sympathetic, and, while aglow with spirituality, was very human and likeable, with a heart as tender and wistful as a child's. What specially distinguished her, says one who knew her well, were her humility and the width and depth of her love. With diffidence, but in high hope, she went forward to weave the pattern of her service in the Mission Field....

She sailed on August 5, 1876. Two Dundee companions went with her to Liverpool. At the docks they saw going on board the steamer Ethiopia, by which she was to travel, a large number of casks of spirits for the West Coast. "Scores of casks!" she exclaimed ruefully, "and only one missionary!"

SECOND PHASE

1876-1888. Age 28-40.

WORK AND ADVENTURE AT THE BASE

"I am passing through the lights and shadows of life."

CHAPTER I
THE BREATH OF THE TROPICS

There is a glamour like the glamour of the dawn about one's first voyage to the tropics; and as the *Ethiopia* passed out of the grey atmosphere of England into the spring belt of the world, and then into a region where the days were a glory of sunshine and colour and the nights balmy and serene, Miss Slessor, so long confined within the bare walls of a factory, found the experience a pure delight in spite of a sense of loneliness that sometimes stole over her. Her chief grievance was that Sunday was kept like other days. Trained in the habits of a religious Scottish home it seemed to her extraordinary that no service should be held. "My very heart and flesh cried out for the courts of God's house," she wrote. Some of the crew comforted her by saying that there was always a Sabbath in Calabar.

It was not until the headland of Cape Verde was sighted and passed, and she saw in succession stretches of green banks, white sands upon which the surf beat, and long grey levels of mangrove, that she began to realise the presence of Africa. From the shore came hot whiffs of that indescribable smell so subtly suggestive of a tropical land; while the names of the districts—the Ivory Coast, the Gold Coast, the Slave Coast—conjured up the old days of adventure, blood-red with deeds of cruelty and shame. This Gulf of Guinea was the heart of the slave trade: more vessels loaded up here with their black cargo than at any other port of the continent, and the Bight of Biafra, on which Calabar is situated, was ever the busiest spot. Mangrove forests, unequalled anywhere for immensity and gloom, fringe the entire sweep of the Gulf. Rooted in slime, malodorous and malarious, they form a putrescent paradise for all manner of loathly creatures.

Out of the blue waters of the Atlantic the *Ethiopia* ran, on Saturday, September 11, into the mud-coloured estuary of the Cross and Calabar Rivers. On the left lay the flat delta of the Niger, ahead stretched the landscape of mangrove as far as the eye could range; to the south- east rose the vast bulk of the Cameroon Mountains. With what interest Mary gazed on the scene one can imagine. Somewhere at the back of these swamps was the spot where she was to settle and work. That it was near the coast she knew, for all that more distant land was unexplored and unknown: most of what was within sight, indeed, was still outside the pale of civilisation; through the bush and along the creeks and lagoons moved nude people, most of whom had never seen a white face. It might well seem an amazing thing to her, in view of the fact that there had been commerce with the coast for centuries. Vessels had plied to it for slaves, spices, gold dust, ivory, and palm oil; traders mingled with the people, and spoke their tongue; and yet it remained a land of mystery.

There were many reasons for this. The country was owned by no European Power. Britain regarded it—somewhat unwillingly at first—as a sphere of influence, but had no footing in it, and no control over the people. These were divided into many tribes and sections of tribes, each speaking a different tongue, and each perpetually at war with its neighbour. The necessities of trade fostered a certain intercourse; there was neutral ground where transactions took place, and products for the traders filtered down to the people at the coast who acted as middlemen. These, for obvious reasons, objected to the white men going inland—they would get into touch with the tribes, their authority would be undermined and their business ruined, and as they controlled the avenues of approach and were masters in their own house their veto could not be disregarded. In any case a journey up-river was full of peril. Every bend brought one to a new tribe, alert, suspicious, threatening. For Europeans it was a foodless country, in which they had to face hunger, fever, and death. Even the missionaries had only been feeling their way very slowly: they explored and planted out stations here and there, as permission was obtained from the chiefs, but their main efforts were directed to the task of establishing a strong base at the coast.

The estuary is about twelve miles in breadth, its banks are lined by mangrove, and here and there its surface is broken by islands. From these, as the steamer passed, parrots flew in flocks. From the sandbanks and mudbanks alligators slid into the water with a splash. Occasionally a shrimp-fisher in his canoe was seen. Higher up were the ruins of the barracoons, where the slaves were penned while waiting for shipment. Some fifty miles from the sea the steamer swung round to the east and entered the Calabar River; the swamps gave place to clay cliffs thick with undergrowth and trees, and far ahead a cluster of houses came into view—this, Mary knew, was Old Town. Then the hulks in the stream, used as stores and homes by the traders, appeared, and the steamer anchored opposite Duke Town. It lay on the right among swamps in a receding hollow of the cliff: a collection of mud-dwellings thatched with palm leaf, slovenly and sordid, and broiling in the hot rays of a brilliant sun.

It was the scene she had often endeavoured to picture in her mind. There was the hill where into the bush the dead bodies of natives used to be cast to become the food of wild beasts, now crowned with the Mission buildings. What memories had already gathered about these! What experiences lay behind the men and women who lived there! What a land was this she had chosen to make her dwelling-place—a land formless, mysterious, terrible, ruled by witchcraft and the terrorism of secret societies; where the skull was worshipped and blood-sacrifices were offered to jujus; where guilt was decided by ordeal of poison and boiling oil; where scores of people were murdered when a chief died, and his wives decked themselves in finery and were strangled to keep him company in the spirit-land; where men and women were bound and left to perish by the water-side to placate the god of shrimps; where the alligators were satiated with feeding on human flesh; where twins were done to death, and the mother banished to the bush; where semi- nakedness was compulsory, and girls were sent to farms to be fattened for marriage. A land, also, of disease and fever and white graves.

There, too, lay her own future, as dark and unknown as the land, full of hard work, she knew, full, it might be of danger and trial and sorrow....

But the boats of the traders and the missionaries came off, the canoes of the natives swarmed around, the whole town seemed to be on the water. With eyes that were bright and expectant Mary stepped from the Mission boat and set foot on African soil.

CHAPTER II
FIRST IMPRESSIONS

The young missionary-teacher was delighted with the novelty and wonders of her surroundings. She revelled in the sunshine, the warmth, the luxuriant beauty, and began to doubt whether the climate was so deadly after all: some of the missionaries told her that much of the illness was due to the lack of proper care, and there was even one who said he preferred Calabar to Scotland.

She was impressed with the Mission. The organisation of church and school, the regular routine of life, the large attendance at the services, the demeanour of the Christians, the quiet and persistent aggressive work going on, satisfied her sense of the fitness of things and made her glad and hopeful. To hear the chime of Sabbath bells; to listen to the natives singing, in their own tongue, the hymns associated with her home life, the Sabbath school and the social meeting; and to watch one of them give an address with eloquence and power, was a revelation. She went to a congregational meeting at Creek Town and heard King Eyo Honesty VII. speaking, and so many were present, and the feeling was so hearty and united that it might have served as a model for the home churches. She was attracted by the King; a sincere kindly Christian man, she found him to be. When she told him that her mother was much interested in him, he was so pleased that he wrote Mrs. Slessor, and the two corresponded—he a negro King in Africa and she an obscure woman in Scotland, drawn to each other across 4000 miles of sea by the influence of the Gospel.

It was true that the results of thirty years' work in Calabar did not seem large. The number of members in all the congregations was 174, though the attendances at the services each Sunday was over a thousand. The staff, however, had never been very large; of Europeans at this time there were four ordained missionaries, four men teachers, and four women teachers, and of natives one ordained missionary and eighteen agents; and efforts were confined to Duke Town, Old Town, Creek Town, Ikunetu, and Ikorofiong— all on the banks of the rivers or creeks—with several out-stations.

Her work at first was simple: it was to teach in the day-school on Mission Hill and visit in the yards, both on week-days and Sundays. Not until the strangeness of things had worn off a little did she begin to see below the surface and discover the difficulties of the situation. What assisted the process was a tour of the stations, which it was thought well she should make in order to become acquainted with the conditions. In the out-districts she came into contact with the raw heathen, and felt herself down at the very foundations of humanity. Most of the journeying was through the bush: there were long and fatiguing marches, and much climbing and jumping and wading to do, in which she had the help of three Kroo boys, but being active in body and buoyant in spirit, she enjoyed it thoroughly. A white "Ma" was so curious a sight in some of the districts that the children would run away, screaming with fright, and the women would crowd round her talking, gesticulating, and fingering, so that the chiefs had to drive them off with a whip. She was a little startled by these demonstrations, but was told the people were merely wishing to make friends with her, and she soon overcame her nervousness.

Her first meeting was held while she was with one of the native agents, John Baillie, and took place in the shade of a large tree beside a devil-house built for a dead man's spirit, and stocked with food. After the agent had spoken in Efik he turned to her and said, "Have you anything to say to them?" She looked at the dark throng, degraded, ignorant, superstitious. All eyes were fixed on her. For once she found it difficult to speak. Asking Mr. Baillie to read John v. 1-24, she tried to arrange her thoughts, but seemed to grow more helpless. When she began, the words came, and very simply, very earnestly—the agent interpreting—she spoke of their need of healing and saving, of which they must be conscious through their dissatisfaction with this life, the promptings of their higher natures, the experience of suffering and sorrow, and the dark future beyond death, and, asking the question, "Wilt thou be made whole?" pointed the way to peace.

As she observed and assimilated, she came to hold a clearer view of the people and the problems confronting the missionaries. She realised that the raw negroes, though savage enough, were not destitute of religious beliefs: their "theology," indeed, seemed somewhat too complicated for comprehension. Nor were their lives unregulated by principles and laws; they were ruled by canons and conventions as powerful as those of Europe, as merciless as the caste code of India; their social life was rooted in a tangle of relationships and customs as intricate as any in the world. The basis of the community was the House, at the head of which was a Master or Chief, independent and autocratic within his own limited domain, which consisted merely of a cluster of mud-huts in the bush. In this compound or yard, or "town" as it was sometimes called, lived connected families. Each chief had numerous wives and slaves, over whom he exercised absolute control. The slaves enjoyed considerable freedom, many occupying good positions and paying tribute, but they could be sold or killed at the will of their master. All belonging to a House were under its protection, and once outside that protection they were pariahs, subject to no law, and at the mercy of Egbo. This secret society was composed of select and graded classes initiated according to certain rites. Its agents were Egbo-runners, supposed to represent a supernatural being in the bush, who came suddenly out, masked and dressed in fantastic garb, and with a long whip rushed about and committed excesses. At these times all women were obliged to hide, for if found they would be flogged and stripped of their clothing. Egbo, however, had a certain power for good, and was often evoked in aid of law and order. Naturally it was the divorcing of superfluous wives, and the freeing of slaves that formed the greatest difficulty for the missionaries—it meant nothing less than breaking up a social system developed and fortified by long centuries of custom. Thus early Miss Slessor came to see that it was the duty of the missionary to bring about a new set of conditions in which it would be possible for the converts to live, and the thought influenced her whole after-career.

The district of Calabar afforded a striking object-lesson of what could be achieved. There was no central native government, and the British consular jurisdiction was of the most shadowy character. So far there had been but the quiet pressure of a moral and spiritual agency at work, but under its influence the people had become habituated to the orderly ways of civilisation, and were living in peace and amity. It was admitted by the officials that the agreements which they concluded with the chiefs had only been rendered possible by the teaching of the missionaries: and later it was largely upon the same sure and solid foundations that British authority was to build.

So, she realised, it was not a case where one could say, "Let there be light," and light would shine. The work of the Mission was like building a lighthouse stone by stone, layer by layer, with infinite toil and infinite patience. Yet she often found it hard to restrain her eagerness. "It is difficult to wait," she said. One text, however, kept repeating itself—"Learn of Me." "Christ never was in a hurry," she wrote. "There was no rushing forward, no anticipating, no fretting over what might be, Every day's duties were done as every day brought them, and the rest was left with God. 'He that believeth shall not make haste.'" And in that spirit she worked.

Her better knowledge of the position made her resolve to acquire a thorough mastery of the language in order to enter completely into the life and thought of the natives. Interpretation she had already found to be untrustworthy, and she was told the tale of a native who, translating an address on the rich man and Lazarus, remarked, in an aside to the audience, that for himself he would prefer to be the rich man! Efik was the tongue of Calabar and of trade and commerce, and was understood more or less over a wide tract of country. She learnt it by ear, and from the people, rather than from the book, and soon picked up enough to take a larger share in the varied work of the Mission.

Life had a piquancy in these days when she lived with the Andersons on Mission Hill. "Daddy" Anderson was a veteran of the Mission, but it was "Mammy" Anderson with whom she came into closest relation. Of strong individuality, she ruled the town from the Mission House, and the chiefs were fain to do her bidding. At first Mary stood somewhat in awe of her. One of the duties assigned to her was to ring, before dawn, the first bell for the day to call the faithful to morning prayer. There were no alarm clocks then, and occasionally she overslept, and the rebuke she received from Mrs. Anderson made her cheeks burn. Sometimes she would wake with a start to find her room flooded with light. Half- dazed with sleep and shamed at her remissness she would hurry out to ring the bell, only to discover that it was not dawn but the light of the moon that was making the world so bright.

At one time when doing duty in Old Town she had to walk along a narrow native track through the bush. To let off the high spirits that had been bottled up in the Mission House she would climb any tree that took her fancy. She affirmed that she had climbed every tree worthy of the name between Duke Town and Old Town. Sometimes her fun made her late for meals, and Mrs. Anderson would warn her that if she offended again she would go without food. She did offend, and then Mr. Anderson would smuggle biscuits and bananas to her, with, she was confident, the connivance of his wife. She had a warm affection for all the members of the Mission staff, but for none more than for "Mammy" Anderson.

There was one of the humbler inmates of the Mission who watched with affectionate interest the young missionary with the soft voice and dancing eyes. This was Mrs. Fuller, a coloured woman who had come over from Jamaica in 1858 with the Rev. Mr. Robb and Mrs. Robb as a nurse, and married and remained after they left to be a help and comfort to many. She remembered the day when the slaves were emancipated in the West Indies. A kindly, happy, unselfish soul, she never spoke ill of any one. Somebody said to her, "Mammy, I believe you would say a good word about the devil himself." "Well," she replied, "at any rate he minds his own business." "Dear old Mammy Fuller," Miss Slessor called her, little dreaming that Mammy would live to throw flowers into her grave.

CHAPTER III
IN THE UNDERWORLD

In the hush of a beautiful Sunday morning the new missionary begins what she calls the commonplace work of the day. Looking out some illustrated texts she sends a few with a kindly message to all the big men, reminding them that Mr. Anderson expects them at service. Then she sets out for the town, and few people escape her keen eye and persuasive words.

"Why are you not going to God's House?" she asks a man who is sitting at the door of his hut. Close by are the remains of a devil-house.

He rocks himself and replies, "If your heart was vexed would you go any place? Would you not rather sit at home and nurse your sorrow?"

Mary learns that his only child has died and has been buried in the house, and according to custom the family is sitting in filth, squalor, and drunkenness. She talks to him of the resurrection, and he becomes interested, and takes her into a room where the mother is sitting with bowed head over the grave, the form of which can be seen distinctly under a blue cloth that covers the ground. A bunch of dirty muslin is hanging from the ceiling. It is a dismal scene. She reads part of John xi., and speaks about life and death and the beyond.

"Well," remarked the man, "if God took the child I don't care so much— but to think an enemy bewitched it!"

To the mother she says, "Do you not find comfort in these words?"

"No," is the sullen reply. "Why should I find comfort when my child is gone?"

Mary pats her on the head, and tells her how her own mother has found comfort in the thought of the reunion hereafter. The woman is touched and weeps: the mother-heart is much the same all the world over.

A few slave-girls are all she finds in the next yard, the other inmates having gone to work at the farms; but she speaks to them and they listen respectfully. Another yard is crowded with women, some eating, some sleeping, some dressing each other's hair, some lounging half- naked on the ground gossiping—a picture of sheer animalism. Her advent creates a welcome diversion, and they are willing to listen: it helps to pass the time. They take her into an inner yard where a fine-looking young woman is being fattened for her future husband. She flouts the message, and is spoken to sternly and left half-crestfallen, half- defiant. It is scenes like this which convince Mary that the women are the greatest problem in the Mission Field. She does not wonder that the men are as they are. If they are to be reached more must be done for the women, and a prayer goes up that the Church at home may realise the situation.

Farther on is a heathen house. The master is dead: the mistress is an old woman, hardened and repulsive, the embodiment of all that is evil, who is counting coppers in a room filled with bush, skulls, sacrifices, and charms. A number of half-starved cowed women and girls covered with dirt and sores are quarrelling over a pipe. The shrill voice and long arms of the mistress settle the matter, and make them fly helter- skelter. They call on Mary to speak, and after many interruptions she subdues and controls them, and leaves them, for the moment, impressed.

She arrives at a district which the lady agents have long worked. The women are cleanly, pleasant, and industrious, but polished hypocrites, always ready to protest with smooth tongue and honeyed words that they are eager to be "god-women," but never taking the first step forwards. Mary, who is learning to be sarcastic, on occasion, gives them a bit of her mind and goes away heart-sick. But she is cheered at the next yard, where she has a large and attentive audience.

In the poorest part she comes upon a group of men selling rum. At the sight of the "white Ma" they put the stuff away and beg her to stay. They are quiet until she denounces the sale of the liquor; then one interrupts:

"What for white man bring them rum suppose them rum no be good? He be god-man bring the rum—then what for god-man talk so?"

What can she answer?

It is a vile fluid this trade spirit, yet the country is deluged with it, and it leaves behind it disaster and demoralisation and ruined homes. Mary feels bitter against the civilised countries that seek profit from the moral devastation of humanity.

She cannot answer the man.

A husband brings his woebegone wife who has lost five children. Can "Ma" not give her some medicine? She again speaks of the resurrection. A crowd gathers and listens breathlessly. When she says that even the twin-children are safe with God, and that they will yet confront their murderers, the people start, shrug their shoulders, and with looks of terror slink one by one away.

She visits many of the hovels, which are little better than ruins. Pools of filth send out pestilential odours. There is starvation in every pinched face and misery in every sunken eye. Covered with sores the inmates lie huddled together and clamour only for food. One old woman says:

"I have prayed and prayed till there is no breath left in me. God does not answer. He does not care."

"To whom do you pray?"

"I don't know, but I call Him God. I tell Him I have no friend. I say 'You see me. I am sick. I am hungry. I am good. I don't steal. I don't keep bread from any one. I don't kill. I don't speak with my mouth when my heart is far away. Have mercy upon me.'"

Mary talks to her lovingly and earnestly, and when she leaves, the heart of the wretched woman is quietened and grateful.

It is afternoon, and time for the Efik service at four o'clock, and Mary, a little tired with the heat and the strain, turns and makes for Mission Hill.

CHAPTER IV
THE PULL OF HOME

It was not long before she had to revise her opinion of the climate. Nature was beautiful, but beneath its fair appearance lurked influences that were cruel and pitiless. "Calabar needs a brave heart and a stout body," she wrote; "not that I have very much of the former, but I have felt the need for it often when sick and lonely." Both the dry and rainy seasons had their drawbacks, but she especially disliked the former-which lasted from December to March-because of the "smokes" or harmattan, a haze composed of fine dust blown from the great African desert, that withered her up and sucked out all the energy she possessed. She was frequently attacked by fever, and laid aside, and on one occasion was at the point of death. But she never lost her confidence in God. Once she thought she had. It was during an illness when she was only semi-conscious, but on recovering the clearness of her mind she realised that she had given herself into His keeping and need not fear, and a sense of comfort and peace stole over her. So many attacks weakened her constitution and made her think oftener of home. She began to have a longing to look again upon loved faces, to have grey skies overhead, and to feel the tang of the clean cool air on her cheek, "I want my home and my mother," she confessed. It was home- sickness, and there is only one cure for that. It comes, however, to pass. It is not so overpowering after the first home-going, and it grows less importunate after each visit. One finds after a short absence that things in the old environment are, somehow, not the same; that there has ceased to be a niche which one can fill; that one has a fresh point of view; and as time goes on and the roots of life go deeper into the soil of the new country, the realisation comes that it is in the homeland where one is homeless, and in the land of exile where one is at home. But at first the pull of the old associations is irresistible; and so when her furlough was due, Mary flew to Scotland as a wandered bird flies wing-weary back to its nest.

She left Calabar in June 1879 and proceeded straight to Dundee. During her stay she removed her mother and sisters to Downfield, a village on the outskirts of the city, and was happy in the knowledge that all was well with them. Friends who listened to her graphic account of Calabar tell that even then she spoke of her desire to go up country into the unworked fields, and especially to the Okoyong district, but "Daddy" Anderson was opposed to the idea. Before returning, she wrote the Foreign Mission Committee and begged to be sent to a station other than Duke Town, though she loyally added that she would do whatever was thought best. She sailed with the Rev. Hugh Goldie, one of the veteran pioneers of the Mission, and Mrs. Goldie, and on arrival at Calabar, in October 1880, found to her joy that she was to be in charge of Old Town, and that she was a real missionary at last.

CHAPTER V
AT THE SEAT OF SATAN

The first sight she saw on entering her new sphere was a human skull hung on a pole at the entrance to the town. In Old Town and the smaller stations of Qua, Akim, and Ikot Ansa, lying back in the tribal district of Ekoi, the people were amongst the most degraded in Calabar. It was a difficult field, but she entered upon it with zest. Although under the supervision of Duke Town, she was practically her own mistress, and could carry out her own ideas and methods. This was important for her, for, to her chagrin, she had found that boarding was expensive in Calabar, and as she had to leave a large portion of her salary at home for the support of her mother and sisters, she could not afford to live as the other lady agents did. She had to economise in every direction, and took to subsisting wholly on native food. It was in this way she acquired those simple, Spartan-like habits which accompanied her through life. Her colleagues attributed her desire for isolation and native ways to natural inclination, not dreaming that they were a matter of compulsion, for she was too loyal to her home and too proud of spirit to reveal the reason for her action.

One drawback of the situation was the dilapidated state of the house. It was built of wattle and mud, had a mat roof and a whitewashed interior. She did not, however, mind its condition; she was so absorbed in the work that personal comfort was a matter of indifference to her. Her household consisted of a young woman and several boys and girls, with whose training she took endless pains, and who helped her and accompanied her to her meetings. School work made large drafts on her time at Old Town, Qua, and Akim. Young and old came as scholars. At Qua the chief man of the place after the king sat on a bench with little children, and along with them repeated the Sunday School lessons. He set them an example, for he was never absent.

But to preach the love of Christ was her passion. With every visitor who called to give compliments, with every passer-by who came out of curiosity to see what the white woman and her house were like, with all who brought a dispute to settle, she had talk about the Saviour of the world. Sunday was a day of special effort in this direction. She would set out early for Qua, where two boys carrying a bell slung on a pole summoned the people to service. One of the chiefs would fix the benches and arrange the audience, which usually numbered from 80 to 100, She would go on to Akim or Ikot Ansa, where a similar meeting was held. On the way she would visit sick folk, or call in at farms, have friendly conversation with master and dependants, and give a brief address and prayer. By mid-day she would be back at Old Town, where she conducted a large Sunday School. In the evening a regular church service was held, attended by almost the entire community. This, to her, was the meeting of the week. It took place in the yard of the chief. At one side stood a table, covered with a white cloth, on which were a primitive lamp and a Bible. The darkness, the rows of dusky faces just revealed by the flickering light, the strained attention, the visible emotion made up a strange picture. At the end came hearty "good-nights," and she would be escorted home by a procession of lantern-bearers.

Such service, incessant and loving, began to tell. The behaviour of the people improved; the god of the town was banished; the chiefs went the length of saying that their laws and customs were clearly at variance with God's fashions. Mr. Anderson reported to the Church at home that she was "doing nobly." When two deputies went out and inspected the Mission in 1881-82, they were much impressed by her energy and devotion. "Her labours are manifold," they stated, "but she sustains them cheerfully— she enjoys the unreserved friendship and confidence of the people, and has much influence over them." This they attributed partly to the singular ease with which she spoke the language. Learning that she preferred her present manner of life to being associated with another white person—they were unaware, like others, of the real reason which governed her—they recommended that she should be allowed to continue her solitary course.

It was at Old Town that she came first into close contact with the more sinister aspects of mission work, and obtained that training and experience in dealing with the natives and native problems which led her into the larger responsibilities of the future. Despite the influence of the missionaries and the British Consul, many of the worst heathen iniquities were being practised. A short time previously the Consul had made a strong effort to get the chiefs to enforce the laws regarding twin-murder, human sacrifice, the stripping and flogging of women by Egbo-runners, and other offences, and an agreement had been reached; but no treaty, no Egbo proclamation could root out the customs of centuries, and they continued to be followed, in secret in the towns and openly in the country districts.

The evil of twin-murder had a terrible fascination for her. A woman who gave birth to twins was regarded with horror. The belief was that the father of one of the infants was an evil spirit, and that the mother had been guilty of a great sin; one at least of the children was believed to be a monster, and as they were never seen by outsiders or allowed to live, no one could disprove the fact. They were seized, their backs were broken, and they were crushed into a calabash or water-pot and taken out—not by the doorway, but by a hole broken in the back wall, which was at once built up—and thrown into the bush, where they were left to be eaten by insects and wild beasts. Sometimes they would be placed alive into the pots. As for the mother, she was driven outside the bounds of decent society and compelled to live alone in the bush. In such circumstances there was only one thing for the missionaries to do. As soon as twins were born they sought to obtain possession of them, and gave them the security and care of the Mission House. Some of the Mission compounds were alive with babies. It was no use taking the mother along with them. She believed she must be accursed, for otherwise she would never be in such a position. First one and then the other child would die, and she would make her escape and fly to the bush.

Mary realised that the system was the outcome of superstition and fear, and she could even see how, from the native point of view, it was essential for the safety of the House, but her heart was hot against it; nothing, indeed, roused her so fiercely as the senseless cruelty of putting these innocent babes to death, and she joined in the campaign with fearless energy.

She could also understand why the natives threw away infants whose slave-mother died. No slave had time to bring up another woman's child. If she did undertake the task, it would only be hers during childhood; after that it became the property of the master. The chances of a slave-child surviving were not good enough for a free woman to try the experiment, and as life in any case was of little value, it was considered best that the infant should be put out of the way.

The need of special service in these directions made her suggest to the Foreign Mission Committee that one of the woman agents should be set apart to take care of the children that were rescued. It was impossible, she said, for one to do school or other work, and attend to them as well. "If such a crowd of twins should come to her as I have to manage, she would require to devote her whole time to them." More and more also she was convinced of the necessity of women's work among the women in the farming districts, and she pressed the matter upon the Committee. She was in line with the old chief who remarked that "them women be the best man for the Mission."

Another evil which violated her sense of justice and right, and against which she took up arms, was the trade attitude of the Calabar people. Although they had settled on the coast only by grace of the Ekois, they endeavoured to monopolise all dealings with the Europeans and prevent the inland tribes from doing business direct with the factories. Often the up-river men would make their way down stealthily, but if caught they were slain or mutilated, and a bitter vendetta would ensue. She recognised that it would only be by the tribes coming to know and respect each other, and by the adoption of unrestricted trade with the stores that the full reward of industry could be secured. She accordingly took up the cause of the inland tribes. When Efik was at war with Qua, sentries were posted at all the paths to the factories, but the people came to her by night, and she would lead them down the track running through the Mission property. At the factory next to the Mission beach they would deliver their palm oil or kernels, and take back the goods for which they had bartered them. In this way she helped to open up the country. It was not, perhaps, mission work in the ordinary sense any more than much of Dr. Livingstone's work was missionary work, but it was an effort to break down the conditions that perpetuated wrong and dispeace, and to introduce the forces of righteousness and goodwill. In all this work she had the sympathy of the traders, who showed her much kindness. She was a missionary after their own heart.

CHAPTER VI
IN ELEPHANT COUNTRY

The spirit of the pioneer would not allow her to be content with the routine of village work. She began to go afield, and made trips of exploration along the river. The people found her different from other missionaries; she would enter their townships as one of themselves, show them in a moment that she was mistress of their thought and ways, and get right into their confidence. Always carrying medicine, she attended the sick, and so many maimed and diseased crowded to her that often she would lose the tide twice over. In her opinion no preaching surpassed these patient, intimate interviews on the banks of the river and by the wayside, when she listened to tales of suffering and sorrow and gave sympathy and practical help. Sometimes she remained away for nights at a time, and on these occasions her only accommodation was a mud hut and her only bed a bundle of filthy rags.

A larger venture was made at the instance of a chief named Okon, a political refugee whom she knew. He had settled at a spot on the western bank of the estuary, then called Ibaka, now James Town, and had long urged her to pay the place a visit. It was only some thirty miles away, but thirty miles to the African is more than two hundred to a European, and Old Town was in a state of excitement for days before she left. Nine A.M. was the hour fixed for departure, but Mary knew local ways, and forenoon found her calmly cooking the dinner. The house was crowded with visitors begging her to be careful, and threatening vengeance if anything happened to their "Ma." At 6 P.M. came word that all was ready, and, followed by a retinue comprising half the population, she made way to the beach. Women who were not ordinarily permitted to be viewed by the public eye waited at every yard to embrace hers and to charge all concerned to look well after her comfort.

A State canoe sent by the King lay at the water-side. It had been repainted for the occasion in the gayest of colours, while thoughtful hands had erected a little arch of matting to seclude her from the paddlers and afford protection from the dew, and had arranged some rice-bags as a couch. The pathos of the tribute touched her, and with a smile and a word of thanks she stepped into her place and settled the four house-children about the feet of the paddlers. More hours were lost in one way or another. Darkness fell, and only the red gleam of the torches lit up the scene. Alligators and snakes haunted the spot, but she had no fear so long as the clamour of the crowd continued.

At last, "Sio udeñ!" The command was answered by the "dip-dip" of thirty-three paddles, and the canoe glided into the middle of the river and sped onwards. In her crib she tried to read by the light of a candle, while the paddlers extemporised songs in her honour, assigning to her all the virtues under the sun—

Ma, our beautiful, beloved mother, is on board, Ho! Ho! Ho!

The gentle movement, the monotonous "tom-tom-tum" of the drummer, and the voice of the steersman, became mingled in a dreamy jumble, and she slept through the night as soundly as on a bed of down. Ten hours' paddling brought the craft to its destination, and at dawn she was carried ashore over golden sand and under great trees, and deposited in the chief's compound amongst goats, dogs, and fowls. She and the children were given the master's room—which always opens out into the women's yard—and as it possessed no door a piece of calico was hung up as a screen. The days were tolerable, but the nights were such as even she, inured to African conditions, found almost unbearable. It was the etiquette of the country that all the wives should sit as close to the white woman as was compatible with her idea of comfort, and as the aim of each was to be fatter than the other, and they all perspired freely, and there was no ventilation, it required all her courage to outlast the ordeal. Lizards, too, played among the matting of the roof, and sent down showers of dust, while rats performed hop, skip, and jump over the sleepers.

Crowds began to pour in from a wide area. Many of the people had never looked upon a white woman, and she had to submit to being handled and examined in order to prove that she was flesh and blood like themselves. Doubtful men and women were forcibly dragged to her by laughing companions and made to touch her skin. At meal times she was on exhibition to a favoured few, who watched how she ate and drank, and then described the operations to the others outside.

Day by day she prescribed and bandaged, cut out garments, superintended washing, and initiated women into the secrets of starching and ironing. Day by day she held a morning and evening service, and it was with difficulty that she prevented the one from merging into the other. On Sabbath the yard became strangely quiet: all connected with it were clothed and clean, and in a corner stood a table with a white cloth and upon it a Bible and hymn-book. As the fierce-looking, noisy men from a distance entered they stopped involuntarily and a hush fell upon them. Many heard the story of Christ for the first time, and never had she a more appreciative audience. In the evening the throng was so great that her voice could barely reach them all, and at the end they came up to her and with deep feeling wished her good-night and then vanished quietly into the darkness.

The people would not allow her to walk out much on account of the presence of wild beasts. Elephants were numerous—it was because of the destruction they had wrought on the farms that fishing had become the main support of the township. Early one morning a commotion broke out: a boa constrictor had been seen during the night, and bands of men armed with clubs, cutlasses, and muskets set off, yelling, to hunt the monster. Whenever she moved out she was followed by all the men, women, and children. On every side she saw skulls, rudely carved images, peace-offerings of food to hungry spirits, and other evidences of debased fetishism, while cases of witchcraft and poisoning were frequent.

One day she noticed a tornado brewing on the Cameroon heights, and kept indoors. While sitting sewing the storm burst. The wind seized the village, lifting fences, canoes, trees, and buildings; lightning played and crackled about the hut; the thunder pealed overhead; and rain fell in floods. Then a column of flame leapt from the sky to earth, and a terrific crash deafened the cowering people. Accustomed as she was to tornadoes Mary was afraid. The slaves came rushing into the yard, shrieking, and at the same moment the roof of her hut was swept away, and she was beaten to the ground by the violence of the rain. In the light of the vivid flashes she groped her way through the water, now up to her ankles, and from her boxes obtained all the wraps she possessed. To keep up the spirits of the children she started a hymn, "Oh, come let us sing." Amidst the roar of the elements they caught the tune, and gradually their terror was subdued. When the torrent ceased she was in a high fever. She dosed herself with quinine, and as the shadow of death is never very far away in Africa she made all arrangements in case the end should come. But her temperature fell, and in two days she was herself again.

There was a morning when her greetings were responded to with such gravity that she knew something serious had occurred. During the night two of the young wives of a chief had broken the strictest law in Efik, had left the women's yard and entered one where a boy was sleeping, and as nothing can be hidden in a slave community their husband knew at once.

The culprits were called out, and with them two other girls, who were aware of the escapade, but did not tell. The chief, and the men of position in his compound and district, sat in judgment upon them, and decided that each must receive one hundred stripes.

Mary sought out Okon and talked the matter over. "Ma," he said, "it be proper big palaver, but if you say we must not flog we must listen to you as our mother and our guest. But they will say that God's word be no good if it destroy the power of the law to punish evildoers."

He agreed, however, to delay the punishment, and to bring the judges and the people together in a palaver at mid-day. When all were assembled she addressed the girls:

"You have brought much shame on us by your folly and by abusing your master's confidence while the yard is in our possession. Though God's word teaches men to be merciful, it does not countenance or pass over sin, and I cannot shelter you from punishment. You have knowingly and deliberately brought it on yourselves. Ask God to keep you in the future so that your conduct may not be a reproach to yourselves and the word of God which you know."

Many were the grunts of satisfaction from the people, and the faces of the big men cleared as they heard their verdict being endorsed, while darker and more defiant grew the looks of the girls.

With a swift movement she turned to the gathering:

"Ay, but you are really to blame. It is your system of polygamy which is a disgrace to you and a cruel injustice to these helpless women. Girls like these, sixteen years old, are not beyond the age of fun and frolic. To confine them as you do is a shame and a blot on your manhood: obedience such as you command is not worth the having."

Frowns greeted this denunciation, and the old men muttered:

"When the punishment is severe, neither slave nor wife dare disobey: the old fashions are better than the new."

Much heated discussion followed, but at last she succeeded in getting the punishment reduced to the infliction of ten stripes and nothing more. She had gone as far as she dared. Under ordinary circumstances salt would have been rubbed into the wounds, and mutilation or dismemberment would have followed. She thanked the men, enjoined the wives and slaves to show their gratitude by a willing and true service, and went to prepare alleviations for the victims.

Through the shouting and laughing of the operators and onlookers she heard piercing screams, as strong arms plied the alligator hide, and one by one the girls came running into her, bleeding and quivering in the agony of pain. By and by the opiate did its work and all sank into uneasy slumber.

Fourteen days went by, and it was time for the return journey. The same noise and excitement and delay occurred, and it was afternoon ere the canoe left the beach. The evening meal, a mess of yam and herbs, cooked in palm oil, which had been carried on board smoking hot from the fire and was served in the pot, had scarcely been disposed of when the splendour of the sunset and afterglow was swept aside by a mass of angry cloud, and the moaning of the wind fell threateningly on the ear. "A stormy night ahead," said Mary apprehensively to Okon, who gave a long look upward and steered for the lee of an island. The sky blackened, thunder growled, and the water began to lift. The first rush of wind gripped the canoe and whirled it round, while the crew, hissing through their set teeth, pulled their hardest. In vain. They got out of hand, and there was uproar and craven fear. Sharing in the panic the master was powerless. At the sight of others in peril Mary threw aside her own nervousness and anxiety and took command. In a few moments order was restored and the boat was brought close to the tangle of bush, and the men, springing up like monkeys into the branches, held on to the canoe, which was now being dashed up and down like a straw. Mary sat with the water up to her knees, the children lashed to her by a waterproof, their heads hidden in her lap. Lightning, thunder, rain, and wave combined to make one of the grandest displays of the earth's forces she had ever witnessed.

As quickly as it came the storm passed, and to the strains of a hymn which she started the journey was resumed. She was shaking with ague, and in order to put some heat into her the chief came and sat down on one side, while his big wife sat on the other. As her temperature rose, the paddlers grew alarmed, and pulled as they had never done in their lives. Dawn was stealing over the land when Old Town was reached, and as "Ma" was hardly a fit sight for critical eyes, she was carried up by a bush path to the Mission House.

Ill as she was, her first care was to make a fire to obtain hot tea for the children and to tuck them away comfortably for the night. Then she tottered to her bed, to rise some days later, a wreck of her former self, but smiling and cheerful as usual....

Towards the close of the year 1882 a tornado swept over Old Town and damaged the house to such an extent that she had to make a hasty escape and take refuge in a factory. The Presbytery brought her to Duke Town, but she became so ill as a result of her strenuous life and her experience in the storm, that she was ordered home, and left in April 1888. She was so frail that she was carried on board, and it was considered doubtful whether she would outlive the voyage. With her was a girl-twin she had rescued. She had saved both, a boy and girl, but whilst she was absent from the house for a little, the relatives came, and, by false pretences, obtained possession of the boy, and killed him. She was determined that the girl should live and grow up to confute their fears, and she would not incur the risk of leaving her behind.

CHAPTER VII
WITH BACK TO THE WALL

Many strange experiences came to Mary Slessor in her life, but it is doubtful whether any adventure equalled that which she was now to go through in the quiet places of home, or whether any period of her career was so crowded with emotion and called for higher courage and resource.

She remained for the greater part of the time with her mother and sisters at Downfield, seeing few people, and nursing the little black twin, who was baptized in Wishart Sunday School, and called Janie, after her sister.

One of her earliest visits was to her friends the Doigs in the south side of Edinburgh, and here again her life touched and influenced another life. There was in connection with Bristo Street Church a girl named Jessie F. Hogg, who worked in the mission at Cowan's Close where the "two Marys" had formerly taught. She had heard much about Mary Slessor, and when, one Sunday, a lady friend remarked that she was going to visit the missionary, Miss Hogg declared she would give much to meet her. "Then come with me," said the lady, "I will leave you at the foot of the stair, and if you are to come up I will call you." She was invited up, and was not five minutes in Mary's presence before the latter said, "And what are you doing at home? What is hindering you from going to the mission field?" "There is nothing to hinder me," was the reply. "Then come: there is a good work waiting for you to do." Miss Hogg applied to the Foreign Mission Committee and was accepted, received some medical training, and was in Calabar before Mary herself returned. The anticipations of the latter were fulfilled. For thirteen years, with quiet heroism, Miss Hogg did a great work as one of the "Mothers of the Mission": her name was a household word, both in Calabar and at home: and when, through ill-health, she retired, she left a memory that is still cherished by the natives. There were few of the missionaries then who loved and understood Mary better, and whom Mary loved so well.

Mary's ideas of the qualities needed for work among the ignorant and degraded may be gathered from a letter which she wrote at this time to a friend in Dundee:

Nothing, I believe, will ever touch or raise fallen ones except sympathy. They shrink from self-righteousness which would stoop to them, and they hate patronage and pity. Of sympathy and patience they stand in need. They also need refinement, for the humble classes respect it, and they are sharper at detecting the want of it than many of those above them in the social scale. I am not a believer in the craze for "ticket-of-leave men" and "converted prize-fighters" to preach to the poor and the outcast. I think the more of real refinement and beauty and education that enter into all Christian work, the more real success and lasting, wide-reaching results of a Christian and elevating nature will follow. Vulgarity and ignorance can never in themselves lay hold on the uneducated classes, or on any class, though God often shows us how He can dispense with man's help altogether. Then there is need for knowledge in such a work, knowledge of the Bible as a whole, not merely of the special passages which are adapted for evangelistic services. They know all the set phrases belonging to special services and open-sir meetings. They want teaching, and they will respect nothing else. I am pained often at home that there is so little of depth, and of God's word, in the speeches and addresses I hear. It seems as if they thought anything will do for children, and that any kind of talk about coming to Christ, and believing on Christ, will feed and nourish immortal souls.

In January 1884 she informed the Foreign Mission Committee that her health was re-established and that she was ready to return, and in accordance with her own desire it was arranged to make the house habitable at Old Town and send her back there. Meanwhile she had begun to address meetings in connection with the missionary organisations of congregations, and at these her simple but vivid style, the human interest of her story, and the living illustration she presented in the shape of Janie, made so great an impression that the ladies of Glasgow besought the Committee to retain her for a time in order that she might go through the country and give her account of the work to quiet gatherings of women, young and old. The suggestion was acted upon, and for some months she was engaged in itinerating. It was not in the line of her inclination. She was very shy, and had a humbling consciousness of her defects, and to appear in public was an ordeal. It was often a sheer impossibility for her to open her lips when men were present, and she would make it a condition that none should be in her audience. When some distinguished minister or Church leader had been requisitioned to preside, a situation was created as embarrassing to him as to her. She did not, however, seem to mind if the disturbing factor was out of sight, and the difficulty was usually overcome by placing the chairman somewhere behind. These meetings taxed her strength more than the work in Africa, and she began to long for release. In December the Committee gave her permission to return, but, as conditions in the field had changed, decided to send her in the meantime to Creek Town to assist Miss Johnstone, who was not in good health.

Within a few weeks a situation developed which altered her plans. The severe weather had told on the delicate constitution of her youngest sister Janie, a quiet, timid girl, but bright and intelligent, and somewhat akin to herself in mind and manner; and it was made clear that only a change to a milder climate would save her life. Mary was torn with apprehension. She had a heart that was bigger than her body, and she loved her own people with passionate intensity, and was ready for any further sacrifice for their sake. Never bold on her own behalf, she would dare anything for others. Thinking out the problem how best she could reconcile her affection for her sister and her duty to the Mission, she fell upon a plan which she would have shrunk from proposing had she alone been concerned. If she could take the invalid out with her to Creek Town, and if they were allowed to dwell by themselves, the life of her sister would not only be prolonged, but she herself would be able to continue, by living native fashion, to pay her share of the expenses at home. To the Committee, accordingly, she wrote early in 1885, stating that she would not feel free to go to Creek Town unless she were permitted to take her sister with her, and unless she were allowed, instead of boarding with any of the Mission agents, to build a small mud house for their accommodation.

The Committee received the proposal with a certain mild astonishment. It had many a problem to solve in its administration of the affairs of the Missions, but its difficulties were always increased when it came into contact with that incalculable element, human nature. It could not be supposed to know all the personal and private circumstances that influenced the attitude of the missionaries: it could only judge from the surface facts placed before it; and as a rule it decided wisely, and was never lacking in the spirit of kindness and generosity. But even if the members had known of that fluttering heart in Dundee, they could not, in the best interests of the Mission, have acquiesced in her scheme, and it was probably well, also, for Mary that it was gently but firmly put aside.

For her the way out was found in the recommendation of an Exeter lady whom she had met, who advised her to take her sister to Devonshire. She seized on the idea, and forthwith wrote a letter stating that she felt it to be her duty to remove the invalid to the South of England, where she hoped her health would be restored, and asking whether in the event of her own way being cleared she would be allowed to return to Calabar, or whether she was to consider herself finally separated from the Mission. Nothing could have been more sympathetic than the reply of the Board. It regretted her family afflictions, said it would be glad to have the offer of her services again in the future, and in consideration of her work continued her home allowance till the end of April.

Meanwhile Mary had, in her swift fashion, carried off her sister, and her answer came from Devonshire. She thanked the Committee for its consideration, but, with the independence which always characterised her, accepted the allowance only up to the end of February. Thus voluntarily, and from a sense of duty, but with a sore heart, she cut herself adrift, for the time being, from the service of the Church.

As the climate of Devonshire seemed to suit her sister, they went to Topsham, where a house was secured with the help of a Mr. Ellis, a deacon in the Congregational Church, to whom she was introduced. It was soon furnished, and then her mother was brought down, and for all her toil and self-sacrifice she was rewarded by seeing a steady improvement in the condition of the invalid, and the quiet happiness of both. The place proved too relaxing for her own health, and she was never free from headaches, but she was not one to allow indisposition to interfere with her service for the Master. In the Congregational Church her winning ways made many friends, and she was soon taking an active part in the meetings and addressing large gatherings on her work in Calabar.

And then another event occurred which further complicated the situation. Her sister Susan in Scotland went to pay a visit to Mrs. M'Crindle, and died suddenly on entering her house. Mary had now the full responsibility for the home and its upkeep; she was earning nothing, and she had her mother and sister and the African baby to provide and care for. Happily the invalid continued to improve, and as it was imperative for Mary to be back at work, it was decided that she should apply for reinstatement. She told her mother of her desire to go up-country, and asked whether she would allow her to do so if the opportunity came. "You are my child, given to me by God," was the reply, "and I have given you back to Him. When He needs you and where He sends you, there I would have you be." Mary never forgot these brave words, which were a comfort to her throughout her life. On applying to the Foreign Mission Committee stating that she was willing, if it saw fit, to go back at once, she was gladly reinstated, and Calabar was consulted regarding her location. As there was some talk of a forward movement it was resolved to leave the matter over, and send her in the meantime to Creek Town.

Her friends in Topsham assured her that they would look well after her mother and sister, but all the arrangements she had made for the smooth working of the household collapsed a month before she was booked to sail.

Her mother suddenly failed and took to her bed. Mary grew desperate with strain and anxiety, and like a wild creature at bay turned this way and that for an avenue of escape. In her agony of mind she went to Him who had never failed her yet, and He gave her guidance. Next day a letter was on its way to Dundee to an old factory friend, asking if she would come and take charge of the household. A strange mingling of pathos and dignity, a passionate love and solicitude, marked the appeal, which, happily, evoked a ready assent. Not less moving in its way was the practical letter she sent to her friend, with long and minute directions as to travelling; there was not a detail forgotten, the mention of which might contribute to her ease and comfort. Her friend arrived a few days before her departure. On Guy Fawkes' Day Mary wished to take her to a church meeting to introduce her to some acquaintances, but was too afraid to venture out among the roughs—she who was soon to face alone some of the most savage crowds in Africa!

On the sea the past months receded and became like an uneasy dream. She was content simply to lie In her chair on deck and rest her tired mind and body. On arriving it was pleasant to receive a warm welcome from all the Mission friends, and still more pleasant to find that there had been talk of her going to Ikunetu to attempt to obtain a footing among the wild people of Okoyong.

CHAPTER VIII
BEREFT

Despite her happiness in being back at the work she loved, there was an underlying current of anxiety in her life. Her thoughts dwelt on the invalids at home; she wearied for letters; she trembled before the arrival of the mails; even her dreams influenced her. But she would not allow herself to grow morbid. Every morning she went to the houses in the Mission before breakfast to have a chat and cheer up the inmates. On New Year's Eve, fearing the adoption of European customs by the natives, and wishing to forestall them, she invited all the young men who were Christians to a prayer-meeting from eleven o'clock till midnight. They then went up and serenaded Mr. and Mrs. Luke, two new missionaries, whose subsequent pioneer work up-river was a record of toil and heroism. Mr. Luke entered into the spirit of the innovation. He gave out the 2nd Paraphrase and read the 90th Psalm. Prayer was uttered, and the company separated, singing the evening hymn in Efik.

Next morning, the first of the year 1886, she arose early and wrote a letter, overflowing with love and tenderness and cheer, to her mother and sister. It was finished on the third, on the arrival of the home mail. She was at tea with Mrs. Luke before going to a meeting in the church, when the letters came. "I was hardly able to wait for mine," she wrote; "and then I rushed to my room and behaved like a silly body, as if it had been bad news. It brought you all so clearly before me. At church I sat beside the King and cried quietly into my wrap all the evening," The last words in her letter were, "Tell me all your troubles, and be sure you take care of yourselves." She never received a reply. Mrs. Slessor had died suddenly and peacefully at the turn of the year. She had been nursed by loving hands, whilst her medical attendant and the minister of the Congregational Church, and his wife, showed her much kindness. Three months later Janie also passed away, and was laid beside her mother in Topsham cemetery, the deacons and members of the church and many friends attending and showing honour to one whom they had learned to love for her own sake as well as for her sister's.

Mary was inconsolable. "I, who all my life have been caring and planning and living for them, am left, as it were, stranded and alone." A sense of desolation and loneliness unsupportable swept over her. After all the sorrow that had crowded upon her she felt no desire to do anything. "There is no one to write and tell all my stories and troubles and nonsense to." One solace remained. "Heaven is now nearer to me than Britain, and no one will be anxious about me if I go up- country." It was characteristic of her that the same night she heard of her mother's death she conducted her regular prayer-meeting: she felt that her mother would have wished her to do so, and she went through the service with a breaking heart, none knowing what had happened.

She wrote hungrily for all details of the last hours, and specified the keepsakes she wished to have. "I would like something to look at," was her repeated cry. To her friend who had taken charge of the home she was for ever grateful. In the midst of her grief she was thoughtful for her welfare and attended to the minutest details, even repaying the sixpences expended for the postage of her letters to Calabar. All admirers of Mary Slessor will honour this lowly Scotswoman who came to her help in the day of her greatest need, and who quietly and efficiently fulfilled her task....

So the home life, the source of warmth and sweetness and sympathy, was closed down and she turned to face the future alone.

CHAPTER IX
THE SORROWS OF CREEK TOWN

Again three Marys were in close association—Miss Mary Edgerley, Miss Mary Johnstone, and Miss Mary Slessor. During the year, however, the two former proceeded home on furlough, and the last was left in entire charge of the women's side of the work at Creek Town. It was the final stage of her training for the larger responsibilities that awaited her. There was at first little in the situation to beguile her spirits. It was a bad season of rain and want, and she was seldom out of the abodes of sickness and death. So great was the destitution that she lived on rice and sauce, in order to feed the hungry. And never had she suffered so much from fever as she did now in Creek Town.

Her duties lay in the Day School, Sunday School, Bible Class, and Infant Class, but, as usual, the more personal aspect of the work engaged her chief energies. The training of her household, which, as she was occupying a part of Mr. Goldie's house and had less accommodation, was a small one then, took much of her time and thought and wit. First in her affections came Janie, now a big and strong girl of four years, and as wild as a boy, who kept her in constant hot- water. She was a link with the home that had been, and Mary regarded her as specially her own: she shared her bed and her meals, and even her thoughts, for she would talk to her about those who had gone. The child's memory of Britain soon faded, but she never ceased to pray for "all in Scotland who remember us." She was made more of than was good for her, but was always brought to her level outside of Creek Town. Mary had heard that both her parents were dead, but one day the father appeared at the Mission House. She asked him to come and look at his child. He shrugged his shoulders, and said, "Let me look from a distance." Mary seized him and drew him towards the child, who was trembling with terror. In response to a command in Efik the girl threw her arms around his neck, and his face relaxed and became almost beautiful. When he looked into her eyes, and she hid her head on his breast, the victory was complete. He set her upon his knee and would scarcely give her up. Although he lived a long way off he returned every other day with his new wife and a gift of food.

Next came a girl of six years, whose father was a Christian. She also was full of tricks, and, with Janie, was enough for one house. But there was also Okin, a boy of about eight, whose mother was a slave with no voice in his upbringing, but whose mistress wished him to be trained up for God, a mischievous fellow whose new clothes lasted usually about a week, but willing and affectionate and, on the whole, good; and another boy of ten called Ekim, a son of the King of Old Town, whose mother gave him to Mary when she first went out. On her departure for Scotland he had gone back to his heathen home and its fashions, but returned to her when she settled in Creek Town. He was truthful, warm-hearted, and clever, and as a free boy and heir to a responsible position the moulding of his character gave her much thought and care. The last was Inyang, a girl of thirteen, but bigger than Mary herself, possessing no brains, but for faithfulness, truthfulness, honesty, and industry without a peer. She hated to dress or to leave the kitchen, but she washed, baked, and did the housework without assistance, and was kind to the children. These constituted her inner circle, but she was always taking in and caring for derelict children. At this time there were several in the house or yard. Two were twins five months old, whom she had found lying on the ground discarded and forlorn, and who had developed into beautiful children. Their father was a drunken parasite, with a number of wives, whom he battered and beat in turn. Another castaway came to her in a wretched state. The father had stolen a dog, and the mother had helped him to eat it. The owner threw down a native charm at their door, and the woman sickened and died, and as all believed that the medicine had killed her no one would touch the child. The woman's mistress was a daughter of old King Eyo, and a friend of Mary, and she sent the infant, dirty and starved, to the Mission House with her compliments. Mary washed and fed it and nursed it back to decent life, but on sending to the mistress a request that one of the slave women might care for it, she got the reply, "Let it die." She let it live.

In the mornings, while busy with her household, there were perpetual interruptions. Sick folk came to have their ailments diagnosed and prescribed for. Some of the diseases she attended to were of the most loathsome type, but that made no difference in her compassionate care. Hungry people came to her to be fed, those in trouble visited her to obtain advice and help, disputes were referred to her to be settled. When all these cases had been dealt with she would go her round of the yards, the inmates of which had come to look upon her as a mother. She would sit down and chat with them and discuss their homes, children, marketing, illness, or whatever subject interested them, sometimes scolding them, but always leading them to the only things that mattered. "If I told you what I have seen and known of human sorrow during the past months you would weep till your heart ached," she wrote to a friend. Some of her experiences she could not tell; they revealed such depths of depravity and horror that the actions of the wild beasts of the bush were tame in comparison.

At Creek Town, as elsewhere, it was not easy to tabulate what had been achieved, as the fact that women could not make open confession without incurring the gravest penalties kept the missionaries ignorant of the effect of their work. But Mary saw behind the veil; she knew quiet women whose souls looked out of their eyes, and who were more in touch with the unseen than they dared tell; women who prayed and communed with God even while condemned to heathen practices. There was one blind woman whom she placed far before herself in the Christian race:

She is so poor that she has not one farthing in the world but what she gets from us—not a creature to do a thing for her, her house all open to rain and sun, and into which the cows rush at times—but blind Mary is our one living, bright, clear light. Her voice is ever set to music, a miracle to the people here, who only know how to groan and grumble at the best. She is ever praising the Lord for some wonderful manifestation of mercy and love, and her testimony to her Saviour is not a shabby one. The other day I heard the King say that she was the only visible witness among the Church members in the town, but he added, "She is a proper one." Far advanced in spiritual knowledge and experience, she knows the deep things of God. That old hut is like a heaven here to more than me.

"Pray for us here" was the appeal in all her letters to Scotland at this time. "Pray in a business-like fashion, earnestly, definitely, statedly."

For herself she found a friend in King Eyo, to whom she could go at any time and relate her troubles and receive sympathy and support. She, in turn, was often in his State room advising him regarding the private and complicated affairs of his little kingdom and his relations with the British Government. He honoured her in various ways, but to her the dumb affection of a slave woman whom she had saved was more than all the favours which others, high in the social scale, sought to show her.

CHAPTER X
THE FULNESS OF THE TIME

The question of her future location received much consideration. The needs of the stations on the Cross River, the highway into the interior, were urgent, and it was thought by some that the interests of the Mission called for her presence there, but her mind could not be turned from the direction in which she believed she could do the best work. She was essentially a pioneer. Her thoughts were for ever going forward, looking past the limitations and the hopes of others, into the fields beyond teeming with populations as yet unreached. She was of the order of spirits to which Dr. Livingstone belonged. Like him she said, "I am ready to go anywhere, provided it be forward." From the districts inland came reports of atrocity and wrong: accusations of witchcraft, the ordeal of the poison bean, the shooting of slaves, and the destruction of infants; and she felt the impelling call to go and attack these evils. It was not that she did not recognise the value of base-work, of order and organisation and routine.

The fact that she spent twelve years in patient and loyal service at Duke Town, Old Town, and Creek Town demonstrates how important she considered these to be. But they had been years of training meant to perfect her powers before she went forward on her own path to realise the vision given her from above, and they were now ended. For her the fulness of the time had come, and with it the way opened up. The local Mission Committee decided, in October 1886, to send her into the district of Okoyong, and informed the authorities in Scotland of the fact, carefully adding that this was in line with her own desire.

A change had just been made in the relation of the women on the staff of the Mission to the administration at home. The Zenana Scheme of the Church had been constituted as a distinct department of the Foreign Mission operations in 1881, and having appealed to the women of the congregations, had proved a success. It was now thought expedient that the Calabar lady agents should be brought into the scheme, and accordingly, in May 1886, they became responsible to the Zenana Committee, and through them to the Foreign Mission Board. The Zenana Committee recommended that the arrangement regarding Mary should be carried out, and the Foreign Mission Board agreed.

THIRD PHASE

1888-1902. Age 40-54.

THE CONQUEST OF OKOYONG

"I am going to a new tribe up-country, a fierce, cruel people, and every one tells me that they will kill me. But I don't fear any hurt—only to combat their savage customs will require courage and firmness on my part."

CHAPTER I
A TRIBE OF TERRORISTS

Some time in the dim past a raiding force had swept down from the mountains to the east of Calabar, entered the triangle of dense forest-land formed by the junction of the Cross and Calabar Hirers, fought and defeated the Ibibios who dwelt there, and taken possession of the territory. They were of the tribe of Okoyong believed to be an outpost, probably the most westerly outpost, of the Bantu race of Central and South Africa, who had thrust themselves forward like a wedge into negro-land. Physically they were of a higher type than the people of Calabar. They were taller and more muscular, their nose was higher, the mouth and chin were firmer, their eye was more fearless and piercing, and their general bearing contrasted strongly with that of the supine negro of the coast.

To their superior bodily development they added the worst qualities of heathenism: there was not a phase of African devilry in which they did not indulge. They were openly addicted to witchcraft and the sacrifice of animals. They were utterly lawless and contemptuous of authority. Among themselves slave-stealing, plunder of property, theft of every kind, went on indiscriminately. To survive in the struggle of life a man required to possess wives and children and slaves—in the abundance of these lay his power. But if, through incompetence or sickness or misfortune, he failed he was regarded as the lawful prey of the chief nearest him. To weaken the House of a neighbour was as clear a duty as to strengthen one's own. Oppression and outrage were of common occurrence. So suspicious were they even of each other that the chiefs and their retainers lived in isolated clearings with armed scouts constantly on the watch on all the pathways, and they ate and worked with their weapons ready to their hands. Even Egbo law with all its power was often resisted by the slaves and women regardless of the consequences. No free Egbo man would submit to be dictated to by the Egbo drum sent by another. A fine might be imposed, but he would sit unsubdued and sullen, and then obtain his revenge by seizing or murdering some passing victim. But all combined in a common enmity against other tribes, and the region was enclosed with a fence of terrorism as impenetrable as a ring of steel. The Calabar people were hated because of the favoured position they enjoyed on the coast, and their wealth and power; and a state of chronic war existed with them. Each sought to outrival the other in the number of heads captured or the number of slaves stolen or harboured, and naturally there was no end to the fighting. All efforts to bring them together in the interests of trade had been in vain. Even British authority was defied, and messages from the Consul were ignored or treated with contempt.

They had their own idea of justice and judicial methods, and trials by ordeal formed the test of innocence or guilt, the two commonest being by burning oil and poison. In the one case a pot was filled with palm oil which was brought to the boil. The stuff was poured over the hands of the prisoner, and if the skin became blistered he was adjudged to be guilty and punished. In the other case the eséré bean—the product of a vine—was pounded and mixed with water and drunk: if the body ejected the poison it was a sign of innocence. This method was the surest and least troublesome—for the investigation, sentence, and punishment were carried out simultaneously—unless the witch-doctor had been influenced, which sometimes happened, for there were various means of manipulating the test.

These tests were applied when it was desired to discover a thief, or when a village wanted to know whose spirit dwelt in the leopard that slew a goat, or when a chief wished to prove that his wife was faithful to him in her heart, but chiefly in cases of sickness or death. They believed that sickness was unnatural, and that death never occurred except from extreme old age. When a freeman became ill or died, sorcery would be alleged. The witchdoctor would be called in, and he would name one individual after another, and all, bond and free, were chained and tried, and there would be much grim merriment as the victims writhed in agony and their heads were chopped off. The skulls would be kept in the family as trophies. Occasionally the relations of the victims would be powerful enough to take exception to the summary procedure and seek redress by force of arms, and a vendetta would reign for years.

If a man or woman were blamed for some evil deed an appeal could be made to the law of substitution, and a sufficient number of slaves could be furnished as would be equivalent for themselves, and these would be killed in their stead. The eldest son of a free House, for instance, would be spared by the sacrifice of the life of a younger brother.

The fact that a man's position in the spirit-world was determined by his rank and wealth in this one, demanded the sacrifice of much life when chiefs died. A few months before Miss Slessor went up amongst them a chief of moderate means died, and with him were buried eight slave men, eight slave women, ten girls, ten boys, and four free wives. These were in addition to the men and women who died as a result of taking the poison ordeal. Even when death was due to natural decay the retinue provided was the same. After her settlement she made careful enquiry, and found that the number of lives sacrificed annually at the instance of this custom could not have averaged fewer than 150 within a radius of twenty miles, while the same number must have died from ordeals and decapitation on charges of causing sickness. To these had to be added the number killed in the constant warfare.

Infanticide was also responsible for much destruction of life. Twin murder was practised with an even fiercer zeal than it had been in Calabar. Child life in general was of little value.

It was significant of the state of the district that gin, guns, and chains were practically the only articles of commerce that entered it. Gin or rum was in every home. It was given to every babe: all work was paid for in it: every fine and debt could be redeemed with it: every visitor had to be treated to it: every one drank it, and many drank it all the time. Quarrels were the outcome of it. Then the guns came into play. After that the chains and padlocks.

Women were often the worst where drink was concerned, There were certain bands formed of those born in the same year who were allowed freer action than others: they could handle gun and sword, and were used for patrol and fighting purposes, and were so powerful that they compelled concessions from Egbo. They exacted fines for breach of their rules, and feasted and drank and danced for days and nights at a time at the expense of the offenders.

Such lawlessness and degradation at the very doors had long caused the Calabar Presbytery much thought. Efforts had been made to enter the district both from the Cross and the Calabar Rivers. In one of his tours of exploration Mr. Edgerley was seized, with the object of being held for a ransom of rum, and it was only with difficulty that he escaped. Others were received less violently, though every member of the tribe was going about with guns on full cock. Asked why, they said, "Inside or outside, speaking, eating, or sleeping, we must have them ready for use. We trust no man." When they learned of the new laws in Calabar their amazement was unbounded. "Killing for witchcraft prohibited!" they exclaimed. "What steps have been taken to prevent witchcraft from killing?" "Widows not compelled to sit for more than a month in seclusion and filth!—outrageous!" "Twins and their mothers taken to Duke Town—horrible! Has no calamity happened?"

Very little result was achieved from these tours of observation. A Calabar teacher was ultimately induced to settle amongst them, but after a shooting affray was compelled to fly for his life. Missionaries, however, are never daunted by difficulties, nor do they acquiesce in defeat. Ever, like their Master, they stand at the door and knock. Once again the challenge was taken up, and this time by a woman. So difficult was the position, that the negotiations for Miss Slessor's settlement lasted a year. Three times parties from the Mission went up, she accompanying them, only to find the people—every man, woman, and child—armed and sullen, and disinclined to promise anything. "I had often a lump in my throat," she wrote, "and my courage repeatedly threatened to take wings and fly away—though nobody guessed it!"

At last, in June 1888, in spite of her fears, she resolved to go up and make final arrangements for her sojourn.

CHAPTER II
IN THE ROYAL CANOE

She went up the river in state. Ever ready to do her a kindness, King Eyo had provided her with the Royal canoe, a hollow tree-trunk twenty feet long, and she lay in comfort under the cool cover of a framework of palm leaves, freshly lopped from the tree, and shut off from the crew by a gaudy curtain. Beneath was a piece of Brussels carpet, and about her were arranged no fewer than six pillows, for the well-to-do natives of Calabar made larger and more skilful use of these than the Europeans.

The scene was one of quiet beauty; there was a clear sky and a windless air; the banks of the river—high and dense masses of vegetation— glowed with colour; the broad sweep of water was like a sheet of molten silver and shimmered and eddied to the play of the gleaming paddles. As they moved easily and swiftly along, the paddlemen, dressed in loin- cloth and singlet, improvised blithe song in her praise. Strange and primitive as were the conditions, she felt she would not have exchanged them for all the luxuries of civilisation.

She needed sustenance, for there was trying work before her, and this a paraffin stove, a pot of tea, a tin of stewed steak, and a loaf of home-made bread gave her. Wise mental preparation also she needed, for there were elements of uncertainty and danger in the situation. The Okoyong might be on the war-path: her paddlers were their sworn enemies: a tactless word or act might ruin the expedition. As the canoe glided along the river she communed with God, and in the end left the issue with Him. "Man," she thought, "can do nothing with such a people."

Arriving at the landing beach she made her way by a forest track to a village of mud huts called Ekenge, four miles inland. Her reception was a noisy one; men, women, and children thronged about her, and called her "Mother," and seemed pleased at her courage at coming alone. The chief, Edem, one of the aristocrats of Okoyong, was sober, but his neighbour at Ifako, two miles farther on, whom she wished to meet, was unfit for human company, and she was not allowed to proceed. She stayed the night at Ekenge, where she gathered the King's boys about her to hold family worship. The crowd of semi-naked people standing curiously watching the proceedings exclaimed in wonder as they heard the words repeated in unison: "God so loved the world," and so on. At ten o'clock the women were still holding her fast in talk. One, the chiefs sister, called Ma Eme, attracted her. "I think," she said, "she will be my friend, and be an attentive hearer of the Gospel." Wearied at last with the strain she was forced to retire into the hut set apart for her.

A shot next morning startled the village. Two women on going outside had been fired at from the bush. In a moment every man had his gun and sword and was searching for the assailant. Mary went with one of the parties, but to find any one in such a labyrinth was impossible, and the task was given up. Going to Ifako she interviewed the chiefs. The charm of her personality, her frankness, her fearlessness, won them over, and they promised her ground for a schoolhouse. Would, she asked, the same privilege be extended to it as to the Mission buildings in Calabar? Would it be a place of refuge for criminals, those charged with witchcraft, or those liable to be killed for the dead, until their case could be taken into consideration? They assented. And the house she would build for herself— would it also be a harbour of refuge? Again they assented. She thanked them and promptly went and chose two sites, one at Ekenge and one at Ifako, about twenty to thirty minutes' walk apart, according to the state of the track, in order that the benefits of the concession might operate over as wide an area as possible. She foresaw, however, that as they were an agricultural and shifting people, and spread over a large extent of territory, she would require to be constantly travelling, and to sleep as often in her hammock as in her bed.

Rejoicing over the improved prospects, she set out on the return journey to Creek Town. It was the rainy season, and ere long the canoe ran into a deluge and she was soaked. Then the tide was so strong that they had to lie in a cove for two hours. The carcase of a huge snake drifted past, followed by a human body. She was on the outlook for alligators, but only saw crowds of crabs on the rotten tree-stumps and black mud fighting as fiercely as the Okoyong people. She was too watchful to sleep, but she heard the boys say softly, "Don't shake the canoe and wake Ma," or "Speak lower and let Ma sleep." When they were once more out on the river she slumbered, and awoke to find the lights of Creek Town shining through the darkness.

When her friends saw her packing her belongings they looked at her in wonder and pity. They said she was going on a forlorn hope, and that no power on earth could subdue the Okoyong save a Consul and a gunboat. But she smiled and went on with her preparations. King Eyo again offered his canoe and paddlers and a number of bearers for her baggage. By Friday evening, August 3, 1888, all was ready, and she lay down to rest but not to sleep. On the morrow she would enter on the great adventure of her life, and the strangeness of it, the seriousness of it, the possibilities it might hold for her, kept her awake and thoughtful throughout the night.

CHAPTER III
THE ADVENTURE OF TAKING POSSESSION

The dawn came to Creek Town grey and wet. The rain fell in torrents, and the negroes, moving about with the packages, grumbled and quarrelled. Wearied and unrefreshed after her sleepless night, Mary was not in the best of spirits, and she was glad to see King Eyo, who had come to supervise the loading and packing of the canoe: his kind eyes, cheery smile, and sympathetic words did her good, and her courage revived. Few of the natives wished her God-speed. One young man said with a sob in his voice, "I will constantly pray for you, but you are courting death." Not great faith for a Christian perhaps, but her own faith at the moment was not so strong that she could afford to cast a stone at him. As the hours wore on, the air of depression became general, and when the party was about to start Mr. Goldie suddenly decided to send one of the Mission staff to accompany her on the journey. Mr. Bishop, the printer, who was standing by, volunteered, and there and then stepped into the canoe. Mary and her retinue of five children stowed themselves into a corner, the paddlers pushed off, and the canoe swept up the river and disappeared in the rain.

The light was fading ere they reached the landing beach for Ekenge, and there was yet the journey of four miles through the dripping forest to be overtaken. It was decided that she should go on ahead with the children in order to get them food and put them to sleep, and that Mr. Bishop and one or two men should follow with dry clothes, cooking utensils, and the door and window needed for the hut, whilst the carriers would come on later with the loads. As Mary faced the forest, now dark and mysterious, and filled with the noises of night, a feeling of helplessness and fear came over her. What unseen perils might she not meet? What would she find at the end? How would she be received on this occasion? Would the natives be fighting or drinking or dancing? Her heart played the coward; she felt a desire to turn and flee. But she remembered that never in her life had God failed her, not once had there been cause to doubt the reality of His guidance and care. Still the shrinking was there; she could not even move her lips in prayer; she could only look up and utter inwardly one appealing word, "Father!"

Surely no stranger procession had footed it through the African forest. First came a boy, about eleven years of age, tired and afraid, a box containing tea, sugar, and bread upon his head, his garments, soaked with the rain, clinging to his body, his feet slipping in the black mud. Behind him was another boy, eight years old, in tears, bearing a kettle and pots. With these a little fellow of three, weeping loudly, tried hard to keep up, and close at his heels trotted a maiden of five, also shaken with sobs. Their white mother formed the rear. On one arm was slung a bundle, and astride her shoulders sat a baby girl, no light burden, so that she had to pull herself along with the aid of branches and twigs. She was singing nonsense—snatches to lighten the way for the little ones, but the tears were perilously near her own eyes. Had ever such a company marched out against the entrenched forces of evil? Surely God had made a mistake in going to Okoyong in such a guise? And yet He often chooses the weakest things of this world to confound and defeat the mighty.

The village was reached at last, but instead of the noise and confusion that form a bush welcome there was absolute stillness. Mary called out and two slaves appeared. They stated that the chief's mother at Ifako had died that morning, and all the people had gone to the carnival. One obtained fire and a little water, while the other made off to carry the news that the white woman had arrived. She undressed the children and hushed them to sleep, and sat in her wet garments and waited. When Mr. Bishop appeared it was to say that the men were exhausted and refused to bring up anything that night. A woman of weaker fibre and feebler faith would have been in despair: Mary acted with her usual decision. The glow of the fire was cheerful and the singing of the kettle tempting, but the morrow was Sunday, there was no food, the children were naked, and she herself wet to the skin. She gave one of the lads who had arrived with Mr. Bishop a lantern, and despatched him to the beach with a peremptory message that the mea must come at once and bring what they could. But knowing their character she asked Mr. Bishop to collect some of the slaves who had been left to watch the farms, and send them after her as carriers, and then, bootless and hatless, she plunged back into the forest.

She had not gone far before one of the other lads came running after her to keep her company; a touch of chivalry which, pleased and comforted her. So dense was the darkness that she often lost sight of her companion's white clothes, and was constantly stumbling and falling. The shrilling of the insects, the pulsation of the fire-flies, the screams of the night-birds and the flapping of their wings, the cries of wild animals, the rush of dark objects, the falling of decayed branches all intensified the weirdness and mystery of the forest gloom. Even the echo of their own voices as they called aloud to frighten the beasts of prey struck on their ears with peculiar strangeness.

By and by came an answer to their cries, and a glimmer of light showed in the darkness. It was the lad with the lantern. As she had surmised, he had failed in his mission. She moved swiftly to the river, splashed into the water, and, reaching the canoe, threw back the cover under which the men were sleeping, and routed them out, dazed and shamefaced. So skilful, however, was she in managing these dusky giants that in a short time, weary as they were, they were working good-humouredly at the boxes. With the assistance of the slaves who came on the scene they transferred what was needed to Ekenge, and by midnight she felt that the worst was over.

Sunday did not find her in more cheerful mood. Her tired limbs refused to move, and wounds she had been unconscious of in the excitement of the journey made themselves felt, while her feet were in such a state that for six weeks afterwards she was unable to wear boots. Whether it was the persistent rain and the mud and the weariness and the squalid surroundings, or the fact that the tribe she had come to civilise and evangelise were given over to the service of the devil, or that her faith had weakened, or whether it was all of these together, her first Sunday in Okoyong was one of the saddest she ever experienced. More than once she was on the verge of tears.

And yet she was eager to begin work. Prudence, however, held her back from visiting the scene of debauchery at Ifako. A few women had come home with fractious babies, or to procure more food for the revellers, and gathering these about her she held a little service, telling them in her simple and direct way the story of the Christ who came from the Unseen to make their lives sweeter and happier.

It was the first faint gleam of a better day for Okoyong.

CHAPTER IV
FACING AN ANGRY MOB

The room allotted to Mary was one of those in the women's yard or harem of Edem the chief, and had been previously used by a free wife, who had left its mud floor and mud walls in a filthy state. At one entrance she caused a door to be hung, while a hole was made in the wall and a window frame fitted in. The work was rude and gaps yawned round the sides, but she ensured sufficient privacy by draping them with bedcovers. The absence of the villagers at Ifako gave her time to complete the work, and with her own hands she filled in the spaces with mud. She also cleared a portion of the ground set apart for her and circled it with a fence, and within this did her washing. But soon there were calls upon her.

"He took a little child and set him in the midst." Her work began with a child. In a fight between Okoyong and Calabar a man of Ekenge had been beheaded. His head was recovered and sent home, thus removing the disgrace, but his wife did not survive the shock, and left a baby girl, which was now brought to Mary. It had been fed on a little water, palm oil, and cane juice, and looked less like an infant than a half- boiled chicken. Its appearance provoked mirth in the yard, but she stooped down and lifted it and took it to her heart, resolving to give it a double share of the care and comfort of which it had been defrauded. As she carried it about in her arms, or sat with it in her lap, she was regarded with a kind of amused astonishment. But the old grandmother came and blessed her. At first the child rallied to the new treatment: it grew human-like: sometimes Mary thought it looked bonnie: but in a few days it drooped and died.

The bodies of children were usually placed anywhere in the earth near the huts or under the bush by the wayside, but she dressed the tiny form in white and laid it in a provision box and covered it with flowers. A native carried the box to a spot which she had reserved in her ground: here a grave was dug, and she stood beside it and prayed. The grandmother knelt at her feet, sobbing. Looking on at a distance, curious and scornful, were the revellers from Ifako; they had heard of the proceedings, and had come to witness the white woman's "witchcraft." All that they said in effect when they saw the good box and the white robe was, "Why this waste?" And so the work in Okoyong was consecrated by the death and Christian burial of a little child.

When the people came crowding back from the devil-making they sought out a young lad who had detached himself from the orgies and remained in the village, where he had been very attentive to Mary. They accused him of deserting their ancient customs. She saw him standing in their midst near a pot of oil which was being heated over a fire, and noticed the chief, in front going through some movements and the lad holding out his arms, but was unaware of what was taking place until she saw a man seize a ladle, plunge it into the boiling oil, and advance to the boy. In a moment the truth flashed upon her and she darted forward, but was too late. The stuff was poured over the lad's hands, and he shuddered in agony. It was doubtful whether her intervention at that early period would have done any good. They were following the law of the country, and if she had managed to prevent the act they would probably have resorted to the ordeal thereafter in secret; and her object was to show them a better way.

Immediately after this the men of the village left on an expedition of revenge against a number of mourners with whom they had quarrelled. A week of rioting followed. Then a freeman died in the neighbourhood, and once more the village was deserted. Mary, meanwhile, moved hither and thither, making friends with the women, healing the sick, tending the children, and doing any little service that came in her way.

The return to normal conditions brought her into active conflict with the powers of evil. The mistress of a harem in the vicinity bought a good-looking young woman whom the master coveted, and she became a slave-wife. She appeared sullen and unhappy. One afternoon Mary saw her mudding a house that was being built for a new free-born wife, and spoke to her kindly in passing. A few minutes later the girl made her way to one of her master's farms, and sat down in the hut of a slave. The latter was alarmed, knowing well what the consequences would be, but she refused to move. The man went off to his work, and she walked into the forest and hanged herself. Next morning the slave was brought in heavily ironed, and at a palaver the master and his relatives decreed he must die; they had been degraded by being associated in this way with a common slave.

Mary, who was present, protested against the injustice of the sentence; the man, she argued, had done no wrong; it was not his fault that the girl had gone to his hut. "But," was the reply, "he has used sorcery and put the thought into the girl's mind, and the witch-doctor has pronounced him guilty." She persisted. The crowd became angry and excited; they surged round her demanding why a stranger who was there on sufferance should interfere with the dignity and power of free-born people, and clamoured for the instant death of the prisoner. Threats were shouted, guns and swords were waved, and the position grew critical, but she stood her ground, quiet and cool and patient. Her tact, her good humour, that spiritual force which seemed to emanate from her in times of peril, at last prevailed. The noise and confusion calmed down, and ultimately it was decided to spare the man's life. She had won her first victory.

But the victim was loaded with chains, placed in the women's yard, starved, and then flogged, and his body cruelly cut in order to exorcise the powers of sorcery that were in him. When Mary went to him he was a bruised and bleeding heap of flesh lying unconscious by the post to which he was fastened. The women in the yard were sitting about indifferent to his plight.

CHAPTER V
LIFE IN HAREM

For many weeks she was an inmate of the harem, a witness of its degraded intimacies, enduring the pollution of its moral and physical atmosphere, with no other support than hallowed memories and the companionship of her Bible. Her room was next that of the chief and his head wife: the quarters of five lesser wives were close by; other wives whose work and huts were at the farms shared the yard with the slaves, visitors, and children; two cows—small native animals that do not produce milk— occupied the apartment on the other side of the partition; goats, fowls, cats, rats, cockroaches, and centipedes were everywhere. In her own room the three boys slept behind an erection of boxes and furniture, and the two girls shared her portion. Every night her belongings had to be taken outside in order to provide sufficient accommodation for them all, and as it was the wet season they had usually to undergo a process of drying in the sun each day before being replaced.

There was a ceaseless coming and going in the yard, a perpetual chattering of raucous voices. The wives were always bickering and scolding, the tongue of one of them going day and night, her chief butt being a naked and sickly slave, who was for ever being flogged. There was no sleep for Mary when this woman had any grievance, real or imaginary, on her mind.

Both wives and visitors conceived it their duty to sit and entertain their white guest. To an African woman the idea of loneliness is terrible, and good manners made it incumbent that as large a gathering as possible should keep a stranger company. All is implied in the word "home," its sacredness and freedom, its privacy, lies outside the knowledge and experience of polygamists. Kind and neighbourly as the women were, they could not understand the desire of Mary to be sometimes by herself. She needed silence and solitude; her spirit craved for communion with her Father, and she longed for a place in which to pour out her heart aloud to Him. As often as politeness permitted, she fled to the ground reserved for her, but they followed her there, and in desperation she would take a machete and hack at the bush, praying the while, so that her voice was lost in the noise she made.

One woman of mark was Eme Ete—Ma Eme as she was usually called—a sister of the master, the same who had attracted her attention on the previous visit. She was the widow of a big chief, and had just returned from the ceremonies in connection with her husband's death, where she had undergone a terrible ordeal. All his wives lay under suspicion, and each brought to the place of trial a white fowl, and from the way in which it fluttered after its head was cut off the judgment was pronounced. The strain was such that when the witch-doctor announced Ma Eme free from guilt she fainted. Big-boned and big-featured, she had been fattened to immensity. One day Mary pointed to some marks on her arms and said, "White people have marks like these," showing the vaccination cicatrice on her own arm. Ma Eme simply said, "These are the marks of the teeth of my husband." In that land a man could do as he liked with his free-born wife—bite her, beat her, kill her, and nobody cared. When consorting with the others Ma Eme had the coarse tone common to all, but as she spoke to Mary or the children her voice softened and her instincts and manners were refined and gentle. A mother to every one, she scolded, encouraged, and advised in turn, and when the chief was drunk or peevish she was always between him and his wives as intercessor and peacemaker. She watched over Mary, brought her food, looked after her comfort, and helped her in every way, and did it with the delicacy and reserve of a well-bred lady. Unknown to all she constituted herself Mary's ally, becoming a sort of secret intelligence department, and, at the risk of her life, keeping her informed of all the underground doings of the tribe. "A noble woman," Mary called her, "according to her lights and knowledge."

The wives appeared to have less liberty than the slaves. How carefully guarded their position was by unwritten law Mary had reason to know. A girl-wife employed a slave-man to do work for a day. His master unexpectedly sent for him, and he asked the girl for the food which was part of his wage. She at first declined; her husband was absent, and it was against the law of the harem, but as he insisted she yielded and handed him a piece of yam. When this became known she was seized, bound, and condemned to undergo the ordeal of the burning oil. It was an occasion for feasting and merriment, and as the fun progressed the cords were gradually tightened until she screamed piteously with the pain. Mary went and faced the crowd and pled for her release. There was the usual uproar, but she succeeded in carrying off the victim, who was kept chained to her verandah until the dancing and rioting ended with the dawn.

Conditions in the harem were not favourable to child life. The mothers were ignorant and superstitious, and there was no discipline or training. Infants were often given intoxicating drink in order that fun might be made of their antics and foolish talk. As they grew up they learned nothing but what was vile. The slave children became thieves— they had to steal in order to live. But if caught they would be chained to a post and starved or branded with fire-sticks. They became deceitful—they had to lie in order to gain favour. In this they simply followed the instinctive impulses of their nature and of the lower nature about them. As the insects mimicked inanimate objects to escape injury or death, so they simulated the truth to save themselves a beating or mutilation. The free-born children did not require to steal, but lying was in the air like a contagion, and none could avoid its influence. Of the older boys and girls Mary wrote: "They are such a pest to every one that it is almost impossible to love them." Yet with a divine pity she gathered them to her and mothered them.

Her earlier observations of the character of the African women were confirmed by her sojourn in the harem. Hard and callous, as a result of centuries of bush law and outrage, their patience and self-repression under the most terrible indignities were to her a marvel. They were not devoid of fine feeling, and beneath the surface of their nature the flow of affection and pity often ran pure and sweet. On one occasion a large number of prisoners were chained previous to undergoing the ordeal of the poison bean. There were mothers with infants in their arms, who throughout a hot day lay on the ground in torture and terror. At dusk the guards left them for a time, and seizing the chance a few of the older women stole tremblingly towards them with water, which they gave to the children and divided the remainder among the mothers. Anticipating such an opportunity Mary had had some rice cooked, and this also the women smuggled to the prisoners. Had they been discovered their lives would have been forfeited.

Bands of women of the special class already described came from a distance to see the white "Ma," always more or less under the influence of drink; loose in speech, and destitute of modesty, these Amazons made her angry. They would appear at night and demand admittance to the yard in the hope of obtaining rum and other good things from the wealthy white woman. When barred out they threatened reprisals. The chief, who never allowed his wives to go out of the yard to dance even with his own relatives, stood on guard all night before his guest's room, and it was only after sunrise, when all were astir, that they were admitted. Haggard after their night's debauch, they presented a sorry sight, their bare bodies painted and decked with beads, coloured wools, and scraps of red and yellow silk, and many with babies at their side. Mary regarded them with pity, but all they could extract from her was disapproval and rebuke, and they left with threats to make her position untenable.

Some of the scenes she witnessed in the harem cannot be described. "Had I not felt my Saviour close beside me," she said, "I would have lost my reason." When at home the memory of these would make her wince and flush with indignation and shame. She had no patience with people who expounded the theory of the innocence of man outside the pale of civilisation—she would tell them to go and live for a month in a West African harem.

CHAPTER VI
STRANGE DOINGS

The sound of native voices chanting came through the brooding stillness of the hot afternoon. With the wild war-song of Okoyong the forest familiar, but words were strange and wonderful;

> *Jesus the Son of God came down to earth*
> *He came to save us from our sins.*
> *He was born poor that He might feel for us.*
> *Wicked men killed Him and hanged Him on a tree,*
> *He rose and went to heaven to prepare a place for us....*

They were sung with a tremendous force, and as each voice fell into the part which suited it, the result was a harmony that thrilled the heart of the white woman who listened.

It was Mary Slessor's day school.

For a people possessing no written language, no literature, no knowledge beyond that handed down from father to son, the first step towards right living, apart from the preaching of the Gospel, is education. Schools go hand in hand with churches in missionary effort. Mary began hers before she had the buildings in which to teach, one at Ekenge and the other at Ifako. The latter was held in the afternoon in order that she might be back in her yard by sunset. The schoolroom was the verandah of a house by the wayside; the seats were pieces of firewood; the equipment an alphabet card hung on one of the posts.

At first the entire population turned out and conned the letters, but as novelty wore off and the men and women returned to their work the attendance dropped to thirty. Good progress was made, and ere long the dark-skinned pupils were spelling out words of one and two syllables. The lesson ended with a scripture lesson, a short prayer, and the singing of the sentences she taught. The last was so much enjoyed that it was often dark before she could get away.

The school at Ekenge was held in the outer yard of the chief's house in the evening, when all the wives and slaves were at leisure. Men and women, old and young, bond and free, crowded and hustled into the yard, amidst much noise and fun. After a lesson on the alphabet and the multiplication-table she conducted worship. It was a weird scene—the white woman, slim and slight, standing bareheaded and barefooted beside a little table on which were a lamp and the Book; in front, squatting on the ground, the mass of half-naked people as dark as the night, their shining faces here and there catching the gleam of the light; the earnest singing that drowned the voices of the forest, and the strange hush that fell, as in grave sweet tones the speaker prayed to what was to them the Unknown God.

The tale of such doings was carried to every corner of Okoyong, and invitations began to arrive from chiefs in other parts. Some, who were known as "the terror of Calabar," came personally to ask her to visit their villages, and all laid down their arms at the entrance to her yard before entering into her presence. But her own chief warned her against acting too hastily, and she would probably have followed his advice and sought to strengthen her position at Ekenge and Ifako had the matter not been taken out of her hands.

CHAPTER VII
FIGHTING A GRIM FOE

The principal wife of a harem in close neighbourhood to Mary went to pay a visit to her son and daughter at a village in the vicinity of the Cross River, some eight hours distant from Ekenge. She found the chief so near death that the head man and the people were waiting outside, ready for the event. Hastening into the harem she spoke of the power of the white "Ma" at Ekenge. Had she not cured her grandchild who had bees very ill? Had she not saved many others? Let them send for her and the chief would not die. Her advice was acted upon, and a deputation was despatched with a bottle and four rods—about the value of a shilling— to secure Mary's aid. She was called to the private room of her chief, where she found the messengers. "What is the matter with him?" she asked. As no one knew she decided to go and see for herself. Edem and Ma Eme objected—the length of the journey, the deep streams to be crossed, the heavy rains, made the task impossible. "I am going to get ready," was her reply. Finding her immovable, the chief turned with a face of gloom to the deputation and sent, them back with a demand for an escort of freewomen and armed men. Mary imagined he was merely endeavouring to mark time until the death took place: in reality he saw the district given over to violence and murder, and she in the midst and her life imperilled.

She passed a sleepless night. Was she right, after all, in taking so great a risk? She laid the matter where she laid all her problems, and came to the conclusion that she was. With the morning appeared the guard of women, who intimated that the armed men would join them outside the village. The rain was falling as they set out later came down in torrents, continuous, and pitiless. Her boots were soon abandoned; then her stockings; next her umbrella, broken in battle with the vegetation, was thrown aside. Bit by bit her clothes, too heavy to be endured, were transferred to the calabashes carried by the women on their heads, and in the lightest of garments she struggled on through the steaming bush.

Three hours of trudging brought her to a market-place where, in the clearing atmosphere, hundreds of natives were gathering. They gazed at her in amazement. Feeling humiliated at her appearance, she slunk shyly and swiftly through their midst and went on, wondering if she had "lost face" and their respect. Afterwards she learnt that the self-denial and courage which that walk in the rain exhibited had done more than anything else to win their hearts. Others, however, were not so well- disposed. At one town the old chief was anything but courtly, and only with reluctance allowed her to pass.

When she reached the sick man's village and looked into the grim expectant faces of the armed crowd, she felt as if she were walking into a den of wild beasts. At any moment the signal might be given, and the slaughter of the retinue for the spirit-land begin. The women, silent and fear-stricken, carried off her wet clothes to dry. She was cold and feverish, but went straight to the patient and tended him as well as she could. Then she turned to the pile of odds and ends of garments which had been collected for her, and looked at them with a shudder. But there was no alternative, and, arraying herself in the rags, she went forth to meet the critical gaze of the crowd.

The medicine she had brought had proved insufficient, and more must be obtained; many lives, she knew, depended upon it. To go back to Ekenge was out of the question. Was there, she asked the people about her, a way to Ikorofiong? The Rev. Alexander Cruickshank was stationed there, and he would supply what was needed. They confessed that there was a road to the river and a canoe could be got to cross, but they dared not go there, they would never come back, they would be seized and killed. Some one told her that a Calabar man, whose mother was an Okoyong woman and who came to trade, was living in his canoe not far off. "Seek him," said she. He was found, but would not land until assured that it was a white woman who wanted him. Mary prevailed upon him to undertake the journey; and he returned with all she required and more. With the thoughtfulness and kindliness of pioneer missionaries Mr. and Mrs. Cruickshank sent over tea and sugar and other comforts and, what she valued not less, a letter of cheer and sympathy. Hot with fever, racked with headache, she brewed the tea in a basin, and it seemed to her a royal feast. The world of friends had drawn nearer, she felt less lonely, her spirits revived.

The patient drew back from the valley of death, regained consciousness, and gathered strength; and the women looking on in wonder, became obedient and reliable nurses; the freemen thought no more of sacrifice and blood; the whole community had visions of peace; they expressed a wish to make terms with Calabar and to trade with the Europeans and learn "book." She was engaged all day in answering questions. Morning and evening she held a simple service, and seldom had a more reverent audience. Much worn out, she left them at last with regret, promising to be always their mother, to try and secure a teacher, and to come again and see them.

Her faith and fearlessness had been justified, and she had her reward, for from that time forward Okoyong was free to her.

CHAPTER VIII
THE POWER OF WITCHCRAFT

The belief in witchcraft dominated the lives of the people like a dark shadow more menacing than the shadow of death. Taking advantage of their superstition and fear the witch-doctors—some of the cunningest rogues the world has produced—held them in abject bondage, and Mary was constantly at battle with the results of their handiwork.

The chief of Ekenge was lying ill. Since she had taken up residence in his yard he had treated her with consideration, and guarded her interests and well-being, and now came the opportunity to reciprocate his kindness. She found him suffering from an abscess in his back, and gave herself up to the task of nursing and curing him. All was going well, when one morning, as she entered with his tea and bread, she saw a living fowl impaled on a stick. Scattered about were palm branches and eggs, and round the neck and limbs of the patient were placed various charms. The brightness of her greeting died away. Edem was suspiciously voluble and frank, flattered the goodness and ability of the white people, but said they could not understand the malignity of the black man's heart. "Ma, it has been made known to us that some one is to blame for this sickness, and here is proof of it—all these have been taken out of my back." He held out a parcel which, on opening, she found to contain shot, powder, teeth, bones, seeds, egg-shells, and other odds and ends.

On seeing the collection the natives standing around shook with terror, and frantically denounced the wickedness of the persons who had sought to compass the death of the chief. Mary's heart sank, she knew what the accusation meant. At once, before her eyes, men and women were singled out, and seized and chained and fastened to posts in the yard. Remonstrance, rebuke, argument were in vain. The chief at last became irritated with her importunity, and ordered his retainers to carry him to one of his farms, whither he was accompanied by his wives, those of note belonging to his house, and the prisoners. He forbade "Ma" to follow, and enjoined secrecy upon all, in order that no tales might be carried back to her. But she had her own means of obtaining intelligence of what was going on, and she heard that many others were being chained, as they were denounced by the witch-doctors.

The chief became worse, and stronger measures were decided on: all the suspected must die. Mary was powerless to do more than send a message of stern warning. Days of suspense and prayer followed. On the last night of the year she was lying awake thinking of the old days and the old friends, her heart homesick, and the hot tears in her eyes, when the sound of voices and the flash of a lantern made her start up. It was a deputation from the farm. They had learnt that the native pastor, the Rev. Esien Ukpabio, at Adiabo—the first native convert in Calabar —was skilled in this form of disease, and would "Ma" give them a letter asking him to come over and see the chief? The letter was quickly given, and she returned to her rest and her memories.

When the native pastor asked what was the matter, the reply was that "Some one's soul was troubling the chief." "In that case," he said, "I can do nothing," and no persuasion or bribe could move him from his position. His sister, however, thought it might be well for her to go and see what she could do, and he consented. Under her care the abscess broke and the chief recovered, and all the prisoners were released with the exception of one woman, who was put to death.

Aware of the uncanny way in which his guest heard of things the chief sent his son to forestall any tale-bearer. "No one has been injured," she was assured. "Only one worthless slave woman has been sold to the Inokon." As it was the custom to dispose of slaves who were criminals and incorrigible to this cannibal section of the Aros for food at their high feasts the story was plausible, but she knew better, and when the son added that the three children of the victim had been "quite agreeable," she thought of the misery she had witnessed on their faces. She pretended to believe the message, however, for to have shown knowledge of the murder would have been to condemn scores to the poison ordeal, in order that her informant might be discovered.

When the chief was convalescent it was announced by drum that he would emerge on a certain day from his filth—for the natives do not wash during illness—and that gifts would be received. His wives and friends and slaves brought rum, rods, clothes, goats, and fowls, and there ensued a week of drinking, dancing, and fighting, worse than Mary had yet seen.

In the midst of it all she moved, helpless and lonely, and somewhat sad, yet not without faith in a better time,

CHAPTER IX
SORCERY IN THE PATH

A more extraordinary instance of superstition occurred soon after. A chief in the vicinity, noted far and wide for his ferocity, intimated that he was coming to Ekenge on a visit. It meant trouble for the women, and she prayed earnestly that he might be deterred from his purpose. But he duly appeared, and throwing all her anxiety upon God, she faced him calm and unafraid. Days and nights of wild licence followed, accompanied by an outcrop of disputes, most of which were brought to her to settle.

One morning she found the guest drunk to excess, but determined to return at once to his village. His freemen and slaves were beyond control, and soon the place was in an uproar: swords were drawn, guns were fired, the excitement reached fever heat. With a courage that seemed reckless she hustled them into order and hurried them off and accompanied them for the protection of the villages through which they must pass. She was able to prevent more drink being supplied to them, and all went well until, at one point on the bush track, they came upon a plantain sucker stuck in the ground, and, lying about, a cocoanut shell, palm leaves, and nuts. The fierce warriors who had been challenging each other and every one they came across to fight to the death, were paralysed at the sight of the rubbish, and turning with a yell of terror rushed back the way they had come. Mary sought forcibly to restrain them, but, frantic with fright, they eluded her grasp, and ran shrieking towards the last town they had passed to wreak vengeance on the sorcerers. She ran with them, praying for swiftness and strength: she passed them one by one, and breathlessly threw herself into the middle of the path, and dared them to advance. She felt she was almost as mad as they were, but she relied on a Power Who had never failed her, and He did not fail her now. Her audacity awed them: they stopped, protested, argued, and gradually their hot anger, resentment, and fear died down, and eventually they retraced their steps. She took up the "medicine" they dreaded, and pitched it into the bush, ironically invoking the sorcery to pass into her body if it wanted a victim. But nobody could persuade them to proceed that way, and they made a long detour.

Unfortunately drink was smuggled to the band, and fighting began. She induced the more sober to assist her to tie a few of the desperadoes to trees. Leaving these, the company went on dancing, brandishing arms, embracing each other, and committing such folly that she felt that she could bear it no longer. As the swift twilight fell she called her few followers and returned, releasing on the way the delinquents bound to the trees, but sending them homewards with their hands fastened behind their backs. On passing the scene of the sorcery she picked up the plantain sucker, laughingly remarking that she would plant it in her yard, and give the witchcraft it possessed an opportunity of proving its powers.

Nothing is hidden in an African community, news travels swiftly. Next morning came a messenger from the chief she had escorted home. It had been a terrible night, he said; the native doctor had come to his master and had taken teeth, shot, hair, seeds, fish-bones, salt, and what not, out of his leg, If they had been left in the body they would have killed him. It was the plantain sucker that was to blame, and his master demanded it back. Mary read the menace in the request: the plant was to be used as evidence against some victim. Argument and sarcasm alike failed, and she was obliged to hand it over, Edem was standing by. "That," he grimly remarked, "means the death of some one."

On the arrival of the sucker native oaths were administered to all in the village accused of the sorcery, ordeals of various kinds were imposed on young and old, slave and free, and the life-blood of a man was demanded by way of settlement of the matter. Strong in their innocence the people resisted the claim, but by guile the chief's myrmidons caught and handcuffed a fine-looking young man belonging to one of the best families and dragged him into hiding. Any attempt to effect a rescue would have meant his murder, and in their dilemma the people thought of the white "Ma" and sent and begged her to come and plead with the chief for the life and liberty of the prisoner.

She had never a more unpleasant task, for she detested the callous savage, but there was nothing else to do; and she went depending less upon herself than upon God. She walked tremblingly into the man's presence, but her fear soon passed into disgust and indignation. He was the personification of brutality, selfishness, and cowardice. Laughing at her entreaties he told her to bring the villagers and let them fight it out. She pointed out that neither he nor his House had suffered by what had happened; that the accused people had taken every oath and ordeal prescribed by their laws; and that his procedure was therefore unjust and unlawful, "It is due to your presence alone that I escaped," he retorted; "they murdered, me in intention if not in fact." His head wile backed him up, and both became so rude and offensive to Mary that it took all her grace to keep her temper and her ground. As she would not leave the house the chief said he would, and walked out, remarking that he was going to his farm on business. Swallowing her pride she followed him and begged him humbly as an act of clemency to free the young man. He turned, elated at her suppliant attitude, laughed loudly, and said that no violence would be used until all his demands had been complied with.

She returned to her yard, and days of strain followed. The situation developed into a quarrel between the truculent chief and Edem, and every man went armed, women crept about in fear, scouts arrived hourly with the latest tidings. Her life was a long prayer....

One day the young man was set free, without reason or apology being given or condition exacted, and told to go to his people. With his safety all desire for revenge was stilled, and matters resumed their normal course. The heart of Mary once more overflowed with gratitude and joy.

CHAPTER X
HOW HOUSE AND HALL WERE BUILT

She was impatient to have a house of her own, but the natives were slow to come to her assistance. They thought the haste she exhibited was undignified, and smiled compassionately upon her. There was no hurry— there never is in Africa. If she would but wait all would be well. When argument failed, they went off and left her to cut down the bush and dig out the roots herself. Lounging about in the village they commiserated a Mother who was so strongheaded and wilful, and consoled themselves with the thought of the work they would do when once they began. She could make no progress, and there was nothing for it but to tend the sick, receive visitors, mend the rags of the village, cut out clothing for those who developed a desire for it, and look after her family of bairns.

One day, however, the spirit moved the people and they flocked to the ground. She constituted herself architect, clerk of works, and chief labourer. Her idea was to construct a number of small mud-huts and sheds, which would eventually form the back buildings of the Mission House proper. Four tree-trunks with forked tops were driven into the ground, and upon them were laid other logs. Bamboos, crossed and recrossed, and covered with palm mats, formed the roof and verandah. Upright sticks, interlaced and daubed with red clay, made the walls. Two rooms, each eleven feet by six with a shaded verandah, thus came into existence. Then a shed was added to each end, making three sides of a square. Fires were kept blazing day and night, in order to dry the material and to smoke it as a protection against vermin. Drains were dug and the surrounding bush cleared.

In one of the rooms she put a fireplace of red clay, and close to it a sideboard and dresser of the same material. Holes were cut out for bowls, cups, and other dishes, and rubbed with a stone until the surface was smooth. The top had a cornice to keep the plates from falling off, and was polished with a native black dye. Her next achievement was a mud-sofa where she could recline, and a seat near the fireside where the cook could sit and attend to her duties.

In the other room she deposited her boxes, books, and furniture. Hanging upon the posts were pots and pans and jugs, and her alphabet and reading-sheets. In front stood her sewing-machine, rusty and useless after its exposure in the damp air. There also at night was a small organ, which during the day occupied her bed.

Such was the "caravan," as Mary called it, which was her dwelling for a year: a wonderful house it seemed to the people of Okoyong, who regarded it with astonishment and awe. To herself it was a delight. Never had the building of a home been watched with such loving interest. And when it was finished no palace held a merrier family. At meals all sat round one pot, spoons were a luxury none required, and never had food tasted so sweet. There were drawbacks—all the cows, goats, and fowls in the neighbourhood, for instance, seemed to think the little open yard was the finest rendezvous in the village.

Her next thought was for the church and schoolhouse. A mistress of missionary strategy, she wished to build this at Ifako, in order that she might control a larger area, but the chiefs for long showed no interest in the matter. One morning, however, an Ifako boy sought her with the message, "My master wants you." She thought the command somewhat peremptory, but went. To her surprise she found the ground cleared; posts, sticks, and mud ready, and the chiefs waiting her orders. She designed a hall thirty feet by twenty-five, with two rooms at the end for her own use, in case storm or sickness or palaver should prevent her going home. Work was started; and not a single slave was employed in the carrying of the material or in the construction. King Eyo sent the mats, some thousands in number, for the roof, and free women carried them the four miles from the beach, plastered the walls, moulded the mud-seats, beat the floor, and cleared up, and all cheerfully, and without thought of reward. Doors and windows were still awanting, but she asked for the services of a carpenter from Calabar to do this bit of work; and meanwhile the humble building, the first ever erected for the worship of God in Okoyong, was formally opened.

It was a day of days for the people. Mary had prepared them for it, and all appeared in their new Sunday attire, which, in many cases, consisted of nothing more than a clean skin. But the contents of various Mission boxes had been kept for the occasion, and the children, after being washed, were decked for the first time in garments of many shapes and colour—"the wearing of a garment," said Mary, "never fails to create self-respect." It was a radiant and excited company that gathered in the hall. There was perhaps little depth in their emotion, but she regarded the event as a step towards better things. Her idea was to separate the day from the rest, and to make it a means of bringing about cleanliness and personal dignity, while it also imposed upon the people a little of that discipline which they so much needed.

The chiefs were present, and they voluntarily made the promise before all that the house would be kept sacred to God and His service, that the slave-women and children would be sent to it for instruction, that no weapon of warfare would be carried into it, and that it would be a sanctuary for those who fled to it for refuge.

Services and day school were now held regularly in the hall. The latter was well attended, all the pupils showing eagerness to learn "book," and many making rapid progress.

The larger Mission House, which Mary intended to occupy the space in front of the yard at Ekenge, was a stiffer problem for the people, and for a time they hung back from the attempt to build it.

CHAPTER XI
A PALAYER AT THE PALACE

Perhaps the greatest obstacle to Christian truth and progress was not superstition or custom, but drink. She had seen something of the traffic in rum and gin at the coast, but she was amazed at what went on in Okoyong. All in the community, old and young, drank, and often she lay down to rest at night knowing that not a sober man and hardly a sober woman was within miles of her. When the villagers came home from a drunken bout the chief men would rouse her up and demand why she had not risen to receive them. At all hours of the day and night they would stagger into the hut, and lie down and fall asleep. Her power, then, was not strong enough to prevent them—but the time came.

The spirit came up from Calabar and was the chief article of trade. When a supply arrived processions of girls carrying demijohns trooped in from all quarters, as if they were going to the spring for water. At the funeral of one big man seven casks of liquor were consumed, in addition to that bought in small quantities by the poorer classes. A refugee of good birth and conduct remarked to Mary once that he had been three days in the yard and had not tasted the white man's rum. "Three days!" she replied, "and you think that long!" "Ma," he said, in evident astonishment, "three whole days! I have never passed a day without drinking since I was a boy."

She fought this evil with all her energy and skill. Her persuasion so wrought on the chiefs that on several occasions they agreed to put away the drink at palavers, with the result that those who had come from a distance departed, sober and in peace, to the wonderment of all around.

She saw that the people were tempted and fell because of their idleness and isolation; for they still maintained their aloofness from all their neighbours, and there was yet no free communication with Calabar. If a missionary happened to pay her a visit he would be stopped on the forest track by sentries who, after satisfying themselves as to his identity, "cooeed" to other watchers farther on. Dr. Livingstone believed that the opening up of Central Africa to trade would help to stamp out the slave traffic, and in the same way she was convinced that more legitimate commerce and the development of wants among the people would to some extent undermine the power of drink. All the ordinary trade she had seen done so far was the sale of five shillings' worth of handkerchiefs and a sixpenny looking-glass. She urged the chiefs to take the initiative, and was never tired of showing them her possessions, in order to incite within them a desire to own similar articles. They were greatly taken with the glass windows and doors, and one determined to procure wood and "shut himself in." Her clock, sewing-machine, and organ were always a source of wonder, and people came from far and near to see them. The women quickly became envious of her household goods, and she could have sold her bedcovers, curtains, meat-safe, bedstead, chest of drawers, and other objects a score of times. More promising still was their desire to have clean dresses like their "Ma," and she spent a large portion of her time cutting out and shaping the long simple garment that served to hide their nakedness.

She also sent down to Calabar and asked some of the native trading people whom she knew to come up with cloth, pots, and dishes, and other useful articles, guaranteeing them her protection; but so great was their fear of the Okoyong warriors and so poor their faith in her power, that they refused point blank—they would as soon have thought of going-to the moon. "Well," said Mary, "if they won't come to us we must go to them." She had been seeking to familiarise the minds of the chiefs with the idea of settling their disputes by means of arbitration instead of by fighting, and had been cherishing the hope that she might persuade some of them to proceed to Creek Town and discuss the subject with King Eyo. She now proposed to the King that he should invite them to a palaver at his house, and at the same time she would endeavour to have some produce sent down direct to the traders.

The King had never ceased to take an interest in her work: he frequently sent up special messengers to enquire if all was well, and always reminded her that he was willing to be of service to the Okoyong people. A grandson of the first King Eyo also sent men occasionally, with instructions to do anything they could for the white Mother, and to bring down her messages to Calabar. Such kindly thought often took the edge off her loneliness.

The King at once sent the invitation, and, trusting more in the word of Mary than in that of the King, all the chiefs in her neighbourhood accepted the offer and an expedition to Creek Town was organised. A canoe was obtained, and heaped with yams and plantains, gifts for the King, and with bags of palm-kernels and a barrel of oil, the first instalment of trade with the Europeans. Alas! the natives know nothing about a load-line, and as the tide rose the canoe sank. It was not an unmixed pleasure setting out with men who were ignorant of the management of canoes, but another day was fixed and another canoe was found. The whole of Okoyong seemed to be at the beach, and every man, woman, and child was uttering counsel and heartening the intrepid voyagers. Several of the chiefs drew back and disappeared, and of the half-dozen who remained only two could be persuaded to embark when they learnt that guns and swords must be left behind.

"Ma, you make women of us! Did ever a man go to a strange place without his arms?" "Ma" was inexorable. She sat down and waited, and after a two hours' palaver swords were ungirt and handed with the guns to the women. Those who still declined to go were received back with rejoicing, and farewells were made with those who went, amidst wailings and tears. A start was made, but the craft proved to be ill-balanced, and the cargo had to be shifted. As this was being done she detected a number of swords hidden below the bags of kernels. Her eyes flashed, and the people scattered out of the way as she pitched the arms out on the beach. With a meekness that was amusing the men scrambled into their places and the canoe shot into the river, Mary taking a paddle and wielding it with the best of the men. The journey was made through dense darkness and drizzling rain, and occupied twelve hours.

But she was rewarded by the result. Nothing could exceed the kindness of King Eyo. He bore himself as a Christian gentleman, listened courteously to the passionate and foolish speech of the Okoyong representatives, reminded the supercilious Calabar chiefs that the Gospel which had made them what they were had only just been taken to Okoyong, and in giving the verdict which went against them, he gently made it the finding of righteousness, according to the laws of God. When all had been settled he asked Mary to take the chiefs over his palace, and invited them to a meeting in the church in the evening, where he spoke words of cheer and counsel from the words, "To give light to them that sit in darkness and in the shadow of death, to guide our feet into the way of peace."

This experience made a great impression upon the chiefs: they left with a profound reverence for the King and a determination to abide by his decisions in the future, whilst Mary had added much to her dignity and position. This was proved the morning after they returned to Ekenge. She was awakened by a confused noise, and on looking out was astonished to find several chiefs directing slaves, who were working with building material. "What is the matter?" she asked in wonder. Instead of answering her one of the chiefs who had accompanied her to Calabar turned to the crowd and, in a burst of eloquence, described all he had seen at Creek Town, how the Europeans lived, and how King Eyo and every chief and gentleman had treated their Mother as a person superior to them, and given her all honour. They in Okoyong must now treat her as befitted her rank and station, and must build her a proper house to live in, Mary was hard put to it to preserve her gravity. Soon afterwards a young slave, for whom she had often pled, began to wash his hands in some dirty water in a dish outside: his master ran at him with a whip, and it was all she could do to prevent him being lashed. Opening out again and again he called the lad a fool for daring to touch a dish used by their Great White Mother.

But what was more important than all was the fact that the way had at last been opened up for trade relations with Calabar. The people began to make oil and buy and sell kernels, and to send the produce down the river direct to the factories. As she had foreseen, they had now less time for palavers, and less inclination for useless drinking, and still more useless quarrelling and fighting.

CHAPTER XII
THE SCOTTISH CARPENTER

The story of the settlement in Okoyong and of the building of the hut and hall was related by Miss Slessor in the *Missionary Record* of the Church for March 1889. The hall she described as "a beautiful building, though neither doors nor windows are yet put in, as we are waiting for a carpenter. And," she added, "if there were only a house built, any other agent could come and take up the work if I fail." In the same number of the *Record* there appeared an appeal by the Foreign Mission Committee for "a practical carpenter, with an interest in Christian work," for Calabar.

There happened to be in Edinburgh at this time a carpenter named Mr. Charles Ovens, belonging to the Free Church, who was keenly interested in foreign missions. As a boy he had wished to be a missionary, but believing that only ministers could hold such a post he relinquished the idea. He was an experienced tradesman of the fine old type, a Scot of Scots, with the happy knack of looking on the bright side of things. Having been in America on a prolonged visit he was about to return there, and had gone to say good-bye to an old lady friend, a United Presbyterian. The latter remarked to him, "I see Miss Slessor wants a man to put in her doors and windows—why don't you go to Calabar?" He had never heard of Miss Slessor, but the suggestion struck him as good, and he straightway saw the Foreign Mission Secretary, and then went and changed the address on his baggage. He left in May, and on his arrival in Calabar was sent up to finish the work Mary had begun. All his speech at Duke Town was of America and its wonders, but when he returned some months later he could talk of nothing but Okoyong.

He found Mary attired in a simple dress, without hat or shoes, dining at a table in the yard in the company of goats and hens. She sprang up with delight on hearing the Scots tongue, and welcomed him warmly. The conditions were most primitive, and his room was only eight feet long and five feet wide, but he possessed much of her Spartan spirit. Although ignorant of the native language he was of great assistance to her during his stay, while his humour and irresistible laugh lightened many a weary day.

As he worked he sang "auld Scots sangs," like the "Rowan Tree" and "The Auld Hoose." When she heard the latter tears came into her eyes at the memories it recalled. Even Tom, his native assistant, was affected. "I don't like these songs," he said, "they make my heart big and my eyes water!"

The Mission House had progressed well under Mary's superintendence. She had aimed at making it equal to any at the big stations, and had planned an "upstairs" building with a verandah six feet above the ground, and a kitchen and dispensary. She had mudded the walls, and the mat roof was being tied on, and now that Mr. Ovens was at work all was promising well, when an event occurred which put a stop to operations for months.

CHAPTER XIII
HER GREATEST BATTLE AND VICTORY

One morning, when nature was as lovely as a dream, Mr. Ovens was working at the new house, and Miss Slessor was sitting on the verandah watching him. Suddenly, from far away in the forest, there came a strange, eerie sound. Ever on the alert for danger, Mary rose and listened.

"There is something wrong," she exclaimed.

For a moment she stood in the tense attitude of a hunter seeking to locate the quarry, and then, swiftly moving into the forest, vanished from sight. Mr. Ovens sent Tom, his boy, off after her to find out what was the matter. He returned with a message that there had been an accident, and that Mr. Ovens was to come at once and bring restoratives. As the ominous news became known to the natives standing around a look of fear came into their faces.

Mr. Ovens found her sitting beside the unconscious body of a young man. "It is Etim, the eldest son of our chief, Edem," she explained. "He was about to be married, and had been building a house. He came here to lift and bring a tree; when handling the log it slipped and struck him on the back of the neck, and paralysis has ensued."

He glanced at her face as if surprised at its gravity. She divined what he thought, and speaking out of her intimate knowledge of the people and their ways she said, "There's going to be trouble; no death of a violent character comes apart from witchcraft…. Can you make some sort of a litter to carry him?"

Divesting himself of part of his clothing, and obtaining some strong sticks, he made a rough stretcher, on which the inert form was laid conveyed to Ekenge.

For a fortnight Mary tended the patient in his mother's house, hoping against hope that he would recover, and that the crisis she dreaded would be averted, but he was beyond human help. One Sunday morning he lay dying, and the news sent a spasm of terror throughout the district. Hearing the sound of wailing Mary rushed to the yard and found the lad being held up, some natives blowing smoke into his nostrils, some rubbing ground pepper into his eyes, others pressing Ms mouth open, and his uncle, Ekpenyong, shouting into his ears. Such treatment naturally hastened the end. When life was fled, the chief dropped the body into her arms and shouted, "Sorcerers have killed and they must die. Bring the witch-doctor."

At the words every man and woman disappeared, leaving only the mother, who, in an agony of grief, cast herself down beside the body. When the medicine-man arrived he laid the blame of the tragedy upon a certain village, to which the armed freemen at once marched. They seized over a dozen men and women, the others escaping into the forest, and after sacking all the houses returned with the prisoners loaded with chains, and fastened them to posts in the yard, which had only one entrance.

Anxious to pacify the rage of the chiefs, father and uncle, Mary undertook to do honour to the dead lad by dressing him in the style befitting his rank. Fine silk cloth was wound round his body, shirts and vests were put on, over these went a suit of clothes which she had made for his father, the head was shaved into patterns and painted yellow, and round it was wound a silk turban, all being crowned with a tall black and scarlet hat with plumes of brilliant feathers. Thus attired the body was carried out into a booth in the women's yard, where it was fastened, seated in an arm-chair, under a large umbrella. To the hands were tied the whip and silver-headed stick that denoted his position, while a mirror was arranged in front of him, in order that he might enjoy the reflection of his grandeur. Beside him was a table, upon which were set out all the treasures of the house, including the skulls taken in war, and a few candles begged from Mary.

When the people were admitted and saw the weird spectacle they became frenzied with delight, danced and capered, and started on a course of drinking and wantonness.

"You'll have to stop all work," Mary said to Mr. Ovens, who felt as if he were moving in some grotesque fantasy of sleep; "this is going to be a serious business. We can't leave these prisoners for a moment. I'll watch beside them all night and you'll take the day."

And time and time about in that filthy yard, through the heat of the day and the chill of the night, these two brave souls kept guard opposite the wretched band of prisoners, with the half-naked people, armed with guns and machetes, dancing drinking about them. As one barrel of rum was finished another was brought in, and the supply seemed endless. The days went by, and Mr. Ovens lost patience, and declared he would go and get a chisel and hammer and free the prisoners at all costs. "Na, na," replied Mary wisely, "we'll have a little more patience."

One day she went to Mr. Ovens and said, "They want a coffin."

"They'll have to make one," he retorted.

"I think you'd better do it," she rejoined; "the boy's father has some wood of his own, of which he was going to make a door like mine, and he is willing to use it for the purpose."

They proceeded to the yard to obtain measurements, and as they entered Mary caught sight of some eséré beans lying on the pounding stone. She shivered. What could she do! She returned to her hut. Prayer had been her solace and strength during all these days and nights, and now with passionate entreaty she beseeched God for guidance and help in the struggle that was to come. When she rose from her knees her fear had vanished, and she was tranquil and confident. Reaching the yard she took the two brother chiefs aside, and told them that there must be no sacrifice of life. They did not deny that the poison ordeal was about to take place, but they argued that only those guilty of causing the death would suffer. She did not reply, but went to the door of the compound and sat down: from there she was determined not to move until the issue was decided. The chiefs were angry. To have a white woman— and such a woman—amongst them was good, but she must not interfere with their customs and laws. The mother of the dead lad became violent. Even the slaves were openly hostile and threatening. The crowd; maddened by drink, ran wildly about, flourishing their guns and swords. "Raise our master from the dead," they cried, "and you shall have the prisoners."

Night fell. Mr. Ovens gathered up the children and put them to bed. Mary scribbled a note to Duke Town and gave it to the two native assistant carpenters, and directed them in English to steal in the darkness to the beach and make their way down the river. There was distraction within the yard as well as without. Three of the women were mothers with babies, who were crying incessantly from hunger and fear. Another, who had chains round her neck and bare limbs, had an only daughter about fifteen years of age, who was a cousin of the dead lad, and the betrothed wife of his father. The girl clung to her mother, weeping piteously. Sometimes she would come and clasp "Ma's" feet, beseeching her to help her, or waylay the chiefs, and offer herself in servitude for life in exchange for her mother's freedom.

Mr. Ovens had gone to the hut, and Mary was keeping vigil when a stir warned her of danger. Several men came and unlocked the chains on one of the women—a mother—and ordered her to the front of the corpse to take the bean. Mary was in a dilemma. Was it a ruse to get her out of the yard?

If she followed, would they bar the entrance and wreak their vengeance on the others who remained? "Do not go," they cried, and gazed at her pleadingly. But she could not see a woman walk straight to death.

One swift appeal to God and she was after the woman. The table was covered with a white cloth, and upon it stood a glass of water containing the poison. As the victim was in the act of lifting the glass she touched her on the shoulder and whispered, "*'Ifehe!*" (run). She gave a quick glance of intelligence into the compelling eyes and off both bounded, and were in the bush before any one realised they were gone. They reached the hut. "Quick," Mary cried to Mr. Ovens, "take the woman and hide her." In a moment he had drawn her in and locked the door, and Mary flew back to the yard. "Where is she?" the prisoners cried. "Safe in my house," she answered. They were amazed. She herself wondered at her immunity from harm. It might be that the natives were stupefied with drink—but she thought of her prayer.

Finding that she was not to be moved, the chiefs endeavoured to cajole and deceive her. "God will not let anybody die of the bean if they are not guilty," they said. They released two of the prisoners, substituting imbiam, the native oath, for the poison ordeal, and later, five others. She still stood firm, and two more obtained their freedom. There they stopped. "We have done more for you than we have ever done for any one, and we will die before we go further." Three remained. One woman, with a baby, they would not release. "Akpo, the chief of her house, escaped into the bush, and the fact of his flight proves his guilt," they argued; "we cannot ransom her." The other two, a freeman and the woman named Inyam with the daughter, were relatives of the bereaved mother, and also specially implicated, and they were seized and led away. Mary hesitated to follow, but hoping that the girl might be able to keep her informed of what was going on she decided to remain with the woman with the infant.

Another dawn brought visitors from a distance, who only added to the rioting and her perplexity. They told her that Egbo was coming, and advised her to fly to Calabar. She replied that he could come and play the fool as much as he pleased, but she would not desert her post. The father stormed and threatened, and declared he would burn down the house. "You are welcome," she said, "it is not mine." In a blazing passion he cried that the woman would die. So terrified and exhausted was the victim that she begged "Ma" to give in. At this point Ma Eme came to the rescue: kneeling to her brother she besought him to allow Mary to have the prisoner in the meantime—she could be chained to the verandah of the hut, and could not possibly escape with such a weight of irons. Mary caught at the plan, and declared that she would give a fair hearing to the charges against the house which she represented.

To her infinite surprise the chiefs gave in. "But," said they, "if she is sent out of the way to Calabar, you pay a heavy fine, and leave here for ever." Fearing they would repent, she hastily called for the keys to unlock the chain, but the slaves pretended ignorance, said they could not find them, and denounced the liberation of the murderers. Patience and firmness again succeeded, the keys were produced, the locks were opened. Mary gathered up the long folds of chain, and Ma Eme, also trembling with eagerness, pushed them out in order that they might escape the crowd. They ran through the scrub to the hut, and here the mother and child were housed in a large packing-case, while a barricade was put up to make the position more secure.

During the afternoon two of the Calabar missionaries arrived, and added the weight of their influence to Mary's, giving a magic-lantern exhibition in the open, and in other ways endeavouring to lend prestige to the funeral, in order to compensate for the lack of human sacrifice. A quieter night followed, though the vigil was unbroken. In the morning the father of the dead lad called her aside, and in a long harangue justified his desire to do his son honour by giving him a retinue in the spirit-land. Then calling to his retainers he ordered them to bring the freeman. Dragging him forward, limping and dazed, he presented him formally to "Ma," saying, "This further act of clemency must satisfy you. The woman who is left must take the poison: you cannot object—she will recover if she is innocent."

She thanked him warmly, but renewed her entreaties for the release of the woman also. The chief turned away in anger and disgust, and the battle went on. As the missionaries were obliged to return to Calabar she and Mr. Ovens were again left alone. All day she followed the chief, coaxing and pleading. Sometimes he ignored her; sometimes he brusquely showed his annoyance; sometimes he looked at her in pity, as if he thought she were crazed. But he gave her no hope. When a whisper came to her ears that the burial would take place that night in the house of the chief she was heart-sick with dread.

Late in the evening, as she was busy with her household, she heard a faint cry at the barricade:

"Ma, Ma, make haste, let me in."

Noiselessly she pulled aside the planks, and Inyam, heavily ironed, crawled on her hands and knees into the room. Her story was that she had managed by friction to cut one of the links of the chain which bound her, and had escaped by climbing the roof. Mary looked at the thick chain hanging about her, and guessed whose were the kindly black hands that had given her aid, but she kept her thought to herself. The last of the prisoners was now safe, the funeral in the house of the chief had taken place, and only a cow had been placed in the coffin, and her joy was great. But her troubles were not over.

A party of natives coming to the funeral met another party returning drunk with excitement and rum. Recalling some old quarrel the latter killed one of the men they met, cut off his head, and carried it away as a trophy. Fighting became general between the factions, and many were seriously wounded.

One afternoon the village went suddenly mad with panic. All the women and children and all the men without arms rushed frantically about. Mothers clutched their babies, wives and slaves seized what belongings they could carry, children screamed and held on to the first person they met. They had heard sounds that heralded the advance of the dreaded Egbo. Then, by a common impulse, all rushed for the protection of the white woman's yard. She pulled down the barricade, packed as many children and women into her room as it could hold, and ordered the others into the bush at the back. The women were almost insane with terror, and the manacled prisoner begged to be killed. As the beating of the drum and the shouting of the mob drew near Mary trembled, but again prayer restored her to calm. Even when the village was invaded and shouting began, she was without fear. And, strange to say, the mob remained but a short time, and not a shot went home. They had set fire to every house in the village from which the prisoners had been taken, and wrecked another and burned the stock alive. As no powerful chief submitted to Egbo sent out by another House, Edem's village also ran amok, and for over a week the population haunted the forest, shooting down indiscriminately every man and woman who passed. It was not until much blood had been shed that the various bands became tired of the struggle and returned to their dwellings.

For three weeks the prisoners were kept in the hut, and then "Ma's" pressure on the chiefs succeeded, and the chained woman was released on condition that if her chief Akpo were caught he would take the poison ordeal, whilst Inyam, taking advantage of all the people being drunk one night, stole out into the forest and escaped. What became of her Mary never knew, until one day, months after, when travelling, she passed a number of huts in the bush, and was accosted by name and found herself face to face with the refugee.

This was the longest and severest strain to which she was subjected; it was her worst encounter with the passions of the natives, her greatest conflict with the most terrible of their customs, and she came out of it victorious. For the first time in the dark history of the tribe the death and funeral of one of the rank of a chief had occurred without the sacrifice of life. In some mysterious way she had been able to subdue these wild people and bend them to her will. Her fame went far and wide throughout Okoyong and beyond into regions still unexplored, and many thought of her with a kind of awe as one possessing superhuman power. There were, indeed, some amongst those who knew her who had a lurking suspicion that she was more than woman.

CHAPTER XIV
THE AFTERMATH

Various incidents came as an aftermath to these happenings. One afternoon the women came running to "Ma" saying that the elder chief, Ekpenyong, was bent on taking the poison ordeal. When she reached his yard she found him in a fury, shouting and threatening, the women remonstrating, the slaves weeping. It was some time ere she could learn the cause of the uproar. A man from a neighbouring village had been about whispering that Ekpenyong had slain his nephew, in order that his own son might absorb the inheritance. Ekpenyong was determined to undergo the test, and in accordance with native law, which gave the right to a freeman to call others of equal rank to share the trial with him, he demanded that his brother Edem—who it was alleged had instigated the man to make the accusation—should also take the poison.

When Mary had grasped the situation she ridiculed the attitude of the chief, scolded him unmercifully, and at last secured his promise not to carry out his threat. As a guarantee of his good faith she claimed possession of the eséré beans. He denied that he had any. With the help of his womenkind she made a secret search, and found eleven beans at the bottom of a basket, which she conveyed in the darkness to her hut. As more beans could not be obtained until the morning she felt that all was well for the night. Shouting, however, made her run back. Mad with drink the chief was clinging to a bag which the women were endeavouring to seize. He was hitting out at them with his heavy hand, and most of them were bleeding. "There is poison in that bag," they cried. "No, Ma, only my palm-nuts and cartridges." Quietly, firmly, persistently, she demanded the bag. He threw it at her. Opening it she found palm-nuts and cartridges. For a moment she looked foolish, but diving deeper she pulled out no fewer than forty of the deadly beans. "I'll take the liberty of keeping these," she said coolly, but with a swiftly beating heart. "No, no," he shouted, and his followers joined him in protest. Outwardly calm she walked between the lines of armed men, ironically bidding them take the bag from her. But their hands were held, and she passed safely through, reached her hut, handed the beans to Mr. Ovens, and returned to the scene to pacify the crowd.

Next morning she learnt to her consternation that Ekpenyong had risen stealthily during the night and gone off on his errand of death. Fortunately a chief some miles off detained him by force until she arrived. She stuck resolutely to him, and as all the more powerful chiefs came over to her side from sheer admiration of her pluck, he had eventually to abandon his purpose. After taking the native oath he betook himself to another part of the forest, where he built up a new settlement.

One more episode remained to round off the sequence of events. The murderer of the young man in the funeral party was the oldest son of a House noted for bloody deeds, and the act roused the slumbering fury of its neighbours. War was declared and fighting began. Mary interfered and pressed for arbitration, and both sides at last acceded to her request, and asked her to conduct the palaver. Aware that the man was a triple murderer and the penalty death, she shrank from the duty, and begged them to put the matter into the hands of a Calabar chief. This they did, and went to Ikunetu on the Cross River, where "blood for blood" was the verdict. Fines and death by substitution of slaves were offered and refused; the youngest son, a mere baby, was sent in atonement and rejected; then the second son, a lad of twenty, was despatched, and it was agreed that his death would redeem his brother. Mary's distress was acute, especially as she had declined to act as judge, but she was relieved on learning that the prisoner had escaped, and was being sheltered by one of the slave-traders across the river. She wished to get him into her own yard, but the weeping mother said it was too dangerously near home.

One morning, early, she heard the sound of rapid firing, and in alarm she sent messengers to enquire the cause. The lad had been betrayed, brought back, filled with gin, and amidst discharge of guns, beating of drums, singing and dancing, had been strangled and hung in the presence of his mother and sister. These two alone mourned the dead, the others were glad that the matter had been so easily settled, and for a week the loafers and drunkards in the district held high carnival.

As time passed and the heat of the persecution cooled, Mary made tentative proposals that Akpo, the escaped chief, and his family, should be allowed to return. "I will go and fetch them myself if their safety be guaranteed," she said. Edem, the father of the dead lad, replied, "Very well, Ma, you can say that all thought of vengeance is gone from our heart, and if he wishes to come to his own village or live in your home or go anywhere in Okoyong he is at liberty to do so." But trust is rare in Africa, and suspicion dies hard, and Akpo could not bring himself to believe that Edem wished him well, and he elected to remain where he was. Again she paid the exile a visit, taking with her an elderly man, who was betrothed to his daughter, but he could not overcome his fears. In his heart he and his friends were incredulous that the chiefs of Okoyong would listen to a woman. A third time the patient Mary went to him, and succeeded in bringing him and his son back with her, the women remaining behind until a new house could be built.

The home-coming was fall of pathos. House, farm, clothing, seed-corn, yams, goats, fowls, all had vanished. But as the chief stood amidst the familiar surroundings his gloom and silence fell away, and he knelt and clasped "Ma's" feet, and with eyes filled with tears vowed that he and his house would be under yoke to her for ever, and that they would never rebel against any commands she gave or do anything contrary to her wishes. Most people, white and black, occasionally felt disposed to dispute her rulings, and more than once her will and that of the chief clashed, but he stood to his word, and there was no family in the district who gave her message a more loyal hearing.

Edem acted nobly. He not only arranged for the housing of the two men, but gave them a piece of ground and seed for food plants. When she went to tell him all had been done, he simply said, "Thank you, Ma." But in the evening he came alone to her, knelt and held her feet, and thanked her again and again for her wonderful love and courage, for her action, in forbidding them to take life at his son's death, and for all the peaceful ways which she was introducing. "We are all weary of the old customs," he said, "but no single person or House among us has power to break them off, because they are part of the Egbo system."

And one by one, secretly and unknown to each other, the free people came to her and thanked her gratefully for the state of safety she was bringing about, and charged her to keep a stout heart and to go forward and do away with all the old fashions, the end of which was always death.

CHAPTER XV
THE SWEET AND THE STRONG

Meanwhile the Mission House had evolved into what was in her eyes a thing of beauty. She could at any rate boast that it was the finest dwelling in Okoyong, and it was a happy day when she removed "upstairs." Nor was the house all that was accomplished during these troublous times. Mr. Goldie had made her a gift of a canoe; but without a boathouse it was exposed to rain and ants and thieves, and she planned a shelter at the beach that would do both for it and for herself. Ma Eme brought her people to the spot, the men cut down trees and erected the framework, and the women dug the mud and filled in the walls, and Mr. Ovens made a door and provided a padlock.

Thus, in the course of a short time, she had built a hut; a good house with accommodation for children, servants, and visitors; a dispensary; a church; and a double-roomed boathouse. All the native labour had been given cheerfully and without idea of money, but from time to time she distributed amongst the workers a few gifts from the Mission boxes, or a goat or a bag of rice. In addition to her house at Ekenge she had a room in several of the villages, where she put up on her journeys; and it was characteristic of her that she secured these not for her own convenience but for the sake of the people, in order that they might feel that they were being looked after.

It was, indeed, for the people she lived. Mr. Ovens states that she was at their beck and call day and night; she taught in the schools, preached in the church, and, as he puts it, "washed the wee bairnies herself," and dressed the most loathsome diseases, all with tenderness and gay humour. "I never saw a frown on her face," he says. She was always ready for anything and equal to any emergency. "One morning," he recalls, "she came to me. 'Twins,' she said, 'and we have to go.' When we arrived at the spot we found that the bairns had been murdered by the grandmother, and the mother was lying on the bare ground in a hut some distance away. Miss Slessor sent her a bed and pillow, and told her husband to be kind to her. The man took her back into the house— such a thing had never been known before."

It was at this time that the plump and pretty infant referred to by Miss Kingsley in her *Travels in West Africa* was saved. The mother died a few days after the birth, and as there was a quarrel between her family and that of the father the child was thrown into the bush by the side of the road leading to the market, and lay there for five days and six nights.

This particular market is held every ninth day, and on the succeeding market-day, some women from the village by the side of Miss Slessor's house happened to pass along the path and heard the child feebly crying: they came into Miss Slessor's yard in the evening, and sat chatting over the day's shopping, and casually mentioned in the way of conversation that they had heard the child crying, and that it was rather remarkable that it should be still alive. Needless to say Miss Slessor was off, and had that waif home. It was truly in an awful state, but just alive. In a marvellous way it had been left by leopards and snakes, with which this bit of forest abounds, and, more marvellous still, the driver ants had not scented it. Other ants had considerably eaten into it one way and another; nose, eyes, etc., were swarming with them and flies; the cartilage of the nose and part of the upper lip had been absolutely eaten into, but in spite of this she is now one of the prettiest black children I have ever seen, which is saying a good deal, for negro children are very pretty with their round faces, their large mouths not yet coarsened by heavy lips, their beautifully-shaped flat little ears, and their immense melancholy deer-like eyes, and above these charms they possess that of being fairly quiet. This child is not an object of terror, like the twin children; it was just thrown away because no one would be bothered to rear it—but when Miss Slessor had had all the trouble of it the natives had no objection to pet and play with it, calling it "the child of wonder," because of its survival. This child was named Mary after the house mother, and completed the number of those who for long constituted the inner circle of the family. The others were Janie, Alice—a rescued twin of "royal" blood, and Annie—the child of the woman who took a native oath to prove that she did not help her husband to eat a stolen dog. These four were to grow up and become a comfort to their white "Mother," and will reappear from time to time in the course of the story. Another helper in the house at this time was Mana, a faithful girl, who had been caught by two men when going home from a spring, and brought to Okoyong and sold to Ma Erne. Other children there were, all with more or less tragic histories, and all were looked after and trained and loved.

But Mary could be as stern and strong as her native granite when combating evil. Mr. Ovens saw her repeatedly thrust brawny negroes away from the drink, taking them round the neck, and throwing them back to the ground. An intoxicated man, carrying a loaded gun, once came to see her. She ordered him to put the weapon in a corner of the verandah. He declined. She went up, wrested the gun from him, placed it in a corner, and defied him to touch it. He went away, and came back every day for a week before she gave it up. Another man came to her for medicine, and after he had described his symptoms she brought a bottle of castor oil and told him to open his mouth. Fearful that it might be some sort of witchcraft, he demurred. "Ma" simply gave him a smart box on the ear and repeated the order, whereupon he meekly took the stuff and went ruefully away. About this time, also, she went and prevented two tribes from fighting: although her heart was beating wildly she stood between them and made each pile their guns on opposite sides of her, until the heaps were five feet high. On another occasion she stopped and impounded a canoe-load of machetes that were going up-river to be used in a war.

Mr. Ovens was struck by her mental power and wide outlook. Despite her incessant preoccupation with matters about her she never ceased the cultivation of intellectual interests. She was a loving student of the Bible, a wide and discriminating reader, and she followed with a brooding mind the development of world affairs throughout the world.

Before his work was finished Mr. Ovens began to suffer from the exposure, and she nursed him day and night through a serious illness. When he returned to Duke Town she missed his cheery company; her isolation and loneliness seemed intensified, and she was only sustained by her faith in the efficacy of prayer and by her communion with the Father, "My one great consolation and rest," she wrote, "is in prayer." So invariably was she comforted: so invariably was she preserved from harm and hurt, that her reliance upon a higher strength became an instinctive habit. It conquered her natural nervousness and apprehension. She had frequently to take journeys through the forest with the leopards swarming around her. "I did not use to believe the story of Daniel in the lions dens" she often said, "until I had to take some of these awful marches, and then I knew it was true, and that it was written for my comfort. Many a time I walked along praying, 'O God of Daniel shut their mouths,' and He did." If she happened to be travelling with bearers or paddlers, she would make them sing and keep them singing; "And, *Etubom*" (Sir, Chief, or White Man), she would say, when telling her experiences, "ye ken what like their singing is— it would frighten any decent respectable leopard." And yet in some things she was as timid as a child. When travelling in the Mission steam-launch she would bury her head in her hands and cry out in fear if the engine gave a screech or if the vessel bumped on a sandbank. She was in terror all the time she was on board.

It was not possible for her to go on expending so much nervous force without a breakdown, and as attacks of fever were coming with increasing frequency she began to think of her furlough. The difficulty was to fill her place. In 1890 Mr. Goldie reported that only she or a man could fill it; no native agent could go from. Calabar on account of tribal unfriendliness. But she thought otherwise. "No person connected with me need fear to come to Okoyong, or suffer from lack of hospitality." Okoyong was a very different place from what it had been in 1888. There was greater order and security, and much less drinking among the younger people, many of whom were at school; none dared to use the slightest freedom with, her; they might come as far as the verandah but no farther. The people were becoming ashamed of their superstition, and were ready to inform her secretly when palavers and sacrifices were in contemplation. Chiefs came voluntarily and requested her to sit in the seat of judgment and adjudge their disputes. The tribe, as a whole, was also working better, and developing a regular trade with the Europeans. The problem was solved by another woman with a stout heart, who voluntarily agreed to occupy the station during her absence. This was Miss Dunlop. The Home Board were anxious as to her safety, and recommended frequent communications with her; and later, Miss Hutton, who had just arrived from Scotland, was appointed to keep her company. When Miss Dunlop went up before "Ma" left, she was met by what she thought was a crowd of peaceful, cheerful—people, eager only to greet her and to help her. She modified her opinion later: a "wild and lawless class," she called them, "boasting of their wildness," and who came to the services drunk. When she spoke of God's love they would say, "Yes, Ma Slessor tell us that plenty times." But she bravely held the fort.

CHAPTER XVI
WAR IN THE GATES

At the last moment she was busy packing when messengers arrived from a far-off township with intelligence that a young freeman had accidentally shot his hand while hunting, and a request that she would come to him with medicine. She was weak and ill: she was expecting tidings of the steamer; she was beset with visitors from all parts who had come to bid her farewell. Telling them what to do, and asking them to let her know only if serious symptoms set in, she gave them what was needed. Almost immediately came secret news that the man had died, that his brother had wounded one of the chiefs, and that all the warriors of the latter had been ordered to prepare for fighting on the morrow. She never knew how this message had come or who had brought it. She made up her mind to proceed to the spot, but the chief people about her opposed the idea. They pointed to her weakness, and the probability of her missing the steamer. They enlarged on the savage character of those concerned. "They own no authority"; "They will insult you in their drunken rage"; "The bush will be full of armed men, and they will fire indiscriminately;" "The darkness will prevent them recognising you." But they could not prevail upon her to relinquish what she thought was a duty to those who had sought her aid. She, however, compromised by consenting to take two armed attendants with lanterns, and to call at a chief's place some eight miles distant, and secure a freeman to beat the Egbo drum before her, thus letting the people in the fighting area know that a free protected person was coming.

She reached their village about midnight. The chief was reported to be at his farm, and she was urged to lie down until the morning, She suspected that he was not many yards away, and she persuaded a messenger to carry an urgent request to him for an escort and drum. The reply was in the language of diplomacy all the world over:

"I have heard of no war, but will enquire regarding it in the morning. If, in the event of there being war, you persist in going on you prove your ignorance of the people, who from all time have been a war-loving people, are not likely to be helped by a woman."

This put her on her mettle.

"In measuring the woman's power," she responded, "you have evidently forgotten to take into account the woman's God."

She decided to go on. The people were astonished, not so much at her folly in risking her life as in daring to disobey the despot, who held their fate in the hollow of his hand. Somewhat chilled by her unsympathetic reception she started, without much enthusiasm, on her journey, but with her faith in God as strong as ever.

Reaching the first town belonging to the belligerents she found it so silent and dark that she began to imagine the chief was right, and she had come on a wild-goose chase. She crept quietly up to the house of an old freewoman whose granddaughter had once lived with her: there was a cautious movement within and a whispered, "Who's there?" She had barely answered, when she was surrounded by a band of armed men, whose dark bodies were like shadows in the night. In a few moments they were joined by scores of others, and the greatest confusion prevailed. She was asked what her business was and who were her informants, but ultimately the chiefs permitted her to remain, and the women saw to her comfort.

After conferring together the chiefs thanked her for coming at such discomfort to herself, and promised that no fighting, so far as they were concerned, would take place until she heard the whole story.

"All the same," they averred, "we must fight to wipe out the disgrace that has been put on us-see here are men badly wounded. Now, Ma, go to bed, and we shall wake you at cock-crow, and you can accompany us."

This meant an hour's rest, which she urgently needed. At second cock-crow she was called, but before she was steady on her feet they were off and away down the steep hillside and through the stream at the foot like a herd of wild goats. The women were at every house.

"Run, Ma!" they cried.

Run! Was she not running as fast as her weak and breathless state allowed her? But she soon lost sight of the warriors, and could only fall back upon prayer.

A hundred yards from the village of the enemy she came upon the band in the bush making preparations for attack: the war-fever was at its height, and the air resounded with wild yells. Walking quietly forward she addressed them as one would speak to schoolboys, telling them to hold their peace and behave like men and not like fools. Passing on to the village she encountered a solid wall of armed men. Giving them greeting, she got no reply. The silence was ominous. Twitting them on their perfect manners she went up to them, and was about to force a passage. Then a strange thing happened.

From out of the sullen line of dark-skinned warriors there stepped an old man, who came and knelt at her feet.

"Ma, we thank you for coming. We admit the wounding of the chief, but it was the act of one man and not the fault of the town. We beg you to use your influence with the injured party in the interests of peace."

It was the chief whom she had travelled in the rain to see and heal when she first came to Okoyong. Her act of self-sacrifice and courage had borne fruit after many days.

She was so thankful that her impulse was to run back to their opponents in the forest and arrange matters there and then; but she restrained herself, and, instead, purposely told the men with an air of authority to remain where they were while her wants were attended to.

"I am not going to starve while you fight," she said, "and meanwhile you can find a comfortable seat In the bush where I can confer with the two sides; choose two or three men of good address and good judgment for the purpose."

They obeyed her like children.

When the two deputies from the other side came forward, two chiefs laid down their arms and went and knelt before them and held their feet saying it was foolish and unjust to punish the whole district for the action of a drunken boy, begging them to place the matter before the White Ma, and expressing their willingness to pay whatever fine might be imposed. She, too, knelt and begged that magnanimity might be shown, and that arbitration might be substituted for war. So novel a proposal was not agreed to at once. The next few hours witnessed scenes of wild excitement, rising sometimes to frenzy. Bands of men kept advancing from both sides and joining in the palaver, and every arrival increased the indignation and the resolution to abide by the old, manlier way of war. She was well-nigh worn out, but her wonderful patience and tact, coupled with her knowledge of all the outs and ins of their character, again won her the victory. It was agreed that a fine should settle the quarrel, and one was imposed which she thought exorbitant In the extreme, but the delinquents accepted it, and promptly paid part in trade gin.

Here was another peril. As the boxes and demijohns were brought forward and put down the mob began to grow excited at the thought of the drink. She foresaw trouble and disaster, but though her voice was now too feeble to be heard in the babel of sound, she was not yet at the end of her resources. Divesting herself of as many of her garments as was possible, she threw them over the stuff, thus giving it the protection of her own body, according to Egbo law.

It was a custom for providers of spirits which might have been tampered with on the way from the boat, to taste the liquor in order to prove that neither sorcery nor poison had been placed in it, and every man wanted to be the taster on this occasion. As soon as the test had been applied, every man on the other side likewise demanded the gin, and for a time it seemed as if all had gone mad.

Mary seized the one glass which they held, and as each bottle was opened she dealt out to the older and chief men one glass only, resolutely refusing to give more, and placed the bottle under the cover of her garments. No one dared to touch the stuff. There was some jostling around her, but a few of the men constituted themselves into a bodyguard, and by whip and drum kept the mob off. Amidst much tumult and grumbling and laughter at her sallies she got them to agree to leave the spirit in her charge on her declaring that she would be surety for it arriving in their several villages in good time, and untampered with.

She made them promise to go straight home and remain at peace during her furlough (a promise that was loyally kept); but there was one party she was obliged to accompany for a mile or two. They had—declared that they were ashamed to return "like women," without having fought. They begged her to allow them to have a "small scrap," in order to prove they were not cowards. Not till they were safely past the danger zone did she leave them. She remained till night at the village. The feeling was still too disturbed to permit of a regular service, but she spoke to them quietly of Christ as a Saviour: and then ordering all to their rest she set out, tired as she was, on her lonely tramp through the long miles of forest path.

She found her baggage had gone, and that messengers had arrived to take her down to Duke Town.

CHAPTER XVII
AMONG THE CHURCHES

Arriving in England la January 1891 with Janie, who proved a great comfort and help, she went straight to Topsham to view the graves of her mother and sister. She was anxious to spend as much of her furlough as possible amongst the scenes and with the friends associated with her loved ones, and she secured and furnished a house. It possessed a fine garden, and there, with the little black girl, she passed a quiet and restful time until the autumn, when she went to Scotland, making her headquarters at the home of her friend, Mrs. M'Crindle, now at Joppa. For many months she was engaged on the deputation work which missionaries on furlough undertake for the stimulation of the home congregations. She had less liking than ever for addressing meetings, but she did not shirk the duty. "It is a trial to speak," she said; "but He has asked me to, and it is an honour to be allowed to testify for Him in any way, and I wish to do it cheerfully." She wanted also to persuade the women in the Church to give themselves up more whole- heartedly to Christ, and to consecrate themselves to His cause. No trouble was too great if it served that purpose. As a halo of romance was beginning to gather about her she was in great request; wherever she went the interest of the meeting centred in her, and her visits were often followed by the formation of a Zenana Mission Committee.

Not always, however, did she satisfy expectations. She would talk freely at the manse tea-table, especially if children were present, and be led on to give vivid pictures of her life in the bush, so that the company would be still sitting entranced when the bell rang for the meeting. Then a rush would be made to the hall, where impatient people would be waiting to be thrilled by stories of heroic service. And what they heard was an evangelistic address! The minister would look disappointed, feeling that he could have done as well himself. But she sometimes deprecated surface interest, and said that if the heart was right and the life consecrated, mission work would be well supported without any adventitious aid.

After addressing a meeting at Slateford near Edinburgh she was on the way to the station when a woman who had been in the audience took Janie and kissed her and pressed some money into her hand. Next day the minister received a letter inscribed:

"For the lady who gave Janie the money and the kiss on the way to the station.-M. M. Slessor."

Enclosed was a photograph of Janie and a letter in which she wrote:

MY DEAR FRIEND—For such I must call you. Such a true womanly Christian spirit as you showed yesterday is one of the fruits of our holy Christianity—I thank you for loving and kissing the child—God bless you, my dear sister. I may yet see you in the flesh. I will if I go back to Slateford. But I may be sure of meeting you in the Father's house when the shadows flee away and the everlasting glory has dawned.

The recipient kept the photograph and letter and still treasures them as mementoes of one of whom she never ceased to think and for whom she always prayed. It was in such ways that she knit hearts to her.

She made many friends in the manses and in the homes of the members of the Church, and greatly increased the interest in her work in Calabar, with the result that after she returned a larger stream of correspondence and Mission boxes began to flow to Okoyong.

CHAPTER XVIII
LOVE OF LOVER

Aware of her singleness of mind and aim in the service of Christ, and her whole-hearted devotion to the interests of the people of Okoyong, it came as a surprise to her friends to learn that she was engaged to be married. The hidden romance was disclosed at a meeting of the Mission Board in September.

The suitor for her hand was Mr. Charles W. Morrison, one of the teachers on the Mission staff, a young man from Kirkintilloch, Scotland, then in his twenty-fifth year. His career at home had been a successful one; he had been an active Christian worker, and when he applied to the Board for an appointment in Calabar he was accepted at once and sent out to Duke Town. He was a man of fine feeling, with a distinct literary gift. On the few occasions that he had seen Mary he was attracted by the brilliant, unconventional little woman, and when she was ill was very attentive and kind to her. Before she left on furlough they had become engaged on the understanding that he would come and live at Okoyong.

She made it clear to the Board that she had pledged her word to her people not to leave them, and that she would not, even for her personal happiness, break her promise, Mr. Morrison, she believed, would make a very good missionary, and they would be able to relieve each other, as she would remain at Okoyong when he was at home. The Board took time to consider the proposal, and meanwhile Mary received the congratulations of her friends. Her replies indicate that there was no uncertainty in her own mind on the subject:

I lay it all in God's hands, and will take from Him whatever He sees best for His work in Okoyong. My life was laid on His altar for that people long ago, and I would not take one jot or tittle of it back. If it be for His glory and the advantage of His cause there to let another join in it I will be grateful. If not I will still try to be grateful, as He knows best.

Both were a little doubtful as to the action of the Board, and Mr. Morrison asked her whether, in the event of a refusal, she would consent to return to Duke Town, Such a project, however, she would not entertain:

"It is out of the question," she explained to a friend. "1 would never take the idea into consideration, I could not leave my work for such a reason. To leave a field like Okoyong without a worker and go to one of ten or a dozen where the people have an open Bible and plenty of privilege! It is absurd. If God does not send him up here then he must do his work and I must do mine where we have been placed. If he does not come I must ask the Committee to give me some one, for it is impossible for me to work the station alone."

The Board, seemingly, were not sure of the wisdom of the arrangement, and their decision was a qualified refusal. The work which Mr. Morrison was doing at Duke Town, they said, was important, and they could not sanction his transference to Okoyong until full provision was made for carrying it on effectively and to the satisfaction of the Calabar Committee.

When Mary was told the result she merely said, "What the Lord ordains is right," and, apparently, dismissed the subject from her mind.

Mr. Morrison was, shortly afterwards, compelled to return to Scotland on account of his health. A medical specialist advised him against resuming work in Calabar, and he offered for service in Kaffraria, but there was no opening in that field, and to the regret and disappointment of the Committee, who regarded him as an able and valued worker, he resigned. He went later to America and was living in a hut among the balsam woods of North Carolina when a fire took place in which his much-treasured literary papers were consumed. The loss affected him greatly, and hastened his death, which occurred shortly afterwards.

Amongst the few treasured books which Mary left at the end were battered copies of *Eugene Aram* and *Sketches by Boz*. On the fly-leaf of one in her handwriting are the letters:

C. W. M. M. M. S.

On the other are signatures in their respective hands:

C. MORRISON. M. M. SLESSOR.

Love of mother and sister had been lost to her long since, and now love of lover and husband was denied, and again she turned her face, alone, towards the future.

> *Yes, without cheer of sister or of daughter,*
> *Yes, without stay of father or of son,*
> *Lone on the land and homeless on the water,*
> *Pass I in patience till my work be done.*

CHAPTER XIX
A LETTER AND ITS RESULT

A sharp attack of influenza followed by bronchitis cut short her engagements. During her convalescence she one day took up the Missionary Record, and read a letter by the Rev. James Luke entitled "An Appeal for Lay Missionaries for Old Calabar." Like her own writing it had a touch of style and originality, and her comment was "Splendid!" But there was one incidental statement with which she did not agree. Mr. Luke called for two more artisan missionaries—"not to teach the trades; we haven't sufficient men for that, even were Calabar ripe for such instruction." As the result of her own observation and experience she had often felt that something ought to be done to develop the industrial capabilities of the natives. The subject had not been lost sight of by the missionaries and the Mission Board, and the latter had sought, by sending out competent artisans, to attend not only to the work required in connection with the Mission but to train some of the native youths in the various departments of labour. There had, however, been no attempt to establish the work on organised lines, and the remark which Mr. Luke made induced her to place the whole matter before the Church. She penned a long letter, the writing of which so exhausted her that she scarcely knew whether or not the words were rightly spelled. It went to Dr. George Robson, then beginning his long and honourable editorship of the *Record*, and appeared in the next issue under the signature of "One of the Zenana Staff."

It was a letter which displayed all the qualities of missionary statesmanship, was clear, logical, and vigorous in style, and glowed with restrained enthusiasm. She pointed out that it was necessary to help the natives to become an industrial people as well as to Christianise them, and she combated the idea that they were not capable of being taught trades; their weak point no doubt was their want of staying power, their lack of persistence in the face of difficulties, but this could be accounted for by their history; their only rule and mode of life hitherto having been "force of circumstance," The question of training them, however, was too large a problem for the unaided missionary, too large even for the Mission Board; it was a matter for the whole Church to take up. "Let the science of the evangelisation of the nations occupy the attention of our sermons, our congregations, our conferences, and our Church literature, and we will soon have more workers, more wealth, more life, as well as new methods."

So earnest an appeal caused some stir in official circles. The Mission Committee took up the subject, and after interviewing the missionaries who were at home at the time, including herself, referred to Calabar for information. As she had no further connection with the matter the outcome may be briefly noted here. The Calabar Committee were favourable to any scheme of industrial training, and the local Government also expressed their willingness to assist. After the Rev. Dr. Laws, of Livingstonia, and the Rev. W. Risk Thomson, had gone out and reported on the situation and outlook, the proposal rapidly took shape, and the Hope Waddell Training Institute—thus called after the founder of the Mission—came into being, and was soon performing for West Africa the same valuable service that Lovedale and Blythswood were doing for South Africa. She never took any credit for her part in promoting the undertaking, and never made a single reference to it in her letters. She was content to see it realised....

Medical advice sent her down to Devon to recruit. She did not complain or worry about the readjustment of her plans. "We alter things for the good of our children," she said, "and God does the same to us." With Janie she left for Calabar in February 1892, the Congregational Church at Topsham bidding her farewell at a public meeting convened in her honour.

CHAPTER XX
THE BLOOD COVENANT

It was strange, even for her, to pass from the trim, well-ordered life of Britain into the midst of West African heathenism,—to find waiting for her in her yard two refugees who, being charged with witchcraft, had been condemned to be sold and killed and preserved as food,—to be interviewed by a slave woman who had been bought by an Okoyong chief as one of his many wives, after having been the wife of other two men, one of whom had been disposed of to the cannibal tribe, whilst her boy had been carried to Calabar in bondage. Such were the conditions into which she was once more plunged.

The majority of the people admired and trusted hers and gave her implicit obedience, but there were some who avoided and feared her, and sought to undermine her authority and perpetuate the old customs. Her own chiefs remained staunch, and Ma Erne, although a heathen, continued to be her truest friend and best ally. It was to her that Mary was still mainly indebted for news of what was going on. If there was any devilry afoot she would send a certain bottle to the Mission House with a request for medicine. It was a secret warning that she was to be ready to act at a moment's notice. As a result of these hints she was able to prevent many a terrible crime. On one occasion, when the natives were seeking to compass a man's death, she lay down without undressing for a month of nights, ready to set out, and the first night she took off her clothes and endeavoured to obtain a good sleep she was called. And just as she was she set out for the scene. The chiefs began to think it was useless to hoodwink or browbeat the wonderful woman who seemed to know their inmost thoughts and all their hidden plans.

Sometimes, when she received the intimation that a palaver was beginning, and that a fight was imminent, she would not be ready, and would resort to stratagem: she would seize a large sheet of paper and scribble some words—any words—upon it and add some splashes of sealing—wax to make it look important. This she would despatch by a swift runner to the chiefs, and by the time they had discussed the mysterious official—looking document, which none of them, could read, she would come on the scene and allay the excitement and settle the dispute.

One of her favourite devices during palavers was to knit. She fancied that the act kept her from being nervous, as well as from showing fear, while the sight of the knitting going quietly and steadily on, in the midst of uproar, helped to calm the excitement. She used to say that it was only during these long palavers that she could get some knitting done. We can well believe this when we are told by an official that on one occasion she stayed knitting and listening the whole of one day and night, until the opposing powers became hungry, and retired without a fight.

The story of one of these knitting palavers must suffice. Shortly after she returned she wished to settle an important dispute that had been going on for a time between two sections of the Okoyong people. Three years before, a gathering such as she summoned would have been impossible—they would have laid down "medicine" and fought. She trembled to go, and longed for some of the Calabar missionaries to come up and accompany her. But God gave her peace. After a sleepless night she started with her knitting material, and reaching the clearing in the forest passed alone through the guards of armed men. Every chief was there, dressed in all the colours of the rainbow,—thanks chiefly to Mission boxes,—each sitting under a huge umbrella of blue and red and yellow silk, with from twenty to fifty of his men forming a cordon about him, all with guns loaded and swords hanging from their sides.

The sky was sober and grey, and the magnificent foliage overhead made the atmosphere cool and sweet. A chair was placed for her beside the oldest chief, in the centre, with the one party on the right and the other on the left. But first she moved from one group to the other, drawing laughter as she went with her jokes and by-play, and trying to lessen the tension that all experienced. Then she took her seat, started her knitting, and the business began. A word from her was sufficient to check any outburst of feeling, but she only spoke now and then, in order to elicit information or to make clear a bit of evidence.

Time was nothing to these men, and, accustomed to one square meal a day, they did not mind a long sitting; but Mary knew what backache and chill and hunger were and she was often tempted to tell them to keep to the point, but it would have been of no avail.

Night fell, torches were lit, the voices waxed louder, the excitement spread, until Mary felt that matters were getting out of hand, and brought the issue to a head. An old chief summed up, and did so with rare tact and patience and good humour. She gathered up the main points and gave her verdict, which was unanimously adopted with ringing cheers. A native oath had now to be taken to ratify the agreement, and the necessary materials were sent for—a razor, corn, salt, pepper, and rum. A freeman from, each side was called forward, and after divesting themselves of all superfluous clothing they knelt at her feet and clasped each other's fingers. Another made an incision with the razor on the back of their hands, and when the blood had flowed a little salt, pepper, and corn were laid upon the wounds. Then out of courtesy to "Ma," they asked her to say a prayer. But she always witnessed the oath under protest, recognising that they knew no better way, and she would not comply with their request, though she offered no objection to one of the chiefs praying. After the terrible oath formula had been repeated, the two men sucked up the blood-saturated ingredients and swallowed them, and the covenant was ratified. Relieved from the strain, the whole assemblage became suddenly smitten with the spirit of fun. The proceedings were over before midnight, and after a tea hours' sitting Mary began her homeward journey of four miles, tired and hungry, but happy.

CHAPTER XXI
"RUN, MA! RUN!"

Her letters at this time bear witness to the strenuous character of the life she led. They often begin with a description of household events: then a break will occur: the next entry starts with "It is many days since I had to leave off here," and then follows an account of some sudden journey and adventure. Another interruption will take place, caused by some long palaver or rescue: and the end will be a remark such as this: "So, you see, life here, as at home, is just a record of small duties which occupy the time, and task the strength without much to show for it."

Here are some incidents which reveal to us the nature of what she deemed her "commonplace" work:

1. *A Forest Vigil*

"Run, run, Ma! there is something going on!" was the significant message. "Where?" She was told, and went straight off. A chief had died, and the people were administering the poison ordeal at a spot deep in the forest, in order to avoid her interference. She arrived before the proceedings began, and for four days and four nights she remained there constantly on the watch. Her clothes were never off—and only those who have lived in tropical lands know what this means. All the rest she allowed herself was a short half-slumber, as she lay upon some plantain fronds. The men would not leave the spot, hoping to tire her out, and at night they lit fires to keep off the wild beasts of prey, and slept about her. In these long hours she was often afraid, not of the armed men, but of the wild creatures of the bush that came creeping up, and with sombre eyes stared at her for a moment ere they slunk away from the flames. Such courage and endurance could not be withstood,—in the end the people gave in and life was saved.

2. *Egbo*

She was sitting quietly in the house, thinking she was alone, when a stealthy step behind made her look round: it was a woman, followed by others all crowding in as smoothly as tigers. "Run, Ma! run!" they said. The words were no sooner spoken than Mary was down the stair and out in the open "square," where she found a number of men pulling about and frightening the slaves and women. She seized hold of one fellow and locked him in her yard, and the act brought quiet. The mob turned out to be Egbo from a far-off town, come to sue for a debt due by a widow, who had already given up everything to liquidate it. She knew the people, had been kind to them, and had induced them to trade with Calabar. She at once ordered them out of the place, and made them restore the property they had seized, and in a short time the matter was settled,

3. *Robbers*

One day she was busy standing on a box plastering a wall when the warning cry came, "Run, Ma! run!" The villagers had gone off with their arms and were fighting a band of plunderers, who had stolen two slave-girls and two slave-men from Ma Eme's farm. Washing the mud off her hands and face she ran to the scene, and all next day, Sunday, she was sitting in the midst of a drinking mob trying to keep down their passions, and succeeded at last in finding a pacific solution.

4. Twins

Again the cry, "Run, Ma! run!" this time from two boys. It was a case of twins born of a Calabar mother, who had come to Okoyong after trade began. The father and his womenkind were furious, and the mother lay deserted and alone. Mary took the two babies into her lap, and as they were Calabar twins sent word to the elder chief. The answer she received was "Ahem!" But the messenger added, "A big lady said, 'Why don't you take the twins to Calabar?'"

She next sent to the younger chief, and asked him to come and confer with her at a distance.

After two hours' weary waiting the reply was, "I am not coming, what should I come for? Should I tell my Mother what to do? Let her do what she sees fit."

"Well," said Mary, "as one chief says, 'Ahem' and the other gives no command, I shall take the children by a back road to my own house, and during the night the mother can follow, and we will see how things turn round."

On being told that she had brought twins to the house Edem groaned and said, "Then I cannot go to my Mother's house any more. Are they upstairs?"

"Yes," said the messenger, "and they are in her own bed."

He groaned again, "No, no, I cannot ever go any more."

Mary went to his yard to see a sick baby, whom she had nursed back from death's door after the witch-doctors had done their best with their charms and medicine, but the mother held the child tightly in her arms and said, "Ma, you shall not touch her!" She turned away, her heart sore.

On the Sunday rain fell all day, and she could not leave one of the children who was ill, but in the late evening she took two lanterns and went to the roadside and held a short service with the few prepared to come, and who huddled together in the rain. But none of them guessed how near to tears the speaker was. She felt the alienation from her people keenly; it was the greatest trial that had come to her, but she was resolved not to give in.

One of the twins died, and some days later Edem offered her a present of yams, but she declined the gift, as it might be mistaken for a bribe to her conscience. He remonstrated, but she remained firm, although it cost her much. Gradually, however, he and his House showed contrition, and the shadow passed away.

Then a chief from another village came, also with a present of yams. Going on his knees he held her feet and begged her not to give up the child. "You are our Mother; and a woman has proved stronger than all the men of the tribe: we will be able to believe in all you ask us by and by, but have patience with us."

When he was gone a message came: "A chief from a distance wants to see you; come for a little."

This man was from a turbulent part of Okoyong and given to fighting and plundering.

"I live in my house as ever I did," was her spirited reply; "and if any one wishes to see me I am here." She felt pretty sure of her ground, though she could not help trembling for the result.

The strangers arrived, and Edem with them, and chairs and mats were placed for them in the court. To her surprise she was asked for her advice, and the visitor went away convinced that the new ways were better than the old.

The elder chief, Ekpenyong, next sent and begged for forgiveness. "The Mother cannot keep a strong heart against her son. Are you not the hope and strength and counsellor of my life? Forgive me, for it was foolishness, I have not been taught from my youth, and have never seen a twin."

Thus good came out of the trial, and the bonds that bound her to the people were strengthened. What was still more remarkable than the attitude of the chiefs was the fact that the husband took the twin- mother and the surviving child home.

5. *The Poison Bean*

A slave woman of importance who occupied a position of trust died suddenly. When her master was told he flew into a passion and despatched a messenger to Mary with the rude intimation that "somebody hereabouts knew how to kill people." She returned a curt reply, and he sent an apology. The next development was the appearance of some chiefs and a crowd of armed men in her yard. With them was a young man, not a favourite of hers, to whom they attributed the woman's death. She questioned him, and he asserted that he had not seen the woman for months, and knew nothing of the supposed witchcraft; but he would take the poison bean, and, he added vindictively, if he did not die he would see that they paid for the outrage. She sent a message by the chiefs to the owner of the woman to dissuade him from inflicting the extreme test. There was the usual period of uproar, and on her part the usual recourse to prayer, and then back came the chiefs with the astonishing reply:

> "I have heard. I understand that the Mother is determined
> in her way. What can I do but submit."

Instead of death the sequel was a feast, a goat was killed, drink procured, and dancing was indulged in all night. Next day the young man went home to his aged mother.

6. *Runaway Slaves*

One day when she was baking, a man and his wife, slaves of a chief in the neighbourhood, came to the door of the Mission House, and after giving compliments squatted down with the air of people who had come to stay.

"Well, what is the matter?" she asked. She knew the woman had a child, which could not have been left at home.

A long tale was told. The woman had been in the field all morning hoeing grass: as the sun rose she and her child grew hungry and she went home to cook some food. As she was doing so her master, who was not a favourite either with bond or free, unexpectedly appeared, and angrily ordered her back to her work. She protested that she needed food, but, brandishing a sword, he frightened her into flight. Her husband, a palm-oil worker, heard the noise, and came on the scene, stopped her, and told her to return and take the food. "What does it matter?" he remarked, "we are his; he can kill us if he likes; we have nothing to live for." The master, enraged, seized a gun and fired at the man, but missed. Taking hold of the screaming child he declared he would kill it and went off.

It was a simple case, but required delicate handling. She sent one of her girls to the chief with the message that his slaves were in her yard, and that as they were householders and elderly people and parents, she hoped there would be no palaver, and that he would take them back.

"I will come to-morrow," was the reply.

The runaways slept in the yard and held something of the nature of a reception, the other slaves coming and condoling with them as the poor do with each other all the world over. It was like a scene from *Uncle Tom's Cabin*. One moment the company would encourage them cheerily, urging them to have patience, then came a string of doleful tales, then a gush of warm sympathy, and next a burst of laughter, followed by a shower of tears.

Next day their master did not appear, and they went to work on the station grounds. The woman was fretting for her child, and Mana, one of the girls, was sent with another message, to the effect that if he could not come himself he must, for the woman's sake, send on the babe. The messenger brought back the news that he was on his way, but was tipsy, and breathing out dire threats against everybody. When Mary heard that three of his wives were with him, and that her own chief had joined the party, her mind was at ease.

His first act was to lie down at her feet. "Ma," he said, "you are the owner not only of my head but of all my house and my possessions. These wretched slaves did well to come to you"—and so forth.

She sent for a chair and a palaver of several hours began. The master sometimes lost control of himself and charged the slave with being full of sorcery and responsible for all the deaths of recent years. Shaking his fist in the man's face he cried:

"If it wasn't sfor the reign of the white woman I would cut you in two! The white woman is your salvation."

The slave biased with passion, but Mary entreated him to be calm. She set the matter in the best light. Both had been angry and behaved as angry people usually do, saying and doing things which in their saner moods they would have avoided. Alternately scolding and beseeching, and throwing in a few jokes occasionally, she at last said both must go home, the master to restrain himself, and the slaves to work faithfully and not to provoke him, as he had troubles of which they were unaware.

Thus with wise words she pacified them, and when she had given them a few presents they went off in great good humour. The slaves found that during their absence thieves had stolen their goats and fowls, but the return of the child compensated for the loss, and in their gratitude they sent "Ma" a gift of food.

7. Spoilt Fashions

A woman was seized on the assumption that she was concerned in the death of a girl, and Mary watched day and night until the burial was over. A goat was killed and placed in the grave, along with cloth, dishes, pots, salt, a lamp, a lantern, and a tin case of cooked food. But her presence prevented any one being murdered to bear the dead company. "Ma!" said a freeman reproachfully, "you have spoiled our fashions. Before you came, a person took his people with him: now one must go alone like this poor girl; you have confused Okoyong too much." The woman who was seized was allowed to take the native oath, praying that if she had a hand in the girl's death *mbiam* should eat her and corrupt her body until she died.

8. The Cost

Mr. W. T. Weir, who had joined the Mission staff, paid her a visit one day, and they were enjoying a cup of tea when she suddenly became alert and said, "There's something wrong, they will be here in a moment." The words were hardly spoken when they heard the pit-pat of bare feet running towards the house. A number of natives appeared, and placing their hands on the floor shouted, "Ma! come! come! come!"

She said to her guest, "Come on." They reached a large compound filled with people excitedly shouting and gesticulating. On one side of the yard lay a girl on a mud slab who seemed to be ill, and opposite was her mother, in appearance a fiend incarnate. It appeared that the girl, the daughter of an old chief, had taken a fainting fit, and the mother, who had once been a refugee in "Ma's" yard, was blaming people for taking her life.

Mr. Weir examined the girl, and said there was nothing much wrong, but she was terribly excited with the noise. Mary at once said, "I'll get quietness," and springing into the middle of the compound she seemed to exert her utmost will-power, and, crying in the native manner, "*Soi, wara do*" (Shoo, go out there!), pointed to the door. In a moment, men, women, and children, including the staid old chief of the village, and the girl's mother, struggled with each other to get out of the compound. The scene reminded Mr. Weir of nothing so much as a lot of sheep being hurried through a gate by a dog. She then came to where he stood. She was trembling from head to foot, and as she sat down she remarked, "I am done for this day." The girl was taken over to the Mission House, and under her care made a quick recovery....

Never in all her dealings with the tribes was she molested in any way. Once only, in a compound brawl, in which she intervened, was she struck, but the native who wielded the stick had touched her accidentally. The cry immediately went up that "Ma" was hurt, and both sides fell on the wretched man, and would have killed him had she not gone to the rescue.

CHAPTER XXII
A GOVERNMENT AGENT

In these years far-reaching changes were taking place in regard to the political status and destiny of the country. Hitherto the British Government had exercised only a nominal influence over the coast districts. A consul was stationed at Duke Towns but he had no means of exercising authority, and the tribes higher up the Cross River would war upon one another, block the navigation, and murder at will. In 1889 the Imperial Government took steps to arrange for an efficient administration, and despite difficulties incidental to the absence of a central native authority succeeded in obtaining the sanction of the principal chiefs to the establishment of a protectorate—the Niger Coast Protectorate. In 1891 Sir Claude Macdonald, who had carried out the negotiations, was appointed Consul—General. No man was better fitted to lay the foundations of British authority in so backward a territory. The period of transition from native to civilised rule brought to the surface many delicate and perplexing problems requiring tact, skill, and unwearied patience, but the task was successfully accomplished, though not without an occasional display of force. It was a special cause of thankfulness to the missionaries that Sir Claude was in full sympathy with their work, and co-operated with them in every scheme for the benefit of the people. When he was promoted to Pekin, the Foreign Mission Board in Scotland expressed their sense of the value of his efforts in promoting the welfare of the native population.

Sir Claude appointed vice-consuls for the various districts, and was proposing to send some one to Okoyong. Miss Slessor knew that her people were not ready for the sudden introduction of new laws, and that there would be trouble if an outside official came in to impose them. Sir Claude took her point of view, and recognising her unique position and influence, empowered her to do all that was necessary, and to organise and supervise a native court. He then left her very much to herself, with the result that the inevitable changes were felt least of all in Okoyong, where they were made through a woman whom the chiefs and people implicitly trusted. Her position was akin to that of a consular agent, and she conducted all the public affairs of the tribe. She presided at the native court. Cases would be referred to her from Duke Town, and she would travel over Okoyong to try these, taking with her the consular messenger, who carried back her decision to headquarters for official signature. Crowds of the natives also visited her to consult her regarding the readjustment and co-ordination of their customs with the new laws, and she was able to settle these matters so quietly that little was heard of her achievements. Although she rendered great service in this way, creating public opinion, establishing just laws, and protecting the poor, it was a work she did not like, and she only accepted it because she thought it in line with her allegiance to Christ.

Her duties brought her in contact with the officials of the country. Government men came to see her, and were not only amazed at her political influence, but charmed with her original qualities. One of these, Mr. T. D. Maxwell, for whom she had a great regard—"a dear laddie" she called him—writes:

What sort of woman I expected to see I hardly know; certainly not what I did. A little frail old lady with a lace or lace-like shawl over her head and shoulders (that must, I think, have been a concession to a stranger, for I never saw the thing again), swaying herself in a rocking-chair and crooning to a black baby in her arms. I remember being struck—most unreasonably—by the very strong Scottish accent. Her welcome was everything kind and cordial. I had had a long march, it was an appallingly hot day, and she insisted on complete rest before we proceeded to the business of the Court. It was held just below her house. Her compound was full of litigants, witnesses, and onlookers, and it was impressive to see how deep was the respect with which she was treated by them all. She was again in her rocking-chair surrounded by several ladies-and babies-in-waiting, nursing another infant.

Suddenly she jumped up with an angry growl: her shawl fell off, the baby was hurriedly transferred to some one qualified to hold it, and with a few trenchant words she made for the door where a hulking, overdressed native stood. In a moment she seized him by the scruff of the neck, boxed his ears, and hustled him out into the yard, telling him quite explicitly what he might expect if he came back again without her consent. I watched him and his followers slink away very crestfallen. Then, as suddenly as it had arisen the tornado subsided, and (lace shawl, baby, and all) she was again gently swaying in her chair. The man was a local monarch of sorts, who had been impudent to her, and she had forbidden him to come near her house again until he had not only apologised but done some prescribed penance. Under the pretext of calling on me he had defied her orders—and that was the result.

I have had a good deal of experience of Nigerian Courts of various kinds, but have never met one which better deserves to be termed a Court of Justice than that over which she presided. The litigants emphatically got justice—sometimes, perhaps, like Shylock, "more than they desired"—and it was essential justice unhampered by legal technicalities. One decision I recall—I have often subsequently wished that I could follow it as a precedent. A sued B for a small debt. B admitted owing the money, and the Court (that is "Ma") ordered him to pay accordingly: but she added, "A is a rascal. He treats his mother shamefully, he neglects his children, only the other day he beat one of his wives with quite unnecessary vehemence, yes and she was B's sister too, his farm is a disgrace, he seldom washes, and then there was the palaver about C's goat a month ago. Oh, of course A didn't steal it, he was found not guilty wasn't he?—all the same the affair was never satisfactorily cleared up, and he did look unusually sleek just about then. On the other hand, B was thrifty and respectable, so before B paid the amount due he would give A a good sound caning in the presence of everybody."

CHAPTER XXIII
"ECCENTRICITIES," SPADE-WORK, AND DAY-DREAMS

Does it seem as if we were watching the career of a woman of hard, self-reliant, and masculine character, capable of living by herself and preferring it, and unconscious of the natural weakness of her sex? In reality Mary was a winsome soul, womanly in all her ways, tremulous with feeling and sympathy, loving love and companionship, and not unacquainted with nervousness and fear.

When people saw, or heard of her, toiling with her hands they were apt to imagine that she possessed a constitution of iron, never realising that her life was one long martyrdom. She was seldom free from illness and pain. Whether her methods of life were partly responsible for this cannot be stated. In any case, she seemed able to do things that would have proved fatal to other people. She never used mosquito-netting, which is considered to be indispensable for the security of health in the tropics. She never wore a hat, which seems a miracle to those who know the strength of the sun in these regions. Her hair she kept cut close, partly because it was a cleanlier fashion, and partly because it was less trouble to look after. Shoes and stockings, also, she never wore, although jiggers and snakes and poisonous plants were common in the bush pathways. Mr. James Lindsay, who was the engineer of the Mission at this time, says, "I walked many miles with her through the bush, and only once did I know her to be troubled with her feet. She had been to Duke Town, attending Presbytery, and made some small concession to the conventions by wearing a pair of knitted woollen slippers. On returning to Okoyong through the bush, small twigs and sticks penetrated the wool and pricked her feet. With an expression of disgust she took the slippers off and threw them into the bush. That was the only time I saw her other than barefoot." She never boiled or filtered the water she drank, two precautions which Europeans do not omit without suffering. She ate native food, and was not particular when meals were served. Breakfast might be at seven one morning and at ten the next; dinner might be an hour or two late; but this was, of course, mainly due to the constant calls upon her time, for she was often afoot most of the night, and her days were frequently taken up with long palavers.

These habits, so seemingly eccentric to people lapped In the civilised order of things, grown naturally out of the circumstances into which she had been forced In pursuit of the task she had set herself. She had deliberately given up everything for her Master, and she accepted all the consequences that the renunciation, involved. What she did was for Him and as she was not her own and had taken Him at His word and believed that He would care for her if she kept in line with His will, she went forward without fear, knowing that she might, through inadvertence, incur suffering, but willing to bear it for His sake and His cause. Her faith devotion led her into strange situations, and these shaped the character of her outward life and habits. She shed many conventions, simply because it was necessary in order to carry out the will of Christ. She knew there were some people like the official who saw her pushing a canoe down to the river and preferred not to know her; but she was always sustained by the knowledge that she was acting in her Master's spirit. She found in her New Testament that He ignored the opinion of the world, and she was never afraid to follow where He led. "What," says Mr. Lindsay, "she lost in outward respectability she more than gained in mobility and usefulness. She kept herself untrammelled in the matter of dress that she might be ready for any emergency. In of a sudden call in the night to some distant village where twin children had been thrown out or a bloody quarrel was imminent, she was literally ready to leave at a moment's notice." The one thing essential to her was her work, and anything that hampered her freedom of action was dropped.

Not that she was thoughtlessly reckless of her health. She frequently wrote about the need of conserving her strength, and stated that she was taking all due care. She apologised for reading her Bible in bed on Sunday mornings; it gave her a rest, she said, before she began her day's work. As her Sunday began at 5.30 A.M. and ended at 7 P.M., and during the greater part of that time she was walking, preaching, and teaching, she might well allow herself the indulgence. It may be noted that she sometimes misplaced Sunday. "I lost it a fortnight ago," she wrote, "and kept it on a Saturday. Never mind, God would hear all the prayers and answer them all the same." On another occasion she was discovered on a Sunday on the roof of the house executing repairs, thinking it was Monday.

Mr. Ovens relates that once when he went up on a Monday to do some work he found her holding a service. She was glad to see him; "but what," said she, "is Duke Town coming to when its carpenter travels on the Sabbath Day?"

"Sabbath Day!" he echoed. "It's Monday."

"Monday! why, I thought it was Sabbath. Well, we'll have to keep it as Sabbath now."

"Na, na," he replied, "it's no Sabbath wi' me. I canna afford two Sabbaths in a week."

"Ah, we must though," she said; adding in a whisper, "I was whitewashing the rooms yesterday."

Realising that he must "save her face," he took part in the service and started his work next morning.

In one of Mr. Goldie's letters to a friend at this time there is a delightful touch. "I am at Okoyong," he wrote, "and am not sure of the date."

Her womanly sympathy and tenderness were never better exhibited than in her relations with her dark sisters about her. She entered into their lives as few have been able to do. She treated them as human beings, saw the romance and tragedy in their patient lives, wept over their trials, and rejoiced in their joys. There was one little idyll of harem life which she liked to tell.

Some slave-dealers arrived at Ekenge, and among their "bargains" was a young and handsome girl, whom Edem bought for one of his chief men. Ma Erne, who heard of the transaction but paid no attention to it, had a respectable slave-woman at one of her farms whom she ordered to come and live in her own yard. The woman obeyed somewhat unwillingly, and in the village began to grumble to others about her enforced removal. The new slave-girl was cooking her master's food when she heard the voice. As she listened memories were stirred within her and she ran out and gazed at the woman, then went nearer and stared closely into her face. The woman demanded what she was looking at. The girl screamed and caught her round the neck and uttered a word in a strange language. It was the name of the woman, who, in turn, stared at the girl. When the latter called out her own name the two embraced and held each other in a grip of iron. The daughter had found a mother who had been stolen many years before. Both went into the yard and sat on the ground discussing their experiences and receiving the warm congratulations of the other women in the village.

There was trouble at the time in the district, and Mary had occasion to see Ma Eme after midnight. She found the two sitting beside some burning logs, with Ma Eme on the other side, all three talking over the mystery of life and its pain and parting and sorrow. She squatted down beside them, and gradually the girl told her story. How she had prayed to the great God for some one to capture her so that she might have a chance of finding her mother when the traders went to Calabar. She believed that among the crowds at Duke Town she would see her face, and when they left there she almost lost hope.

But "Ma" craved the companionship of her kind, and she enjoyed going down to Duke Town to the various meetings, and seeing the ladies of the Mission. She would not leave the children behind, and as the whole family would descend unexpectedly on a member of the Mission staff, some embarrassing situations occurred. One missionary, a bachelor, was preparing to turn in about 10 P.M. when he heard people crowding up the stairs of the verandahs and a babel of voices. It was "Ma" and all her boys and girls and babies come to lodge with him for a week. Fortunately he knew his guests, and, as he surmised, they were content with the floor. When the household grew, and she could not leave the children so often, she would sometimes walk with them to Adiabo on the Calabar River, taking provisions with her, and there, halfway, would meet and picnic with the Calabar lady agents.

It was about this time that the sense of her loneliness grew upon her to such, an extent that she could not sleep at nights, "I feel dreadfully lonely," she wrote, "and want a helper, and I have made up my mind to ask the Committee at next meeting for a companion." But when she went to Duke Town and realised the depleted state of the Mission caused by illness and death, and the manner in which the staff was overworked, she could not find the heart to prefer her request, and instead she thanked God for being able to hold on. She added her appeal to the other requests for workers that were so constantly sent home then, and her idea of the kind of woman most suited for the Calabar field is of interest:

… Consecrated, affectionate women who are not afraid of work or of filth of any kind, moral or material. Women who can nurse a baby or teach a child to wash and comb as well as to read and write, women who can tactfully smooth over a roughness and for Christ's sake bear a snub, and take any place which may open. Women who can take everything to Jesus and there get strength to smile and persevere and pull on under any circumstances. If they can play Beethoven and paint and draw and speak French and German so much the better, but we can want all these latter accomplishments if they have only a loving heart, willing hands, and common sense. Surely such women are not out of our reach. There are thousands of them in our churches, and our home churches have no monopoly of privilege in choosing to keep them. Spare us a few. Induce them to come forward. If there be the call from the Holy Spirit do not let mere accomplishments be a *sine qua non*. Help them to come forward. Take them to your own homes and let them have the benefit of all the conversation and refinement and beauty which fill these, and so gently lead them out of their timidity and accustom them to society that they may meet out in the world, and hand them on to us. Up in a station like mine they want to teach the first principles of everything, and they need to help in times of trouble in the home or in the town palaver. They will not need fine English, for there is none to admire it. No one knows other than native languages, and I would gladly hail any warm-hearted woman from any sphere if she would come to me. I cannot pretend to work this station: the school work is simply a scramble at the thing, mostly by the girls of the house. I can't overtake it. It is because I am not doing it efficiently that I am grieved.

On her visits to Calabar she was an object of much interest. One who knew her then says: "She had the power of attracting young men, and she had great influence with them. Whether they were in Mission work, or traders, or government men, they were sure to be attracted by her vigorous character and by the large-hearted, understanding way she would talk to them or listen to their talk of their work or other interests. She loved to stir them to do great things."

It was sometimes remarked by visitors that her surroundings had not the spick-and-span appearance which usually characterises a Scottish Mission station. She had, nevertheless, a real appreciation of order and beauty, and liked to have everything clean and tidy about her. How to accomplish this was her daily problem, and perhaps only those who have lived in tropical lands can understand the position. The difficulty there is not how to make things grow, but how to prevent them growing. She waged as fierce and incessant a war with vegetation as she did with man, but it proved too much for her strength. "I think," she wrote, "if I left alone some of the outdoor work, even it the place did go to bush and dirt, I would not be so tired, and I could do more otherwise. But I can't help it. I must put my hands in wherever there is work to be done." The task had not become easier for her, for the new trade with Calabar had brought about a demand for Okoyong yams, and the people were so busy planting at their farms that she was unable to hire labour. The bush would creep up swiftly and stealthily to the edge of the dwellings and become a covering for beasts of prey, and, then she and her girls would sally out and cut it down and burn it and dig out the roots. And in its place would be planted corn and cocos and yams and other products, the children each having a plot to tend. A private pathway to the spring which she had constructed in order that the girls might not mix with the village women and hear their talk had also to be kept clear. It was hard work in the hot sunshine, and she and her bairns literally watered the soil with their perspiration. But no tears were shed at the work save those caused by merry jokes and laughter. She often surveyed the scene with pride, revelling in the wild beauty of form and colour, the brilliancy of the flowering trees, the tender green of the yams on their supports, the starry jasmine with its keen perfume. She loved flowers, and taught her scholars to bring them to school. They had never been conscious of these before, and the fact that they began to appreciate them was, she considered, a step forward in their educational development.

Often she longed for the power to bring out thousands of the slum people from the cities at home to enjoy the open life, and to work the rich lands. Not that she used the word "slum"; it seemed to reflect on the poor, many of whom she regarded as the heroes and heroines of God; in her humility she believed that many of them would have been far ahead of her if they had had the same advantages. One of her day-dreams was to inherit a fortune and to spend it all on the poor. "If only" — but she would check herself and say, "Mary Slessor! as if God does not know what to give and how to give it, and as if He did not love and think for all these poor creatures who are so mercilessly pushed aside in the race of life."

CHAPTER XXIV
MAIDEN-MOTHER AND ANGEL-CHILD

Of all the tasks to which she put her hand the sweetest as well as the saddest was the care of the babes of the bush. Her house was the refuge of little children: sickly ones that were left with her to nurse and return; discarded ones that were taken to her; outcast ones that she rescued from injury and death. So many came, received names, were described in her letters, and then passed out of sight, that her friends in Scotland were unable to keep abreast of her efforts in this direction.

They arrived in all stages of sickness, but usually the last. With many a broken body she had never a chance, but with marvellous patience and tenderness she washed them and nursed them and loved them and fought the dark shadow that was ever ready to hover over the tiny forms. Night after night she would sit up watching a face that was wasted and twisted with pain, or walk to and fro crooning snatches of song to soothe a restless mite in her arms. Sometimes a hammock was slung up beside her into which they were placed, so that if they awoke during the night she could touch it with her foot and swing them to sleep again. More than once, when the supply of condensed milk ran out, she strapped her latest baby to her body and tramped the long miles to Creek Town through the bush, and returned next day with the child and the tins.

The children that were brought back to health and strength and restored to their parents it was always a pang to part with. She wished she could have kept them and trained them up away from the degraded influences of their homes. Those who died she dressed and placed among flowers in a box, held a service over them, and buried them in a little cemetery, which by and by became full of tiny graves. She mourned over them as if they had been blood of her blood. Mr. Ovens used to say to her, "Never mind, lassie, you'll get plenty mair" — and indeed there were always plenty,

Of all the African children that passed through her hands none endeared itself so much to her as Susie, her first Okoyong twin. The mother, Iye, was a slave from Bende, light in colour and handsome, and was the property of one of the big women, who treated her with kindness and consideration. When the twins arrived all was changed. Miss Kingsley, who arrived at Ekenge the same day on a visit to Mary, thus describes the scene:

She was subjected to torrents of virulent abuse, her things were torn from her, her English china basins, possessions she valued most highly, were smashed, her clothes were torn, and she was driven out as an unclean thing. Had it not been for the fear of incurring Miss Slessor's anger, she would, at this point have been killed with her children, and the bodies thrown into the bush. As it was, she was hounded out of the village. The rest of her possessions were jammed into an empty gin-case and cast to her. No one would touch her, as they might not touch to kill. Miss Slessor had heard of the twins' arrival and had started off, barefooted and bareheaded, at that pace she can go down a bush path. By the time she had gone four miles she met the procession, the woman coming to her, and all the rest of the village yelling and howling behind her. On the top of her head was the gin-case, into which the children had been stuffed, on the top of them the woman's big brass skillet, and on the top of that her two market calabashes. Needless to say, on arriving Miss Slessor took charge of affairs, relieving the unfortunate, weak, staggering woman from her load and carrying it herself, for no one else would touch it, or anything belonging to those awful twin things, and they started back together to Miss Slessor's house in the forest-clearing, saved by that tact which, coupled with her courage, has given Miss Slessor an influence and a power among the negroes unmatched in its way by that of any other white.

She did not take the twins and their mother down the village path to her own house, for though, had she done so, the people of Okoyong would not have prevented her, yet so polluted would the path have been and so dangerous to pass down, that they would have been compelled to cut another, no light task in that bit of forest, I assure you. So Miss Slessor stood waiting in the broiling sun, in the hot season's height, while a path was being cut to enable her just to get through to her own grounds. The natives worked away hard, knowing that it saved the polluting of a long stretch of market road, and when it was finished Miss Slessor went to her own house by it, and attended with all kindness, promptness, and skill to the woman and children. I arrived in the middle of this affair for my first meeting with Miss Slessor, and things at Okoyong were rather crowded, one way and another, that afternoon. All the attention one of the children wanted—the boy, for there were a boy and a girl—was burying, for the people who had crammed them into the box had utterly smashed the child's head. The other child was alive, and is still a member of that household of rescued children, all of whom owe their lives to Miss Slessor.

The natives would not touch it, and only approached it after some days, and then only when it was held by Miss Slessor or me. If either of us wanted to do or get something, and we handed over the bundle to one of the house children to hold, there was a stampede of men and women off the verandah, out of the yard, and over the fence, if need be, that was exceedingly comic, but most convincing as to the reality of the terror and horror in which they held the thing. Even its own mother could not be trusted with the child; she would have killed it. She never betrayed the slightest desire to have it with her, and after a few days' nursing and feeding up she was anxious to go back to her mistress, who, being an enlightened woman, was willing to have her if she came without the child.

The woman's own lamentations were pathetic. She would sit for hours singing or rather mourning out a kind of dirge over herself: "Yesterday I was a woman, now I am a horror, a thing all people ran from. Yesterday they would eat with me, now they spit on me. Yesterday they would talk to me with sweet mouth, and now they greet me only with curses and execrations. They have smashed my basin, they have torn my clothes," so on, and so on. There was no complaint against the people for doing these things, only a bitter sense of injury against some superhuman power that had sent this withering curse of twins down on her,

The surviving infant, Susie, was not commonplace in feature like the other black children; she was not in reality a negress, but fair, shapely, and clean-skinned, with a nose like a white child's and a sweet mouth—a mouth which Miss Kingsley called the "button-hole." Every one loved her, and she was queen of the household.

When she was fourteen months old Miss Slessor one day went to the dispensary and left her in charge of Mana, who put down a jug of boiling water on the floor beside her. Susie thought it a plaything, and, seizing it, pulled it over upon herself. Instead of calling for "Ma" Mana ran with the child to the bathroom and poured cold water over the wounds. For thirteen days and nights she was never out of Mary's hands. Fortunately Miss Murray, a lady agent who, at her own request, had been stationed at Okoyong for a time, and whose companionship she valued, helped her greatly. "She was like a sister to me," she wrote. Thinking more might be done by a medical man she started off with the child in her arms, arrived at Creek Town at midnight, and woke up the doctor, who, however, said he could not do more than she had done. She returned at once to Ekenge, and again watched the suffering babe by day and night. In the darkness and silence, when all were asleep, she would hear the faint words, "Mem,

Mem, Mem!"—the child's name for her—and the wee hand would be held up for her to kiss. Early one Sunday morning she passed away in her arms. Robed in a pinafore, with her beads and a sash, and a flower in her hand, she looked "like an angel child."

The event caused a strange stir in Okoyong. None of the villagers went to their farms or market while the child was hovering on the brink of death, and when she passed away they came and mourned with "Ma."

She was buried in the cemetery where so many other hapless waifs were already at rest. In her anguish Mary could not conduct the service, but sat at the window and looked out while Miss Murray bravely took her place. The people, respectful and sad, gathered round the grave—the grave of a twin!—and one of the women, a leader in heathenism, praised the white Mother's God for the child, and prayed that they might all have her hope in the Beyond. "Surely," was Mary's comment, "they all felt the vast difference between their burials with all their drink and madness, and ours so full of quiet hope and expectant faith."

The slave-mother had often come to visit her, and had actually got to love the child, and when it died she was heartbroken. "Ma," she said, "don't cry. I have done this. God hates me. I shall go away and not bring any more evil on you." With that she went back to her hut in the bush.

"If I were a wealthy woman," said "Ma," "I would buy her; but I cannot afford it, so we must do our best to cheer her up."

Although she objected to buying slave-women, even to restore them to freedom, on account of the wrong impression it left on the native mind, she made an exception in the case of Iye, and not long afterwards she was able to purchase her liberty for £10, and she became an inmate of the Mission House, Miss Slessor's intention being to train her so that she might be useful to any lady who lived at the station during her absences in Scotland. To the natives Iye was an outcast, and had "no character." "*Etubom*," Mary said to Mr. Ovens, "If a slave-dealer came round I would not get £6 for her." "Why?" said he. "She has no character." "But he would buy her and take her up country." "What for?" "To feed her for chop!"...

For some time she suffered physically from the shock she had received. No mother could have grieved more bitterly over the loss of a beloved child. "My heart aches for my darling," she wrote. "Oh the empty place, and the silence and the vain longing for the sweet voice and the soft caress and the funny ways. Oh, Susie, Susie!"

CHAPTER XXV
MARY KINGSLEY'S VISIT

Miss Kingsley paid her visit to the West Coast in 1893. Like all who travelled in West Africa, she heard of the woman missionary who lived alone among the wild Okoyong, and made a point of going up to see her. Miss Slessor welcomed so capable and earnest a worker, "She gave me," says Miss Kingsley, "some of the pleasantest days of my life." In some respects these two brilliant women were much akin, though they were poles asunder in regard to their outlook on spiritual verities. They had long discussions on religious subjects, and would sit up late beating over such questions as the immortality of the soul. Miss Kingsley was profoundly impressed. "I would give anything to possess your beliefs," she said wistfully, "but I can't, I can't; when God made me He must have left out the part that one believes with."

Nevertheless Miss Slessor said that for all her beliefs and unbeliefs she was one of the most truly Christian women she had ever met. On her return to England Miss Kingsley spoke often of her in terms of affection and admiration, and acknowledged to friends that she had done her much spiritual good. Mary, on her part, poured into her possession all her treasures of knowledge concerning the fetish ideas and practices of the natives, and probably none knew more about these matters than she. Most missionaries confess that they never get to the back of the negro mind, and one who worked in a neighbouring field once said that after nineteen years' careful study he had yet to master the intricacies of native superstition. The information that Mary supplied was therefore of great value, and much of it was utilised in Miss Kingsley's books. In *Travels in West Africa* she gives the following considered view of the missionary:

This very wonderful lady has been eighteen years in Calabar; for the last six or seven living entirely alone, as far as white folks go, in a clearing in the forest near to one of the principal villages of the Okoyong district, and ruling as a veritable white chief over the entire district. Her great abilities, both physical and intellectual, have given her among the savage tribe a unique position, and won her, from white and black who know her, a profound esteem. Her knowledge of the native, his language, his ways of thought, his diseases, his difficulties, and all that is his, is extraordinary, and the amount of good she has done, no man can fully estimate. Okoyong, when she went there alone—living in the native houses while she built, with the assistance of the natives, her present house—was a district regarded with fear by the Duke and Creek Town natives, and practically unknown to Europeans. It was given, as most of the surrounding districts still are, to killing at funerals, ordeal by poison, and perpetual internecine wars. Many of these evil customs she has stamped out, and Okoyong rarely gives trouble to its nominal rulers, the Consuls, in Old Calabar, and trade passes freely through it down to the seaports. This instance of what one white can do would give many important lessons in West Coast administration and development. Only the sort of man Miss Slessor represents is rare. There are but few who have the same power of resisting the malarial climate, and of acquiring the language and an insight into the negro mind, so perhaps after all it is no great wonder that Miss Slessor stands alone, as she certainly does.

With all her robust ability Miss Kingsley's mental range was curiously narrow. She wrote strongly against Protestant missionary aims and methods in West Africa, her views being entirely opposed to those of the White Woman of Okoyong, who had a much greater right to speak on the subject. But the latter, nevertheless, loved her, and when the news of her death came, some years later, she was plunged into grief. "The world held not many so brave and so noble," she wrote. "Life feels very cold and seems grey and sunless." Hearing of a proposed memorial to the intrepid traveller she sent a guinea as her mite towards it.

CHAPTER XXVI
AN ALL-NIGHT JOURNEY

An outburst of fighting had taken place amongst the factions around Ekenge. Women were the cause of it, and a number had been herded into a stockade near the Mission House, where a band of men were proceeding to murder them. Mary came on the scene and held them at bay. All day she stood there and all night, her girls handing her from time to time a cup of tea through the poles of the enclosure. Next night matters had become quieter, a tornado of rain and wind having eased the situation, but she was soaked, whilst the mats of the Mission House had blown up and the interior had been flooded, so that both the girls and herself needed dry garments. Then the condensed milk was nearly done, she was told, and the baby she was nursing would suffer without it. Both clothing and milk could only be procured from Calabar, and as she had no messenger to despatch there, she resolved to go herself.

After dark she stole out of the stockade, placed the child in a basket, secured a woman as guide, and with a lantern started out to walk through the bush to Creek Town. She reached Adiabo on the Calabar River about half-past ten, obtained a cup of tea from the native pastor, and pushed on. Her guide lost the way, a deluge of rain fell, and they wandered aimlessly for a time through the dripping forest, before again striking the track.

Creek Town was reached at four o'clock in the morning. She knocked up Miss Johnstone, who sent her to bed for an hour, and sought for some tins of milk. As soon as two had been procured Mary was eager to be off. Miss Johnstone gave her some changes of clothing, and King Eyo put his canoe and a strong crew at her disposal, and she was soon speeding up-river. On her arrival she found to her satisfaction that her absence had not been discovered, and she was able eventually to restore peace without the shedding of blood.

Two days later a canoe which came down-river to Duke Town brought word that she was ill with dysentery. Dr. Laws of Livingstonia, who was then visiting the Mission as a deputy, happened to be at Creek Town and was asked to go and see her with Mr. Manson, one of the industrial staff, as guide. Their canoe was nearly swamped by rain, and they had to change their clothing when they arrived. She was soon up and through to the hall to provide hospitality for her guests, supporting herself by the table the while. A peremptory order came from Dr. Laws to return to bed at once. She gave him a long curious look, and then without a word went and lay down. He noticed that his companion appeared both astonished and amused, and it was not until he returned to Calabar, and heard Mr. Manson telling how "Ma" Slessor had been taken in charge for once, that he realised how bold he had been. Dr. Laws thought that few women, or even men, could have stood the isolation that she endured.

CHAPTER XXVII
AKOM: A FIRST-FRUIT

Although force of circumstances made her the instrument of law and order her chief aim was to win the people to Christ, and all her efforts were directed to that end. It was for souls she was always hungering, and the lack of conversions was her greatest sorrow. Nevertheless she was making progress. The people were becoming familiar with the name of God and Christ and the principles underlying the Gospel, and there were many who leant more to the new way than to the old, whilst some in their hearts believed. The boys that were being trained at school and service were perhaps the most cheering element in the situation, and upon them she set her hopes.

It was wonderful that she achieved what she did in view of the conditions that prevailed. How difficult it was for a native to break away from habits and customs ingrained in them through centuries of repetition may be gathered from the story of Akom, a freewoman, one of the most self-righteous of the big ladies of the district. She had been betrothed, when a year old, to a young and powerful chief, and had been brought up in the harem and was a zealous upholder of all superstitious practices. On her lord's death she escaped the poison ordeal, and was active in placing wives and slaves into the grave. By and by Ekpenyong made her his wife and mistress of the harem, and for twenty years she held undisputed sway.

When Edem's son was killed by the falling of a log it will be remembered that Ekpenyong was blamed for the event and retired to the bush. Not long afterwards a young chief there fell sick, and the witch- doctor on consulting his oracle declared that he saw Akom and her son dancing the whole night long, and gaily piercing the sick man with knives and spears. Akom was charged with sorcery, and asked to take the poison ordeal. Her friends advised her to flee, and she and her son disappeared during the night and took refuge in Umon, where the people gave them the protection of their *ibritam* or juju.

"Ma" was in Scotland at the time. When she returned Ekpenyong begged her to interfere and have his wife brought back. This she managed to do after Akom had taken *mbiam*—the strongest and most dreaded of native oaths, which included the drinking of blood shed from the wrist. The woman came to see her, but stood outside. "What?" exclaimed "Ma," "you cannot come within my gate?" "No," was the reply; "you had a twin-mother once living in the yard, and I cannot come in lest I touch the place she touched," Those who took the *mbiam* oath, believed that they would die if they came in contact in any way with a twin-mother. "Ma" pretended to be hurt, and said, "If my house is polluted you had better go home, as I do not receive visitors on the road." After a time Akom ventured in, and she was kind to her and gave her an order for mats, at the making of which she was an adept.

She then came regularly and listened intently to "Ma's" teaching, although she said nothing. By and by she began to remark on the purity of the Gospel religion and show increased reverence at the services. Twins came, and she mastered her fear and went into the house. But alas! a mysterious pain straightway developed in her foot, and this surely was *mbiam* punishing her; and when a skin disease followed, her faith nearly failed her, and she wailed and mourned in despair. "Ma" spoke strongly to her; and at last she rose and said, "I am a fool; my God, my Father, listen not to my foolishness. Kill me if Thou wilt, but do not leave me."

The disease was checked, and a native medicine effected a cure. But she stood out against any sacrifice, saying very sensibly, "My Father owns the bush and gives us the knowledge of the medicine, and as the Master knows what He has made He knows also how to bless it apart from any outsider."

Ekpenyong all this while had ignored his wife, expecting that the *mbiam* would do its work. He looked grimly on, and when she injured her foot against a root he believed the end had arrived. All the people watched the struggle between the white woman's prayers and the *mbiam's* power, and when the wound healed they were nonplussed, but quaintly explained the miracle by saying that their Mother was different from other white people, and so had prevailed.

Akom grew in grace despite her surroundings, and found strength in her contact with Christ. An amazing thing to her was that the man who had accused her of witchcraft came and made friends with her.

"Ma," she said, "see what God has wrought. The man who demanded my life comes to tell me his affairs! I sometimes wanted to take revenge, but I have got it from God, and His revenge is of a sweeter kind than that of the Consul."

It was cases like this that coloured Miss Slessor's life with joy. Sometimes, too, she was unexpectedly cheered by evidence of the fruit of her work in past days. In 1894 a lad, an old scholar of hers in Duke Town, turned up in the village. He had made good use of his education, and wherever he went, on farm and on beach, he held worship and got the people to listen. It was not surprising that she regarded the boys as her most hopeful agents, although she was always very careful in choosing them as teachers for bush schools; she thought it belittled the message to send those who were not thoroughly fit for the work.

CHAPTER XXVIII
THE BOX FROM HOME

The most joyous break in the domestic life at Ekenge, both for the house-mother and the children, was caused by the arrival of boxes of gifts from Scotland. So many congregations and Sunday Schools had become interested in her and her work that there was a continuous stream of packages to Okoyong. "I am ashamed at receiving so much," she would say. Her own friends also remembered her; and on one occasion she wrote to a lady who had sent a personal contribution, "It seems like a box from a whole congregation, not from an individual."

She was specially delighted with the articles that came from the children of the Church, and many a letter she wrote in return to the scholars in Sunday Schools. None knew better how to thank them. She would give them a picture of the landing of the boxes at Duke Town, and the journey up the Calabar River in the canoe or in the steamer *David Williamson* — which they had themselves subscribed for and supplied — to the beach, and of the excitement when the engineer came over, perhaps with visitors, to announce the arrival. "White people come, Ma!" The cry by day or night always roused the household. One girl ran to make up the fire and put on the kettle, another placed the spare room in order, a third took the hand parcels and wraps, and "Ma" herself welcomed the guests with a Scottish word or two, and a warm hand-clasp. They would give her home letters, but these she would lay aside until she was more at leisure. Then a whisper would go round that there were goods at the beach, and every man, woman, and child about the place would be eager to be off to bring them up. But the boxes would be too large and heavy to be borne on heads through the forest, and they would be opened and the contents made up into packages, with which the carriers marched off in single file. Depositing them at the house they would return for more until all were safely conveyed. Then the articles would be exposed amidst cries of wonder and delight, and the house become like a bazaar. Sometimes there would be a mix-up of articles, but the loving messages pinned on to each would clear up the confusion. Mary dearly loved to linger over each gift and spin a little history into it, and she would pray with a full heart, "Lord Jesus thou knowest the giver and the love and the prayers and the self-denial. Bless and accept and use all for Thy glory and for the good of these poor straying ignorant children, and repay all a thousandfold."

She was careful in her allocation of the gifts amongst the people in order that they might not be regarded as a bribe to ensure good behaviour or attendance at the services. She would not even give them as payment for work done, as this, she thought, put the service on a commercial basis and made them look again for an equivalent gain. Pictures and texts, like dolls, were somewhat of a problem, as there was a danger of the people worshipping them. But they liked to beautify their squalid huts with them, and she regarded them as an educative and civilising agency not to be despised. Also to a certain extent they gave an indication of those who had sympathy with the new ideas, and were sometimes a silent confession of a break with heathenism.

To one old woman, the first Christian, was given a copy of "The Light of the World." Holding it reverently she exclaimed, "Oh! I shall never be lonely any more. I can't read the Book, but I can sit or lie and look at my Lord, and we can speak together. Oh, my Saviour, keep me till I see you up yonder!" It was explained that the picture was an allegory, and the woman understood; but she simply saw Christ in all the fervour of her newborn love and faith, and Mary trusted to keep her right by daily teaching.

Some of the articles found odd uses. A dress would be given to a girl who was entering into seclusion for fattening; a dressing-gown would go to the chief who was a member of the native Court, and he would wear it when trying cases, to the admiration of the people; a white shirt would be presented to another chief, and he would don it like a State robe when paying "Ma" a formal visit. Blouses she retained, since no native women wore them. The pretty baby-clothes were a source of wonder to the people—they were speechless at the idea of infants wearing such priceless things. It must be confessed that there was something for which "Ma" always searched when a box from her own friends arrived. Like the children she was fond of sweets, and there would be a shriek of delight from more than juvenile lips when the well-known tins and bottles were discovered in some corner where they had been designedly hidden.

CHAPTER XXIX
AN APPEAL TO THE CONSUL

"Religious missions have worked persistently and well, and pointed out to the people the evil of their cruelties and wrongdoing, but there comes a time when their efforts need backing up by the strong arm of the law of civilisation and right."

Sir Claude Macdonald wrote this in the autumn of 1894. Perhaps he had in mind the case of Okoyong. For in that year Miss Slessor came to the conclusion that it was time to invoke the great power which lay behind her in order to put a stop to the practice of killing on charges of witchcraft.

She was busy with a twin-murder case when word suddenly arrived that a man was being blamed for causing his master's death, and that a palaver was going on. She sent some of the children at once to say that when her household had retired she would walk over in the moonlight. But a tornado came on, and the rain poured all night. As soon as it cleared she despatched a message: "Don't do anything till I come—I will come when the bush is drier." On receiving this the accuser rose: "Am I not to give him any ordeal till Ma comes? I will not be able to do it then! She won't be willing. Unlock his chains and take him to Okat Ikan, where he will be beyond her reach."

Seizing the man his henchmen hurried him off, and the chief followed with a grunt of satisfaction at having outwitted the White Mother.

When she heard of the manoeuvre she determined not to go wandering aimlessly in the bush in search of the party. She resolved to do what she had never done before, send down to the Consulate at Duke Town and seek the assistance of the Government not only to rescue this particular victim, but to end the evil throughout the length and breadth of Okoyong.

The house-girls became aware of her intention, and the news that "Ma's" patience, so often and so sorely tried, was at last exhausted, and that she was going to adopt stronger measures, spread swiftly through the villages. In order not to involve any native in the transaction she was the bearer of her own communication to the beach, and she was not long gone on her walk through the forest when the people concerned arrived breathlessly at the Mission House to beg her to forgive them for going beyond her voice.

"Ma is away," announced the children, "and you cannot reach her now."

Sadder and wiser they returned to their village, for they feared the Consul, who was associated in their minds with big guns and burnt towns. She returned late at night, wearied with the journey, yet was up early in the morning again and walked six miles in intense heat to a palaver, carrying a couple of babies. When she arrived she was at the point of fainting.

The next night the slave who had been carried off succeeded in breaking the lock of his chains and escaped to the Mission House. In his baffled rage his master chained all who belonged to him, but fear of the impending visit of the Consul made him reflect, and he sent word later to "Ma" to ask her forgiveness, and to say that all the people had been freed. He asked her to go down to Duke Town and make the Consul come "in peace and not in war." She did so, taking the refugee with her. The Consul adopted her view of the situation, and arranged to visit the district and hold a conference. To this she invited all the chiefs, telling them to free their minds of fear, and preparing them for the subjects that would be dealt with.

It was Mr. Moor, the Vice-Consul, who came, and he brought a small guard of honour which paraded in the village, and gave Okoyong a greater thrill than it had yet experienced. Mr. Moor found "Ma" on the roof of her house repairing the mats which had been leaking, but she was not in the least perturbed, and received him with perfect composure. He was very patient and kind with the chiefs, but sought to impress upon them the necessity for some improvement in their habits. Already Mary had been much impressed with the new stamp of Government official under Sir Claude Macdonald, and this representative of the class she thought one of the best.

As a result of the conference the chiefs promised to abstain from killing at funerals, and to allow "Ma" to have an opportunity of saving twins and caring for them in a special hut. She gave thanks to God; but she knew the African nature, and did not relax her vigilance. A month after the Consul's visit a kinsman of the above chief, older and much more wealthy, died suddenly. "We trembled for their promise to the Consul," she wrote, "but we left them to themselves, believing that it was better to trust them to a great extent, and instead of going and staying with them to watch, we sent our compliments and gifts, and told them we expected they would remember their treaty and the consequences of any breach of faith. After all was over not a slave or vassal was missing, and though there were not wanting idle tongues let loose by the unlimited supply of strong drink, and brawlings, and determinations to take the poison of their own accord in order to prove their innocence, not one person has died as the direct result of the dread event."

Mrs. Weir once spent a week-end at Okoyong, and accompanied her to a village two or three miles away where she was in the habit of going to conduct a service. When they arrived they found that the head of a house had died, and was being buried, according to custom, inside the house. They were taken to the place and saw the dead man's possessions —his pipe, snuff-box, powder-flask, and other articles—placed in the grave in order that they might be useful to him in the other world. Mrs. Weir could not help wondering at their superstition after all the teaching that they had been given. She said nothing; but Mary, with her keen intuition, read her thoughts and said. "You will be thinking they are not very different yet, but when I came to Okoyong, do you think I would have seen men and women moving freely about like this? They would have all been refugees in the bush, and those who had been caught would have been in chains, waiting to be put to death, so that their spirits might accompany the chief."

Towards the end of the year she had what she called one of her descents into the valley of the shadow, and was removed to Duke Town. "Daddy" Anderson, who had retired, but had come out again to Calabar on a visit, walked over to see her; he said very little, but just sat and held her hand. He, himself, was passing into the shadow, but not to return. She was with him at the last, and did her best to comfort him. "Dear Daddy Anderson!" she wrote; "Calabar seems a strange land to me now. All the friends are strangers to the old order. The Calabar of my girlhood is among the things of the past."

Her scepticism regarding the promise of the people was justified, for the killing of twins went on as usual; and in the following year she brought up Sir Claude Macdonald himself to renew the covenant. Sir Claude was all kindness and courtesy, assuring the chiefs that he did not come to take their country, but to guide them into a proper way of governing it, that all, bond and free, might dwell in safety and peace. What he insisted on was their recognition of the claims of justice and humanity. The spokesman, an old greyheaded man, said they wished to retire, in order to consult together. On returning he naively excused their conduct by stating that when they only heard words once they thought the matter unworthy of their consideration, but when they were repeated, they thought there must be something in them, and so they would obey the requirements of the Government this time. As regards twins, they were doubtful, "We are not sure that no evil will happen to us if we obey you; we have our fear, but we will try." They would not, however, consent to keep them in their own homes, and again Mary said that if they would notify her of the births she would be responsible for their welfare.

She had been acting as interpreter, and as the palaver lasted from early morning until after dark she was much fatigued. Her last words were to encourage the chiefs to keep their pledge, and they would enjoy the benefits when she might be no more with them. The very suggestion of farewell alarmed them. "God cannot take you away from your children," they exclaimed, "until they are able to walk by themselves."

CHAPTER XXX
AFTER SEVEN YEARS

Africa is slow to change: the centuries roll over it, leaving scarcely a trace of their passing: the years come and go, and the people remain the same: all effort seems in vain. Could one weak woman affect the conditions even in a small district of the mighty continent?

It had been uphill work for her. At first there had been only a dogged response to the message she had brought. When some impression had been made she found that it soon disappeared. In ordinary life the people were volatile, quick as fire to resent, and as quick to forgive and forget, and they were the same in regard to higher things. They went into rapture over the Gospel, prayed aloud, clasped their hands, shed tears, and then went back to their drinking, sacrificing, and quarrelling. They kept to all the old ways, in case they might miss the right one. "Yes, Ma," they would say, "that is right for you; but you and we are different."

But she never lost hope. "There is not much progress to report," she was accustomed to say, "and yet very much to thank God for, and to lead us to take courage." She was quite content to go on bringing rays of sunshine into the dark lives of the people, and securing for the children better conditions than their fathers had. "After all," she would say, "it comes back to this, Christ sent me to preach the Gospel, and He will look after results." She was always much comforted by the thought of something she had heard the Rev. Dr. Beatt, of her old church in Aberdeen, say in a sermon: she could recall nothing but the heads, and one of these was, "*Between the sower and the reaper stands the Husbandman.*" But results there were of a most important kind, and it is time to take stock of them. Fortunately she was induced at this time to jot down some impressions of her work, and these, which were never published, give the best idea of the remarkable change which had been wrought in the life and habits of Okoyong. It will be noticed that she does not use the pronoun "I." Whenever she gave a statement of her work she always wrote "we," as if she were a co-worker with a Higher Power.

"In these days of high pressure," she says, "men demand large profits and quick returns in every department of our commercial and national life, and these must be served up with the definiteness and precision of statistics. This abnormal and feverish haste has entered to some extent into our religious work, and is felt more or less in all the pulses of our Church. Whatever may be the reasons for such a course in regard to worldly callings, its methods and standards are utterly foreign to the laws of Christ's kingdom, and can only result in distortions and miscalculations when applied to His work. While thanking God for every evidence of life and growth, we shrink from reducing the throes of spiritual life, the development and workings of the conscience, or the impulse and trend toward God and righteousness, to any given number of figures on a table. Hence it is with the greatest reluctance that we endeavour to sum up some tangible proof of the power of God's Word among our heathen neighbours. While to our shame and confusion of face it has not been what it might, and would have been had we been more faithful and kept more in line with the will and spirit of God, it has to the praise of the glory of His grace proved stronger than sin and Satan.

"We do not attempt to give in numbers those who are nominally Christian. Women, lads, girls, and a few men profess to have placed themselves in God's hands. All the children within reach are sent to the school without stipulation. One lady of free birth and good position has borne persecution for Christ's sake. We speak with diffidence; for as no ordained minister has ever been resident or available for more than a short visit, no observance of the ordinances of Baptism or the Lord's Supper have been held and we have not had the usual definite offers of persons as candidates for Church membership, We have just kept on sowing the seed of the Word, believing that when God's time comes to gather them into the visible Church there will be some among us ready to participate in the privilege and honour.

"Of results as affecting the condition and conduct of our people generally, it is more easy to speak. Raiding, plundering, the stealing of slaves, have almost entirely ceased. Any person from any place can come now for trade of pleasure, and stay wherever they choose, their persons and property being as safe as in Calabar. For fully a year we have heard of nothing like violence from even the most backward of our people. They have thanked me for restraining them in the past, and begged me to be their consul, as they neither wished black man nor white man to be their king. It would be impossible, apart from a belief in God's particular and personal providence in answer to prayer, to account for the ready obedience and submission to our judgment which was accorded to us. It seemed sometimes to be almost miraculous that hordes of armed, drunken, passion-swayed men should give heed and chivalrous homage to a woman, and one who had neither wealth nor outward display of any kind to produce the slightest sentiment in her favour. But such was the case, and we do not recollect one instance of insubordination.

"As their intercourse with the white men increased through trade or otherwise, they found that to submit to his authority did not mean loss of liberty but the opposite, and gradually their objections cleared away, till in 1894 they formally met and bound themselves to some extent by treaty with the Consul. Again, later, our considerate, patient, tactful Governor, Sir Claude Macdonald, met them, and at that interview the last objection was removed, and they promised unconditional surrender of the old laws which were based on unrighteousness and cruelty, and cordial acceptance of the just and, as they called it, 'clean' code which he proffered them in return, Since then he has proclaimed them a free people in every respect among neighbouring tribes, and so, placing them on their honour, so to speak, has made out of the roughest material a lot of self-respecting men who conduct their business in a fashion from which Europeans might take lessons. Of course they need superintendence and watching, for their ideas are not so nicely balanced as ours in regard to the shades and degrees of right and wrong, but as compared with their former ideas and practice they are far away ahead of what we expected.

"No tribe was formerly so feared because of their utter disregard of human life, but human life is now safe. No chief ever died without the sacrifice of many lives, but this custom has now ceased. Only last month the man who, for age, wealth, and general influence, exceeded all the other chiefs in Okoyong, died from the effects of cold caught three months before. We trembled, as they are at some distance from us, and every drop of European drink which could be bought from all the towns around was bought at once, and canoes were sent from every hamlet with all the produce at command to Duke Town for some more, and all was consumed before the people dispersed from the funeral. But the only death resulting has been that of a man, who, on being blamed by the witch-doctors, went and hanged himself because the chiefs in attendance—drunk as they were—refused to give him the poison ordeal. Some chiefs, gathered for palaver at our house on the day of his death, in commenting on the wonderful change said, 'Ma, you white people are God Almighty. No other power could have done this.'

"With regard to infanticide and twin-murder we can speak hopefully. It will doubtless take some time to develop in them the spirit of self-sacrifice to the extent of nursing the vital spark for the mere love of God and humanity among the body of the people. The ideals of those emerging from heathenism are almost necessarily low. What the foreigner does is all very well for the foreigner, but the force of habit or something more subtle evidently excuses the practice of the virtue among themselves. Of course there are exceptions. All the evidence goes to show that something more tangible than sentiment or principle determines the conduct of the multitude, even among those avowedly Christian. But with all this there has dawned on them the fact that life is worth saving, even at the risk of one's own: and though chiefs and subjects alike, less than two years ago, refused to hear of the saving of twins, we have already their promise and the first instalment of their fidelity to their promise in the persons of two baby girls aged six and five months respectively, who have already won the hearts of some of our neighbours and the love of all the school children. Seven women have literally touched them, and all the people, including the most practical of the chiefs, come to the house and hold their palavers in full view of where the children are being nursed. One chief who, with fierce gesticulations, some years ago protested that we must draw the line at twins, and that they should never be brought to light in his lifetime, brought one of his children who was very ill, two months ago, and laid it on our knee alongside the twin already there, saying with a sob in his voice, 'There! they are all yours, living or dying, they are all yours. Do what you like with mine.'

"Drinking, especially among the women, is on the decrease. The old bands of roving women who came to us at first are now only a memory and a name. The women still drink, but it is at home where the husband can keep them in check. In our immediate neighbourhood it is an extremely rare thing to see a woman intoxicated, even on feast days and at funerals. None of the women who frequent our house ever taste it at all, but they still keep it for sale and give it to visitors. Indeed it is the only thing which commands a ready sale and brings ready money, and their excuse is just that of many of the Church members at home, that those who want it will get it elsewhere, and perhaps in greater measure. But we have noted a decided stand being taken by several of the young mothers who have been our friends and scholars against its being given by husbands or visitors to their children. We have also thankfully noted for long that on our making an appearance anywhere there is a run made to hide the bottles, and the chief indignantly threatens any slave who brings it into our presence.

"All this points to an improvement in the condition of the people generally. They are eager for education. Instead of the apathy and incredulous laugh which the mention of the Word formerly brought, the cry from all parts is for teachers; and there is a disposition to be friendly to any one who will help them towards a higher plane of living. But it brings vividly before us the failures and weaknesses in our work; for instance, the desultoriness of our teaching, which of necessity stultifies the results that under better conditions would be sure to follow. School teaching has been carried on under great difficulties owing to the scattered population, the family quarrels which made it formerly a risk to walk alone, the fear of sorcery and of the evil spirits which are supposed to dwell in the forest, the denseness of the forest itself, which makes it dangerous for children to go from one place to another without an armed escort, the withdrawing of girls when they have just been able to read in order to go to their seclusion and fattening, and the consequent drafting of them to great distances to their husbands' farms, the irregular attendance of boys who accompany their masters wherever they go, and who take the place of postmen and news-agents-general to the country.

"There have been difficulties on our own side—the distances consume time and strength, the multifarious claims made on the Mission House, the household itself which is usually a large one having in addition to servants those who are training for future usefulness in special spheres—as the Mission House has been until quite lately the only means of getting such training—and having usually one or more of the rescued victims of heathen customs. The Dispensary work calls also for much time and strength, nursing often having to accompany the medicine; the very ignorance and superstition of the patients and their friends making the task doubly trying. Then one must be ever at hand to hear the plaint of and to shelter and reconcile the runaway slave or wife or the threatened victim of oppression and superstition. Visitors are to be received, and all the bothersome and, to European notions, stupid details of native etiquette are to be observed if we are to win the favour and confidence of the people.

"Moreover we must be both able and willing to help ourselves in regard to the wear and tear in our dwelling and station buildings. We must make and keep in repair buildings, fences, drainage, etc., and all amid surroundings in which the climate and its forces are leagued against us.

"Add to all this the cares of housekeeping when there is no baker supply, no butcher supply, no water supply, no gas supply, no coal supply, no laundry supply, no trained-servant supply, nor untrained either for that matter, except when some native can and will lend you a slave to help you or when you can buy one—which, under ordinary circumstances is a very doubtful practice, as, though in buying the person you are literally freeing him, the natives are apt to misinterpret the motive, and unless you are very fortunate in your purchase, the slave may bring you into conflict with the powers that be, owing to their law which recognises no freedom except that conferred by birth. After all this is seen to day by day, where is the time and strength for comprehensive and consecutive work of a more directly evangelistic and teaching type?—specially when the latter is manned year by year by the magnificent total of one individual. Is it fair to expect results under such circumstances?"

CHAPTER XXXI
THE PASSING OF THE CHIEFS

In the year 1896 Miss Slessor realised that she was no longer in the centre of her people. Like all agricultural populations addicted to primitive methods of cultivation, they had gradually moved on to richer lands elsewhere. Even Ma Erne had gone to a farm some distance away. A market had been opened at a place called Akpap, farther inland and nearer the Cross River, and farms and villages had grown up around it, and she saw that it would be necessary to follow the population there. The Calabar Committee—a Committee had succeeded the Presbytery—was at first doubtful of the wisdom of transferring the station, largely owing to the remoteness and inaccessibility of the new site, the nearest landing-place being six miles away, at Ikunetu on the Cross River. There was some advantage in this, however, for the Mission launch was constantly moving up and down the waterway. The voyage was between low, bush-covered banks broken by vistas of cool green inlets, with here a tall palm tree or bunch of feathery bamboos, and there a cluster of huts, while canoes were frequently passed laden with hogsheads of palm oil for the factory, or a little dug-out containing a solitary fisher. The track from Ikunetu to Akpap was the ordinary shady bush path, bordered by palms, bananas, orange trees, ferns, and orchids, but in the wet season it was overgrown with thick grass, higher than one's head, which made a guide necessary, since one trail in the African forest looks exactly like another.

After some consideration it was decided to sanction the change, and to build a good Mission House with a beach shed at Ikunetu. Long before the house was built, however, and even before it was begun, Mary installed herself at Akpap, in conditions similar to those of her first year at Ekenge. Her home consisted of a small shed of two divisions, without windows or floor, into which she and the children and the furniture were packed. And from this humble abode, as from a palace, she ruled Okoyong with all the dignity and power of a queen. Never had her days been so busy or her nights so broken and sleepless. No quarrel, tribal or domestic, no question of difficulty of any kind, was settled other than in the Mission hut. Sometimes the strain was almost greater than she could bear. There was much sickness among the children, and an infectious native disease, introduced by a new baby, caused the death of four. Matters were not mended by an epidemic of small-pox, which swept over the country and carried off hundreds of the people. For hours every day she was employed in vaccinating all who came to her. Mr. Alexander, who was the engineer of the Mission at this time—the natives called him *etúbom ubom nsuñikañ* "captain of the smoking canoe"—remembers arriving when her supply of lymph had run out, and of assisting her with a penknife from the arms of those who had already been inoculated.

The outbreak was severe at Ekenge, and she went over and converted her old house into a hospital. The people who were attacked flocked to it, but all who could fled from the plague-stricken scene, and she was unable to secure any one to nurse the patients or bury them when they died. She was saddened by the loss of many friends. Ekpenyong was seized and succumbed, and she committed his body to the earth. Then Edem, her own chief, caught the infection, and she braced herself to save him. She could not forget his kindness and consideration for her throughout all these years, and she fought for his life day and night, tending him with the utmost solicitude and patience. It was in vain. He passed away in the middle of the night. She was alone, but with her own hands she fashioned a coffin and placed him into it, and with her own hands she dug a grave and buried him. Then turning from the ghostly spot with its melancholy community of dead and dying, she tramped through the dark and dew-sodden forest to Akpap, where, utterly exhausted, she threw herself on her bed as the land was whitening before the dawn.

Towards the village that day two white men made their way,—Mr. Ovens, who was coming to build a Mission House, and Mr. Alexander who had brought him up. When they arrived at the little shed it was eleven o'clock in the forenoon. All was quiet. "Something wrong," remarked Mr. Alexander, and they moved quickly to the hut. A weak voice answered their knock and call, and on gaining entrance they found "Ma" tired and heavy-eyed. "I had only just now fallen asleep," she confessed. But it was not for some time that they learned where she had been and what she had done.

When, two days later, Mr. Alexander went over to bring some material from the old house, he found it full of corpses and not a soul to be seen. The place was never fit for habitation again, and gradually it was engulfed in bush and vanished from the face of the earth.

Conditions were the same far and wide, and her heart was full of pity for the helpless people, "Heartrending accounts," she wrote, "come from up-country, where the people, panic-stricken, are fleeing and leaving the dead and dying in their houses, only to be stricken down themselves in the bush. They have no helper up there, and know of no Saviour. I am just thinking that perhaps the reason God has taken my four bairns is that I may be free to go up and help them. If the brethren say that I should go I shall."

It is not surprising that these events had a depressing effect upon her; she said she had no heart for anything. It was an unusual note to come from her, and indicated that her strength was waning. The presence of Mr. Ovens was a help; his sense of humour seasoned the days, and he made light of difficulty and trial, though he was far from comfortable. One of the divisions in the shed had been turned over to him, she and her children crowding into the other. The place was infested by ants and lizards, and all night the rats used his body as a springboard to reach the roof. There was always one scene in the strange household which touched him with a feeling of pathos and reverence—family worship in the evening. A light from a small lamp illumined the interior. Miss Slessor sat on the mud-floor with her back resting on the wall. Squatting before her in a half-circle were the girls and boys of the house. Behind these were ranged a number of baskets filled with twin babies. "Ma" spoke and prayed very simply and naturally. Then a hymn of her own composition was sung in Efik to the tune of "Rothesay Bay," she accompanying it with a tambourine. If the attention of the girls wandered she would lean forward and tap them on the head with the instrument.

One human solace never failed her—the letters from home. How eagerly she longed for them! How they lifted her out of her surroundings and chased away for a time the moral miasma that surrounded her and often seemed to choke her as if it were physical. Some one wrote about the Synod meetings. "It is easy to be good," she said, "with all the holy and helpful influences about you. Fancy a crowd of Christians that fill the Synod Hall! It makes me envious to read about it. Away up here among heathenism, working away with the twos and the threes and the tens, one almost forgets that there are crowds who would die for Christ. But, with all their imperfections, there are, and we are not in a losing cause at all. I am seldom in Duke Town or Creek Town, and hear little in the way of sermons, and have little of the outward help you have. But Christ is here and the Holy Spirit, and if I am seldom in a triumphant or ecstatic mood I am always satisfied and happy in His love."

Her furlough was overdue, but there was a difficulty in filling her place, and she would not leave the people alone. Meanwhile she kept "drudging away" as well as she could from dawn till dark. People were coming to her now from far-off spots, many from across the river from unknown regions who had never seen a white person before, drawn to her by the fame of her goodness and power. At first they sat outside, and would not cook or eat or drink inside the compound because of the twins, but by and by they gained courage and mixed with the household. The majority of these people were neither bright nor good-looking, but she only saw souls that were precious in the sight of her Master. In one of her letters she describes what was the daily scene: "Four at my feet listening; five boys outside getting a reading-lesson from Janie; a man lying on the ground who has run away from his master and is taking refuge until I get him forgiven; an old chief with a girl who has a bad ulcer; a woman begging for my intervention with her husband; a nice girl with heavy leglets from her knee to the ankles, with pieces of cloth wrapped round to prevent the skin being cut, whom I am teaching; and three for vaccination."

On the last night of the year she wrote: "My bairns have been made happy and myself glad by a handsome Christmas box from the Consul-General and Colonel Boisragon of our Consular staff. They were up with a party, and spent the greater part of three days with me, trying to do good among my people: and they have sent dolls and sweets and fruit and biscuits, and many useful things for the house, and a carpenter to mend my stair, and plane and rehang my doors. He is here now doing odds and ends about the house, so I feel quite cheered up. He (the Consul) must have gone to a steamer and got all these things for us, for there are no such things for sale here, and it shows how much interested he is in mission work. It is seldom, comparatively, that Government officials care for these things."

CHAPTER XXXII
CLOTHED BY FAITH

As Mr. Ovens was at Akpap engaged on the new Mission House the Calabar Committee decided to send her home in 1898 whether they could supply the station or not. "It will be rather trying to get back to the home kind of life and language," she said; "but I shall just want a place to hide in: away from conventionalities and all the paraphernalia of civilisation." Her chief problem was the disposal of the children, whom she dreaded to leave under native influences. There were so few missionaries in the field then that it was difficult to find homes for them. She settled two babies, some of her girls, and the former slave- woman with a lady agent. The rest she made up her mind to take with her. It was a daring thing to do, but doing daring things was her normal habit. She justified herself to a friend by saying that Janie was now a big girl and a great help. Mary was five years old and able to fend for herself; Alice was about three and fairly independent, and Maggie was sixteen months, and could sit about and be easily amused.

The next problem was how to equip both herself and her retinue for the voyage. Her wardrobe had been gradually deplenished in the bush, and during her illnesses ants had eaten up all that remained. She and the children had nothing but the old garments they had on. But she was not dismayed: in the simplicity of her faith she believed that the Master knew her difficulty, and would come to her aid and provide all her needs. And she was not disappointed.

When at Duke Town, preparatory to departure, a box from Renfield Street Church, Glasgow, arrived for her, and she went down to the beach and opened it to see if it contained anything she might require. And everything she required was there, including many knitted and woollen articles—a most uncommon circumstance. There was also a shawl—"I do not know what I should have done without that on the voyage," she said. The ladies of the Mission took the cloth and flannelette and soon had the whole party fitted out. In acknowledging the box she begged the givers not to be vexed at what she had done: the articles had been used in the service of Christ as much as if they had been distributed in Okoyong.

She was so far spent that she was carried on board. On the voyage she received much kindness, and believing that God was behind it all she accepted everything as from Him and was very grateful. Her simple faith in the goodness of her kind was shown by the fact that the telegram she despatched on arriving at Liverpool to Mrs. M'Crindle, Joppa, was the first intimation that lady received that she was coming. And at the railway station she confidingly handed her purse to the porter, asking him to take it and buy the tickets, Mrs. M'Crindle met her at the Waverley Station, Edinburgh. There was the usual bustle on the arrival of a train from the South. The sight of a little black girl being handed down from the carriage caused a mild stir, when another came the interest increased, when a third dropped down a crowd gathered, when a fourth stepped out the cabmen and porters forgot their fares and stared, wondering who the slight, foreign-looking lady could be who had brought so strange a family.

CHAPTER XXXIII
THE SHY SPEAKER

Eagerly looked for after her heroic service in Okoyong she received a warm welcome from her friends in the United Presbyterian Church. For some weeks she lived at Joppa, and then anxious to be independent she took a small house near at hand, where she and Janie managed the work and cooking. It was not a very comfortable *ménage*, and Miss Adam, one of the "chief women" of the Church and Convener of the Zenana Mission Committee, made arrangements for her and the children staying at Bowden, St. Boswells. Here, looking down upon a beautiful expanse of historic border country, she spent a quiet and restful time. As her vitality and spirits came back she began to address meetings, and found that the interest in her work had deepened and extended.

She was, if anything, shyer than ever, and would not speak before men. At a drawing-room gathering in Glasgow the husband of the lady of the house and two well-known ministers were present. She rose to give an address, but no words came. Turning to the men she said, "Will the gentlemen kindly go away?" The lady of the house said it would be a great disappointment to them not to hear her, "Then," she replied, "will they kindly go and sit where I cannot see them?" When she began to speak she seemed to forget her diffidence, and she held the little audience spellbound. At a Stirling meeting a gentleman slipped in. After a slight pause she said, "If the gentleman in the meeting would hide behind the lady in front of him I would be more at my ease." On another occasion she fled from the platform when called on to speak, and it was only with difficulty that she was brought back. When people began to praise her she slipped out and remained away until they had finished.

"She was a most gentle-looking lady," writes one who heard her then, "rather below the average height, a complexion like yellow parchment, and short lank brown hair: a most pleasing expression and winning smile, and when she spoke I thought I had never heard such a musical voice." She went to her home-city, Aberdeen, and addressed a meeting in Belmont Street Church, which her mother had attended; and of her power of speech the Rev. Dr. Beatt, the minister, who was in the chair, says: "It was characterised by a simple diction, a tearful sympathy, a restrained passion, and a pleading love for her people, which made it difficult to listen to her without deep emotion." At one meeting in Glasgow she spent an hour shaking hands. "What a lot of love there is in the world after all," she said gratefully. She received such a reception at a meeting in Edinburgh that she broke down. Recovering herself she earnestly denied that her work was more remarkable than that of any other missionary in Calabar: "They all work as hard or harder than I do." She went on to plead for an ordained missionary for Okoyong. "I feel that my work there is done, I can teach them no more. I would like to go farther inland and make a home among a tribe of cannibals."

Many a stirring appeal she made for workers.

"If missions are a failure," she said, "it is our failure and not God's. If we only prayed and had more faith what a difference it would make! In Calabar we are going back every day. For years we have been going back. The China Inland Mission keep on asking for men, men, men, and they get what they want and more than we get. We keep calling for money, money, money, and we get money—of great value in its place—but not the men and the women. Where are they? When Sir Herbert Kitchener, going out to conquer the Soudan required help, thousands of the brightest of our young men were ready. Where are the soldiers of the Cross? In a recent war in Africa in a region with the same climate and the same malarial swamp as Calabar there were hundreds of officers and men offering their services, and a Royal Prince went out. But the banner of the Cross goes a-begging. Why should the Queen have good soldiers and not the King of Kings?"

Her nervous timidity was often curiously exhibited. She was, for instance, afraid of crowds, and she would never cross a city street alone; and once, when she was proceeding to a village meeting she would not take a short cut through a field because there was a cow in it. Yet she was never lacking in high courage when the need arose. At a meeting in Edinburgh several addresses had been delivered, and the collection was announced. As is often the case the audience drew a sigh of relief, relaxed attention, and made a stir in changing positions. Some began to whisper and to carry on a conversation with those sitting near them. She stood the situation as long as she could, then rose, and spoke, regardless of all the dignitaries about her, and rebuked the audience for their want of reverence. Were they not presenting their offerings to the Lord? Was that not as much an act of worship as singing and praying? How then could they behave in such a thoughtless and unbecoming manner? There was something of scorn in her voice as she contrasted the way in which the Calabar converts presented their offerings with that of the well-educated Edinburgh audience. When she sat down it was amidst profound silence. "That is a brave woman," was the thought of many.

With her bairns she left towards the end of the year (1898), Miss Adam accompanying them to Liverpool to see them safely on board. A more notable person than she realised, she was sought out by a special representative of Reuter's Agency and interviewed. Her story of the superstitious practices connected with the birth of twins in West Africa had the element of horror which makes good "copy," and most of the newspapers in the kingdom next day gave a long description of these customs and of her work of rescue. Incidentally she stated that up to that time she had saved fifty-one twins from destruction. She thought nothing of this talk with the reporter, never mentioning it to any one, and was unaware of the wide publicity accorded to her remarks. She spent Christmas on board the steamer. Again every one was kind to her, the officers and stewards vying with each other in showing her attention. All along the coast she was well known, and invitations came from officials at Government headquarters, but these she modestly declined. She was interested in all things that interested others, and would discuss engineering and railway extension and trade prices and the last new book as readily as mission work and policy. The children she kept in the background, as she had done in Scotland, and would not allow them to be spoiled. On arrival in Calabar they were much made of, and it was only the experienced Janie who did not like the process.

CHAPTER XXXIV
ISOLATION

An exceptionally trying experience followed. Arrangements had been made by the Committee in Scotland for the better staffing of the station, but these broke down, and for the next three years she worked alone, her isolation only being relieved by an occasional visit from the lady missionaries in Calabar. During that long period she fought, single- handed, a double battle in the depths of the forest. She was incessantly at war with the evils that were still rife about her, and she had to struggle against long spells of low fever and sleeplessness. And right bravely did she engage in the task, conquering her ill-health by sheer will-power, and gaining an ever greater personal ascendancy over the people.

1. A Mother in Israel

The gradual pacification of Okoyong brought about by her influence and authority increased rather than diminished her work. As the people settled down to orderly occupations and trade the land became valuable, and disputes were constantly cropping up regarding ownerships and boundaries. There was much underground palavering, of which no one knew but herself, which kept her always on the strain. She had to mother the whole tribe, and it took all her patience and tact to prevent them reverting to their old violent practices. A Government official of that time, who had to enquire into a number of cases over which there had been correspondence with her, says, "I stayed with 'Ma' and had my first lesson in how to deal with natives. It did not require very long for even a 'fresher' to see what a power in the land she was. All came to her in any kind of trouble. As an interpreter she made every palaver an easy one to settle, by the fact that she could represent to each side accurately what the other party wished to convey."

Her fame had gone still farther, and people were now coming from places a hundred miles distant to see the wonderful person who was ruling the land and doing away with all the evil fashions. And what did they see? A powerful Sultana sitting in a palace with an army at her command? No. Only a weak woman in a lowly house surrounded by a number of helpless children. But they, too, came under her mysterious spell. They told her of all the troubles that perplexed their lives, and she gave them advice and helped them. In one week she had deputations from four different tribes, each with a tale of wrong and oppression. Innocent people fled to her to escape the fate decreed by the witch-doctor: guilty people sheltered with her, knowing that they were sure at least of nothing worse than justice. She welcomed them all, and to all she spoke of the Saviour, and strove to bring them to His feet. And none went away without carrying some of the fragrance of that knowledge, and in remote districts unvisited by the white man it lingered for years, so that when missionaries went there later on they would come across a man or a woman who said, "Oh, I know all about Jesus, the White Mother once told me."

She was so interested in these strangers that the desire came to know more about them and their surroundings, and she made numerous trips up the Cross River by Mission steamer and canoe and visited the townships on the banks. On one of these journeys she felt for the first time that death was at her side. A dispute had arisen between Okoyong and Umon, and the Umon people, strong in the belief that she would mete out justice even against her own tribe, begged her to come and decide the quarrel. It was a long day's journey for the best walkers, "but," said she, "if they can do it in a day, so can I." A well-manned canoe was, however, sent for her, and she proceeded in it with some of the twin- children. They were speeding down a narrow creek leading into the river, a man standing with his paddle at the bow to negotiate the canoe past the logs and trees, when a hippopotamus, which was attended by its young, rose immediately in front and attacked it savagely. The man at the bow instantly thrust the paddle into the gaping mouth, and shoved the canoe violently to one side. Mary seized some large tin basins with covers, which the natives used for holding cooked food, and placed them outside in front of the part where the children were sitting, and where the infuriated hippopotamus was trying to grip and upset the canoe. These curious weapons succeeded in baffling the monster. Several times it made a rush and failed. The shouting, the snapping of the jaws, the whirling of the paddles, the cries of the children—"O Abasi ibom Ete nyaña nyin mbok O!" ("O God, Father, please save us, Oh!")—almost unnerved her. The hippo at last made for the stern, where some of the paddlers beat it off and kept it at bay long enough to enable the others to turn the canoe and rush it out of its reach.

But she could not now afford to be long away from her station, for the utmost vigilance was required to combat the evils around her. In spite of British laws and gunboats twin-murder continued in secret. She noticed, however, that where the people came within the influence of the Mission their fears gradually disappeared. What pleased her was that women to whom she had been kind voluntarily brought in twins to her that would otherwise have been killed. One day she and Mr. Alexander were sitting at breakfast when a woman walked in, and without remark placed a large calabash on the table. Mary thought it was a dish of native food and said, "You have come too late, we have just finished." Still the woman was silent. Mary opened the calabash and found that it contained two twin boys.

There were other promising signs. The mother of a twin baby who was saved came to the Mission House and lived there, working at the farm during the day. One master took a twin and the mother home. All his other wives at once gathered up their children and left him, but he remained firm. As the woman had been a neighbour of "Ma's" at Ekenge, it is probable that her influence had told on her then. But the outstanding event in this direction was that a twin boy was taken home by his parents, who were determined to keep him. The affair made a great stir, but she told all the chiefs that she would stand by the parents, and if they dared to say a word or trace any calamity to the family she would "make palaver." They were grimly silent, but could not dispute her word. She believed that their attitude was only due to fear, which would die away if a stand were made.

Her work in school and Bible Class was beginning to tell. Six of the best boys of free birth and good standing whom she was training were now Christians, and working in the villages around. Two, sons of the most powerful chiefs in the district, took the reading and another was the speaker. It was not much to boast of perhaps. "I feel the smallness of the returns" she said, "but is the labour lost? A thousand times No!"

2. *The Cares of a Household*

Her most trying fight during these years was with ill-health. She was now occupying the new house, which she pronounced "lovely," but it was hotter than any she had lived in, and she often sighed for "her lowly mud-hut" again. At one time she was three months in bed, and recovery was always a slow and weary process. The people were afraid she would have to go to Scotland and came and assisted her in every way, while her boy scholars maintained the services. But often she would struggle up and conduct the Sunday meetings herself, although it meant a sleepless night. "I am ashamed to confess," she wrote, "that our poor wee services here take as much out of me as the great meetings at home did." To fill in the wakeful hours she would rise in the middle of the night, light a candle, and answer a batch of correspondence. There were friends to whom she did not require to write often: "Ours is like the life above, we do not need to tell; we can go on loving and praying, but this is a rare thing in the world." Others were not so considerate. Some of her letters at this period are marked "Midnight," "3 A.M.," "Just before dawn," and so on. But more often she was unable to sit up, and was too tired to write, and lay thinking of her last visit home, and particularly of her sojourn at Bowden; "I never had such a time; I live everything all over again during these sleepless nights; it grips me more than my real home life of long ago."

She never grumbled to her correspondents, even when in the grip of nervous debility. Her letters are filled with loving enquiries about people, especially young people, at home. She kept them all in mind, followed their lives with interest, and was always anxious to know if they had consecrated themselves to the service of Christ. "Life is so great and so grand," she would write, and "eternity is so real and so terrible in its issues. Surely my lads out here are not to take the crown from my boys at home."

Now and again, however, a strain of sadness is perceptible in her letters, perhaps due to the state of her health and her isolation, as well as the outlook abroad, which was then unrestful. "All is dark," she said, "except above. Calvary stands safe and sure." Often she wondered what worldlings did in the midst of all their entanglements and the mysteries of life and death without some higher hope and strength. "Life apart from Christ," she would say, "is a dreadful gift."

Her own future loomed uncertain, and the thought of the children began to weigh upon her mind: "It is not likely I shall ever go home again. I feel as if I did not want to. How could I leave the bairns in this dreadful land? Who would mother them in this sink of iniquity?" And soon afterwards she wrote: "I do not think I could bear the parting with my children again. If I be spared a few years more I shall have a bit of land and build a wee house of my own near one of the principal stations, and just stay out my days there with my bairns and lie down among them. They need a mother's care and a mother's love more than ever as they grow up among heathen people, and I could do a little, through them, for the dark homes and hearts around, and it would be a house and home for them when I am gone, where the missionaries could be near them."

Janie, the faithful, unselfish soul who had been with her from babyhood, was at last married. "Her husband," she said, "is my best scholar, and if his social standing is not the highest, he is a real companion to her and to my bairns, who worship him." The ceremony was performed by "Ma," and the entry, in Efik, in a tiny marriage register runs as follows:—

_December 21, 1899.

Janie Annan took oath before Obon (chief), Okon Ekpo, and Erne Ete, that she will marry Akibo Eyo alone, Akibo also took oath that he will marry Jane alone. They went to the farm with Eme Ete.

M.M.S._

The break in the family life gave her much more to do, but Janie—or Jean as she was now more often called—still clung to her, and spent much time at the Mission House attending to the babies as before, her husband not objecting to her handling the twins, and even allowing her to take one home to her house during the day. But difficulty and disappointment came, as they so often do in Africa, and once more Jean became an inmate of the household, in which she was to remain to the end. One day a baby arrived whose mother had died after giving it birth, and she took it and made it her special child. This was Dan MacArthur Slessor—called after a home friend of the Mission—a black boy who was to become almost as well known in Scotland as Jean herself.

By and by with returning strength the house-mother was able to resume her old strenuous ways from cock-crow till star-shine. The cares of her household never grew fewer. "Housekeeping in the bush," she would remark, "means so much more as well as so much less than in Scotland. There are no 'at homes,' no drawing-room ornaments to dust, no starched dresses, but on the other hand there are no butchers or bakers or nurses or washerwomen, and so I have to keep my shoulder to the wheel both indoors and out of doors." There were defects in the situation; she did not need other people to tell her that; she was often overwhelmed with the multitude of her duties, at her wits' end to manage all the children. "I have only three girls at present," she writes, "and I have nine babies, and what with the washing and the school and the palavers and the visitors, you may be sure there are no drones in this house." Sometimes she would stand in a state of pretended distraction and repeat—

"There was an old woman who lived in a shoe, She had so many children she didn't know what to do."

She was not a housewife in the real sense, although she knew domestic economy with the best, and there were days when she arose in her might and introduced order and tidiness, but matters soon fell back into the normal conditions. She was always quite candid about her deficiencies. "I have not an elaborate system or method of work; it is just everything as it comes. I am afraid my mind is not a trained machine. It only works as it chooses."

Yet no family of white children could have been more cared for or loved. She endeavoured to make Sunday a specially pleasant day for them, and tea then was always a happy function. All sat at a big table in the hall— Jean, Mana, Annie, Mary, Alice, and Maggie, with bunches of small boys and girls on the floor. It was then that boxes of delicacies from home were opened and devoured. How grateful she was to all her friends! "The gifts," she would write, "are veiled in a mist of love, real Scottish love, reticent but deep and strong, full of pathos and prayer; the dear love inspired in our strong rugged Scots character by the Holy Ghost and moulded by our beloved Presbyterianism of the olden time; love that does not forget with the passing years." Two years after she returned she related cheerfully that she was still wearing the dress that had been given to her on furlough as her best on the occasions when Government officials called upon her.

She saw pathos in these gifts, but none of that deeper pathos which lay in her own life. She saw nothing to grieve about in her own position, but only in the empty houses along the Cross River. She was not anxious about herself, but desperately anxious about the extension of Roman Catholic influence in Calabar. "To think," she exclaimed, "that all our blood and treasure, love and sacrifice and prayer, should have been given to make a place for them."

From her house in the bush she had been eagerly watching the sweep of that great movement which culminated in 1900 in the union of the United Presbyterian and Free Churches of Scotland. She loved the blue banner of the United Presbyterian Church, and one of her constant admonitions to the younger generation was to carry on the grand old traditions. At first she had been inclined to favour a kind of fraternal federation, each denomination keeping its distinctive principles, but she came to believe in the transfusion of the two streams of spiritual life.

"We must not forget," she wrote, "that the Free Church people were met at the Disruption by an empty exchequer and a confusion and blank that taxed all their energies. It took them such hard work in those days to get churches and homes for themselves that they got a bias that way, and the outlook to the 'other sheep' may not have been so wide as that of our forefathers. These used the little prayer-houses and humble meeting-places for prayer and preaching: they were men nursed in persecution and contempt and poverty, and they reaped God's compensations in a detachment from the world, and in the grit and spirituality and faith and unity which stress and persecution breed. And we have inherited it all, and it is our contribution to the Church life of to-day."

Her hope was that the Union might create a new and enlarged interest in the foreign field and fill up the ranks in Calabar; but she was to be disappointed in this, and she often expressed the view that the Mission to which she had given her heart and life had been swallowed up, and had somehow lost its individuality....

Into the United Free Church the United Presbyterians brought thirty-eight women missionaries and one hundred and eighty-five women agents, and the Free Church brought sixty European women missionaries and ten Eurasians, and nearly four hundred native women agents, making, on the women's side of the work alone, a total missionary staff in round numbers of one hundred European workers assisted by nearly six hundred local agents, and all these were now put under a new body, the Women's Foreign Mission Committee, composed of some of the most gifted and consecrated minds of the Church.

CHAPTER XXXV
EXILED TO CREEK TOWN

A dramatic public event which vitally affected her own life and the course of the mission enterprise brought her seclusion to an end. The story belongs more to the next phase of her career, but may be briefly noticed here. With the extension of British influence into the interior of the continent the form of Government had undergone another development. Two protectorates were formed, Northern and Southern Nigeria, and Sir Ralph Moor was appointed High Commissioner of the latter. The same policy of pacifying and "cleaning up" the country continued; but there were still large stretches practically untouched by the agents of the Government, including the territory lying between the Cross River and the Niger, in the upper part of which slave-raiding and trading went on as it had done for centuries. The Aros, a powerful tribe who controlled the juju worship, were the people responsible for this evil. They would not submit to the new conditions, continued to make war on peaceable tribes, and indulged in human sacrifices, blocked the trade routes, and resisted the authority of the Government. One officer was only able to penetrate fifteen miles west of the Cross River, not without perilous experiences, and then was obliged to beat a rapid retreat to escape being killed and eaten. The Government was very patient and conciliatory; but it became absolutely necessary at last to despatch a small expedition, and a field force was organised at Calabar for the purpose. Dr. Rattray of the Mission staff was attached to it as medical officer. The Aros did not wait for the advance; they raided a village only fifteen miles from Ikorofiong, and, as a precaution, all the missionaries upriver were ordered down to Duke and Creek Towns.

Okoyong was unmoved by these matters, "Ma" Slessor's authority was supreme, but while the Government believed that all would be well, they thought it better that she should also come to Calabar until the trouble was over. Very much against her will she complied. They sent up a special convoy for her, and treated her with all consideration. They even offered to build a house at Creek Town for her and her large family; but she did not wish to become too closely identified with the Government, and declined their kindly assistance. She found accommodation in part of the hospital, where, however, she had no privacy, and was not very comfortable.

It was the first time she had been in Calabar since her arrival three years before, and she was not happy. She was never otherwise than ill, and she longed to get away from the crowd and "the bright, the terribly bright sky." The children also were unwell. But there were compensations. The Okoyong people kept steady during the unrest, and remained true to their Queen. They came down to see her, brought all their disputes for her to settle, and loaded her with gifts of food, which were very acceptable, as prices had risen. Her lads kept on the services, and the people attended regularly. She heard good news of the twins, which the mothers had taken in order to relieve her; they were in four different homes in four different districts, and nothing had been said by the people. One of her oldest friends, the wife of a big chief, a wealthy leisured woman, bore twins. She instantly wrote to the chief telling him to put her into a canoe and send her down to Creek Town. "I am sorry for her," she said, "but we cannot make different laws for the rich and for the poor, and yet one may press too far with a chief, and incite rebellion. After all we are foreigners, and they own the country, so I always try to make the law fit in, while we adjust things between us."

A campaign of three months sufficed to break the power of the Aros, but long before that she was wearying to be back in Okoyong. At last she appealed to the Commissioner. He asked her to wait until a certain movement of troops was completed. Smilingly she replied that she would be off at the first opportunity — and she went.

Her enforced sojourn in Creek Town was followed by the best results. New missionaries had come out in whom she became interested. The one to whom she owed most was the Rev. A. W. Wilkie, B.D., who soon afterwards married a daughter of Dr. George Robson, the Editor of the *Missionary Record*. With these two she formed a friendship which was to prove one of the joys of her life. Mr. Wilkie understood her from the first; his keen insight enabled him to explore a character that was growing ever more complex, and he possessed that quality of understanding sympathy to which alone her sensitive nature responded.

She enjoyed meeting these young workers who had come to carry on the traditions of the Mission; she liked them because of their eagerness and energy and their desire to do things. All her knowledge was at their disposal, and she would tell them of the golden days of the past and describe the characteristics and superstitions of the people as well as speak of the higher things of life. Some of them thought her the most fascinating woman they had ever met. "Her talks," they declared, "are better than medicine." Many a wise bit of counsel she passed on to her sister missionaries. "She gave me at the very beginning of life in Calabar," says one, "a piece of advice that I have never forgotten, and which has comforted me over and over again. I was saying that in a place like Duke Town it was so difficult to know exactly what to do, and she said, '*Do?* lassie, *do?* You've not got to do, you've just got to *be*, and the doing will follow.'" "Make a bold stand for purity of speech and charity of judgment," she told another, "and let none of the froth that rises to the top of the life around you vex or disturb your peace." Many acknowledged that they had their lives enriched, their faith strengthened, and their work helped by contact with her.

CHAPTER XXXVI
PICTURES AND IMPRESSIONS

The younger missionaries began to frequent Akpap, and from the accounts of their visits we obtain some unstudied and vivid pictures of "Ma" and her household. This slight woman with the shrunk and colourless skin, the remarkable deep-set eyes, and the Scots tongue, so poor in the gifts of the world, so rich in the qualities of the spirit, made a deep impression upon them, although it is a question whether they ever fully understood all she was and did. They lived in the European atmosphere, she in the native; they noticed only superficial aspects, she moved deep beneath the surface amongst conditions of which they were only dimly aware.

"We walk for five or six miles along the pleasant bush path," writes one, "and as we near the big trees and the clearing round the Mission House, children's voices cry, 'Ma is coming,' and a sweet, somewhat strident voice inquires, 'What Ma? Jean put the kettle on, Jean put the kettle on.' 'And we'll all have tea,' sings out my friend. 'How are you, Ma?' for we have reached the verandah, and 'Ma,' eagerly hospitable, is giving us a royal welcome." She was usually found barefooted and bareheaded, with a twin-baby in her arms and a swarm of children about her, or on the roof nailing down the sheet-iron which a tornado had shifted, or holding a palaver from the verandah, or sitting in Court, but always busy. "No one can have much time for rest here," was the verdict of one missionary after a short stay. "Her power," wrote another, "is amazing; she is really Queen of the whole of Okoyong district. The High Commissioner and his staff leave the administration of it in her hands. It is wonderful to see the grip she has of the most intricate native and political questions of the country. The people tell me she knows their language better than they do themselves, and that they appeal to her on their own customs and laws. She has done a magnificent work, and the people have a deeper reverence for her than you can imagine. When they speak of her their tones change. One thing I noticed, she never allowed a native to sit in her presence. She keeps them all at a respectful distance, although when they are ill, sometimes with the most loathsome diseases, she will nurse them; and she never shakes hands with them. She told the High Commissioner to do so with some—but for herself, never! When I asked her the reason she looked at me and said simply, 'I live alone.'"

The reference to her command of the language bears out what all competent observers have stated. Some missionaries retain their accent even after long service and speak as foreigners, but she had all the vocabulary, the idioms, the inflections, the guttural sounds, the interjections, and sarcasms, as well as the quick characteristic gestures that belong only to the natives. "She excelled even the natives themselves in their own tongue," says Mr. Luke. "She could play with it and make the people smile; she could cut with it and make them wince; she could pour spates of indignation until they cried out, '*Ekem!* Enough, Ma!' and she could croon with it and make the twins she saved happy, and she could sing with it softly to comfort and cheer." One visitor who accompanied a missionary friend found her haranguing a crowd who had arrived to palaver. She stopped now and again and spoke to the visitors in broad Scots. "Well," said the missionary afterwards, "what do you think of her?" "I would not like her to catch me stealing her chickens!" was the reply.

One of the qualities which astonished her guests was her utter fearlessness. There were no locks on her mission doors. She went everywhere, condemning chiefs, fining them, divorcing them; and came home to her bairns to be a child with them, and to romp and sing to them queer little chants of her own composition. One story of these days her visitors carried away. A murder had been committed, and the slayer was pursued by the people, who intended to follow out their custom and torture him. He was seized and chained. Straining to break loose, his eyes almost bursting from their sockets, he cried, "Beware! You may kill me, but my spirit will come back and spoil you. Ay, it will not be you, the slaves, but you, the chiefs, that will suffer. Beware! I will come if you do not take me to Ma's house."

He was taken to "Ma," who on hearing the evidence ordered him to be conveyed to Duke Town. Then she loosed him from his chains and sat down with him alone in the house for the whole afternoon. The doors and windows were open, and all he had to do was to strike her down and fly. But she showed no fear. At night he was again chained and placed in the prayer-room or store-room underneath until the guard arrived. During the night he managed to slip off his chains and was free to escape into the bush. When she went into the room in the morning with food and called him, there was no sound or reply. It was dark in the place, but she entered and moved around to find the prisoner. At the back of the door she came into contact with his swinging body. He had taken off his loin-cloth and hanged himself.

Her visitors noticed, almost with wonders her devotion to her children and the little morsels of humanity that came pouring in upon her. Miss Welsh, LL.A., thus describes the household: "Jean, the ever-cheerful and willing helper; Annie the drawer of water and hewer of wood, kind willing worker; Mary the smart, handsome favourite; Alice the stolid dependable little body, and Maggie the fusionless, Dannie the imp, and Asoquö who looked with his big innocent eyes a wee angel, and who yet was in constant trouble, chiefly for insisting on sharing the cat's meals. Then there were the babies—a lovely wee twin-girl, whom their mother was nursing, a poor wee boy almost skin and bone lying cradled in a box. Behind the house in a rough shelter was another twin-mother caring none too kindly for her surviving child." Another writes, "I never saw anything more beautiful than her devotion to these black children. She had a poor sick boy in her arms all the time, and nursed him while walking up and down directing the girls. He died at 11.30 and she slept with him in her arms all night. Next morning he was put in a small milk packing-case, and the children dug a grave and buried it and held a service."

And here we have the scene at evening prayers: "We began with an Efik hymn of her own, which she repeated line by line, while the little ones chanted it with a weird intonation. They then sang the whole to the tune *French*. She tested their memory of the morning lesson, and gave them a homely but powerful address, interrupting herself once to tell us how hydrophobia had broken out a few days before, and how she had held one poor lad of ten in her arms until he died. She prayed, and the children bowed down their heads till they rested upon the ground. They next chanted the 'Amen,' and half-chanted the Lord's Prayer, and finished with what she called 'one of the new fanciful English hymns— 'If I come to Jesus.' Then very simply and sweetly she commended us all to the Father's love and care."

Long talks, often prolonged into the night, would follow. "How Ma talked," says Miss Welsh, "and what a privilege it was to listen, what an experience, and what an education! How she made the past vivid as she lived it over again—the days of her girlhood—her mischievous pranks, her love of fun, her early days in Calabar, tales of the old worthies, tales of herself, and her own life, of her early pioneering, of loved ones at home, of kind letters whose messages of cheer she would share, of comfort and help from God's word—from the passage of the day's reading, of new lessons learned, of new light revealed. I can still hear her, still listen with the old fascination, still enjoy her wild indignations, still marvel at her amazing personality, her extraordinary vitality and energy, still feel as I have ever felt her God-given power to draw one nearer to the Lord she loved so well."

When her guests departed she would walk with them a long way, her feet bare, her head uncovered. "No," said a missionary, "I would not like to see other ladies do that, but I would not care to see her different. It is easy to give a false impression of her. She is not unwomanly. She is eccentric if you like, but she is gentle of heart, with a beautiful simplicity of nature, I join in the reverence which the natives show her."

CHAPTER XXXVII
A NIGHT IN THE BUSH

Miss Slessor began to feel that her days in Okoyong were drawing to a close. Her part of the work there was done. The district was civilised, and all that the station required was organisation in detail and steady development. But she was not one to rest in any circumstances in which she was placed. She abated nothing of her devotion in the interests of the peoples and although her strength did not now allow her to take long journeys on foot she never hesitated to answer the call upon her sympathy and courage. She had more than one adventure in these days, but she had passed through so many hard experiences that she made light of them, regarding them as mere incidents in the day's work.

One afternoon, while she was in school, there appeared before her a young man of the superior class of slaves, who said his wife had given birth to twins in the bush more than twelve miles away. All the people had deserted her, a tornado was brewing—would she come and help?

"Ma" thought of her brood of children, and one a sickly baby, but turning them over to the slave twin-mother she had bought, and leaving food with her in her hut, she committed the whole twelve to Providence and set out with Jean.

The young man led them at a breathless pace. "If only you could *dion* the rain-cloud," he cried back. "I am praying that God may keep it back," was all Mary could jerk out. The way seemed endless, and the shadows of night fell swiftly about them, but at last they arrived near the spot and were joined by the mistress of the slave and an old naked woman. They found the mother lying on the ground surrounded by charms. "Ma" pushed these away with her foot. The night was pitch dark, there were occasional raindrops, and the woman was delirious. She ordered the husband and his slave-man to make a stretcher. They regarded the idea with horror, and pleaded that they could never carry her, their belief doubtless being that they would die if they touched the unclean burden. All begged "Ma" to leave the woman to her fate, but she turned upon them with a voice of scorn, and such was her power that the men hastily set to and constructed a rough stretcher of branches and leaves, and even helped to place the woman upon it.

Before leaving, a sad little ceremony had to take place. One of the infants was dead, and Jean took her machete and dug a little cavity in the ground, and upon some soft leaves the child was laid and covered up. She then lifted the other twin, the men raised the stretcher, and the party set off, a fire-stick, red at the point, and twirled to maintain the glow, dimly showing them the way. The rain kept off, but it was so dark that "Ma" had to keep hold of the hem of Jean's dress in order not to lose her. The latter stumbled and fell, bringing down Mary also. "Where are you?" each cried, and then a hand or a foot was held out and gripped. Sometimes the men dropped to their knees, but the jolting brought no cry from the unconscious form they were carrying.

By and by they drew up in the utter solitude, and had to confess they were lost. The men left to grope for signs of the path and the two women were alone. Jean grew depressed, not on her own account but on "Ma's," for she knew that she was utterly exhausted, and could not hold out much longer. "What if they desert us?" she said. "Well," replied Mary, trying to appear as if fatigue and fear and wild beasts had no existence, "we shall just stay here until the morning." Jean's response was something like a grunt. One of the men returned. "Can't find a road," he grumbled, and disappeared again.

What was that? A firefly? No, a light. The other man had discovered a hut, and had procured a lighted palm tassel dipped in oil. Poor as it was the light served to show the way until the path was reached.

After sore toil they gained the Mission yard. The men laid the stretcher in an open shed and, overcome with their exertions, threw themselves down anywhere and went asleep. But there was no rest yet for Mary. Securing some old doors and sheets of iron she patched up a room for the woman, In which she could pass the night.

The children were awakened and crawled out of Iye's hut into the yard crying in sleepy misery. Jean and Annie carried them to the Mission House and put them to bed, and brought back some hot food for the patient, who was constantly moaning, "Cold, cold; give me a fire."

Not till she was fed and soothed did Mary give in. She could not summon sufficient strength to go upstairs, but lay down on the floor where she was, with her clothes on, and all the dirt of the journey upon her, and slept till daybreak.

The baby died next day, and the mother hovered at the point of death. Mary strove hard to save her, but the result was doubtful from the first. None in the yard would give any help save Jean; the woman was a social leper, and all sat at a safe distance, dumb or blaspheming. Conscious at the end, the poor girl cried piteously to her husband not to reproach her. "It is not my fault," she said, "I did not mean to insult you."

"Ma" placed her hand on her hot brow calming her, and prayed that she might find an entrance into a better world than the one which had treated her so badly. When she passed away she thrust aside the leper woman whom her people sent to assist her, and washed the body herself and dressed her so that for once a twin-mother was honoured in her death. She was placed in a coffin of corrugated iron, strengthened with bamboo splints, and beside her were put the spoons and pot and dish and other things which she had used.

Her husband and his slave bore her away into the bush, and there at a desolate spot, where no one was likely to live or plant or build, they left her and stole from the place in terror.

CHAPTER XXXVIII
WITH LOVING-KINDNESS CROWNED

On the fifteenth anniversary of that notable Sunday in 1888 when Mary settled at Ekenge, the first communion service in Okoyong was held. It crowned her service there, and put a seal upon the wonderful work she had accomplished for civilisation and for Christ. Alone, she had done in Okoyong what it had taken a whole Mission to do in Calabar. The old order of heathenism had been broken up, the business of life was no longer fighting and killing, women were free from outrage and the death menace, slaves had begun to realise that they were human beings with human rights, industry and trade were established, peace reigned. Above all, people were openly living the Christian life, and many lads were actively engaged in Church work.

No congregation had been formally organised, but the readiness of the young people to join the Church was brought to the notice of the Rev. W. T. Weir, who was stationed at Creek Town, with the result that he was appointed to go up and conduct the necessary services.

On the Saturday night in August corresponding to the one when she arrived, a preparatory service was held in the hall beneath the Mission House, and in the presence of the people seven young Christians were received into the Church by baptism. More were coming forward, but the fears of their friends succeeded in preventing them. "Wait and see," they urged, "until we know what the thing is." Some of the parents anxiously asked "Ma" whether the ceremony was in any way connected with *mbiam*.

On Sunday came a great throng, which filled the hall and overflowed into the grounds, many sitting on native stools and chairs, and even on gin-boxes. Before the communion service she presented eleven of the children, including six she had rescued, for baptism.

It was a quiet and beautiful day, with the hush that comes with God's rest-day all the world over. As the company gathered to the first Memorial Table in Okoyong, she thought of all the years that lay behind, and was greatly moved. In the stillness the old Scottish Psalm tunes rose thrilling with the gratitude and praise of a new-born people. After the bread and wine had been partaken of, thanks were returned by the singing of the 103rd Psalm to the tune *Stroudwater*. When the third and fourth verses were being sung—

_Kprukpru muquañkpõ ke ima | All thine iniquities who
doth Enye adahado; | Most graciously forgive:
Anam udöñõ okure, | Who thy diseases all and pains
Ye ndutukhö fo. | Doth heal, and thee relieve.

Enye onïm fi ke uwem, | Who doth redeem thy life, that
thou Osio ka mkpa; | To death may'st not go down;
Onyuñ odori fi eti | Who thee with loving-kindness doth
Mfön y'aqua ima_. | And tender mercies crown—

She seemed to be lost In a trance of thought, her face had a far-away look, and tears stood in her eyes. She was thinking of the greatness of God's love that could win even the oppressed people of dark Okoyong.

She could not let the assembly break up without saying a few words. Now that they had the beginnings of a congregation they must, she said, build a church large enough for all who cared to come. And she pled with those who had been received to remain true to the faith. "Okoyong now looks to you more than to me for proof of the power of the Gospel."

In the quiet of the evening in the Mission House, she seemed to dwell in the past. Long she spoke of what the conditions had been fifteen years before, and of the changes that had come since. But her joy was in those who had been brought to confess Christ, and she was glad to think that, after all, the work had not been a failure. And all the glory she gave to her Father who had so marvellously helped her.

For a moment also her fancy turned to the future. She would be no longer there, but she knew the work would go on from strength to strength, and her eyes shone as she saw in vision the gradual ingathering of the people, and her beloved Okoyong at last fair and redeemed.

FOURTH PHASE

1902-1910. Age 54-62.

THE ROMANCE OF THE ENYONG CREEK#

"I feel drawn on and on by the magnetism of this land of dense darkness and mysterious weird forest."

CHAPTER I
THE REIGN OF THE LONG JUJU

Again had come the fulness of the time, and again Mary Slessor, at an age when most women begin to think of taking their ease, went forward to a new and great work for Christ and civilisation. Kind eyes and loving hands beckoned to her from Scotland to come and rest, but she gazed into the interior, towards vast regions as yet unentered, and saw there the gleam of the Divine light leading her on, and she turned with a happy sigh to follow it.

In this case there was no sharp division between the old and new spheres of service. For ten years she had been brooding over the conditions in the territory on the west side of the Cross River, so near at hand, so constantly skirted by missionaries, traders, and officials as they sailed up-river, and yet so unknown, and so full of the worst abominations of heathenism.

Just above Calabar the Cross River bends back upon itself, and here at the point of the elbow the Enyong Creek runs inland into the heart of the territory towards the Niger. At its mouth on high ground stands the township of Itu, of sinister reputation in the history of the West Coast. For there on the broad beach at the foot of the cliff was held & market which for centuries supplied Calabar and the New World with slaves. Down through the forest paths, down the quiet waters of the Creek, countless victims of man's cupidity had poured, had been huddled together there, had been inspected, appraised, and sold, and then had been scattered to compounds throughout the country or shipped across the sea. And there still a market, was held, and along the upper borders of the Creek human sacrifice and cannibalism were practised. Only recently a chief had died, and sixty slave people had been killed and eaten. One day twenty-five were set in a row with their hands tied behind them, and a man came and with a knife chopped off their heads.

It is a strange irony that this old slave creek, the scene of so much misery and anguish, is one of the prettiest waterways in West Africa. It is narrow and still and winding, and great tropical trees covered with the delicate tracery of creepers line the banks, their branches sometimes interlacing above, while the undergrowth is rich in foliage and blossom. Lovely orchids and ferns grow in the hollows of the boughs and old trunks that have fallen; but the glory of the Creek is its water-lilies, which cover the surface everywhere, so that a boat has often to cut its way through their mass. On either hand, side-creeks can be seen twisting among the trees and running deeper into the heart of the forest. The silence of the primeval solitude is unbroken save when a canoe passes, and then a startled alligator will slip into the water, monkeys will scurry chattering from branch to branch, parrots will fly screaming away, blue kingfishers and wild ducks will disappear from their perch, and yellow palm birds will gleam for a moment as they flit through the sunlight. The Creek is beautiful at all times, but in the early morning when the air is cool and the light is misty and the vistas are veiled in dimness, the scene is one of fairy-like enchantment.

Above the Creek all the country between the Cross River and the Niger up to near Lokoja in Northern Nigeria, was occupied by the Ibo tribe, numbering about four millions, of a fairly high racial type, who were dominated by the Aros clan dwelling in some twenty or thirty towns situated close together in the district of Arochuku ("God of the Aros"). A remarkable and mysterious people, the Aros were light- coloured, intelligent, subtle, and cunning. More intellectual and commercial than warlike, they developed two lines of activity—trade and religion—and made each serve the other. Their chief commodity was slaves. Each town controlled certain slave routes, and each had a definite sphere of influence which extended over a wide tract of territory. When slaves were scarce they engaged mercenaries to raid villages and capture them. But they had usually a supply from the Long Juju situated in a secret, well-guarded gorge. The fame of this fetish was like that of the Delphic oracle of old; it spread over the country, and people came far distances to make sacrifices at its shrine, and consult the priests on all possible subjects. These priests were men chosen by the various towns, who were raised to a semi-sacred status in the eyes of the people. Enormous fees and fines were imposed, but the majority who entered the spot never left it alive; they were either sacrificed and eaten, or sold into slavery. The shrine was built in the middle of a stream, which was alive with ugly fish with glaring eyes that were regarded as sacred. When the friends of the man who had entered saw the water running red, they believed that the Juju had devoured him. In reality some red material had been cast in, and the man would be sent as a slave to a remote part of the country.

The priests despatched their emissaries far and wide; they settled in townships, swore blood brotherhood with the chiefs, and took part in local affairs. They planted farms, and traded and acquired enormous power. When disputes arose they got the matter sent for adjustment to the town in Aro within whose sphere of influence they lived, or to the Long Juju. In this way they acted as agents of the slave system. Other men took round the slaves on definite routes. Their usual plan was to leave one on approval, obtaining on their own part so much on each, or a slave of lower value. When the trader returned the bargain would be completed. The usual price of a new slave was 200 or 300 rods and a bad slave. So widespread was the net east by the Aros, and so powerful their influence, that if a chief living a full week's journey to the north were asked, "What road is that?" he would say, "The road to Aro." All roads in the country led to Aro.

A few years before this a party of eight hundred natives had proceeded from the territories about the Niger to consult the Long Juju on various matters. They were led by a circuitous route to Arochuku, and housed in a village. Batches of from ten to twenty were regularly taken away, ostensibly to the Juju, but were either sacrificed or sold into servitude, only a miserable remnant of 130 succeeding in reaching the hands of Government officials.

Of a totally different type were the people living to the south of the Creek, called the Ibibios. They were one of the poorest races in Africa, both morally and physically, a result largely due to centuries of fear and oppression. Ibibio was the chief raiding-ground of the head-hunters, and the people lived in small isolated huts and villages deep in the forest, in order to lessen the risk of capture. In demeanour they were cowed and sullen, gliding past one furtively and swiftly, as if afraid; in language and life they were untruthful and filthy. The women, who wore no clothing save a small piece of native cloth made of palm fibre, were mere beasts of burden. All the young people went naked. Most unpromising material they seemed. Yet they never ceased to draw out the sympathy and hope of the White Mother of Okoyong; there was no people, she believed, who could not be recreated.

She knew a great deal about the Aros and their slave system, more, probably, than any other white person in the country. Indeed few had any knowledge of them. "What is sad about the Aro Expedition," wrote Mr. Luke, one of the Cross River pioneers, "is that nearly all the town names in connection with it are unknown to those of us who thought we had a passable knowledge of Old Calabar. I never heard of the Aros, of Bende, or of Arochuku. It is somewhat humiliating that after over fifty years' work as a mission, the district on the right bank should be so little known to us." Mary had first-hand acquaintance with the people. Refugees came to her from both Ibo and Ibibio with stories of cruelty and wrong and oppression; chiefs from both regions sought her out for advice and guidance; slave-dealers from Arochuku and Bende, with their human wares, called at Ekenge and Akpap, and with many of these she was friendly, and learned from them the secrets of their trade. She told them frankly that she was coming some day to their country, and they gave her a cordial invitation, but hinted that it might not be quite safe. It was not the danger that prevented her. She would have gone before, but the difficulty was providing for Okoyong when she was absent. She would not leave her people unless they were cared for by competent hands. She asked for two ladies to be sent in order that she might be free to carry out her idea of visiting the Aro country, but none could be spared, and so she had, perforce, to wait. It was not easy, but she loyally submitted. "The test of a real good missionary," she wrote, "is this waiting, silent, seemingly useless time. So many who can distinguish themselves at home, missing the excitement and the results, get discontented, morose, cynical, and depreciate everything. Everything, however seemingly secular and small, is God's work for the moment, and worthy of our very best endeavour. To such, a mission house, even in its humdrum days, is a magnificent opportunity of service. In a home like mine a woman can find infinite happiness and satisfaction. It is an exhilaration of constant joy—I cannot fancy anything to surpass it on earth."

Then came the military expedition to break up the slave system and the false gods of Aro. The troops were moved into Arochuku by way of the Creek, and the forces of civilisation encountered the warriors of barbarism in the swamps and bush that edge the waterway. When the troops entered the towns they found juju-houses everywhere, and in almost every home were rude images smeared with the blood of sacrifice. The dreaded Long Juju was discovered in a gloomy defile about a mile from Arochuku. The path to it wound a tortuous way through dense bush, with others constantly leading off on both sides, evidently intended to puzzle the uninitiated. A watch-tower was passed where sentinels had been posted. At the bottom of the valley, between high rocky banks clothed with ferns and creepers, ran a stream which widened out into a pool covered with water-lilies. In the dim light was seen a small island, and upon it a rude shelter surrounded by a fence of gun- barrels. Lying about were gin-bottles, cooking-pots, and human skulls, the witness of past orgies. At the entrance was a white goat starving to death.

Most of the chiefs had never seen-a white man, and when Sir Ralph Moor went up to hold a palaver, their interest was intense. They sat on the ground in a semicircle in the shade of a giant cotton tree, suspicious and hostile, listening to the terms of the Government, which included disarmament, the suppression of the juju-worship, and the prohibition of the buying, pawning, and selling of slaves. After much palaver these were agreed to. Over two thousand five hundred war-guns were surrendered, but sacrifices continued—and still to some extent go on in secret in the depths of the forest. Much work also had still to be done before Government rule was generally accepted. Throughout the whole time occupied by the expedition, but more particularly in the later stages, the important chiefs kept continually in touch with "Ma" Slessor, and one official states that it was to her influence more than all the force and power of the Government emissaries that the final settlement of the country was due....

It is interesting to speculate what might have been the course of events had she been able to carry out her plan before the punitive expedition was called for. Mr. Wilkie goes so far as to say that "had she been settled in the Aro country it is doubtful whether an armed expedition would have been necessary, and it is at least possible that the suppression of the slave-trade would have been achieved by the peaceable means of the Gospel." Primitive peoples often bend more quickly before Christ than break before might of arms.

CHAPTER II
PLANTING A BASE

A large tract of new territory was now open to outside influences. Who was to be the first to settle in it—official, trader, or missionary? Mary studied the situation again in the light of the new conditions, obtaining information first-hand from officials and natives. There were two stations on the west of the Cross River—Ikorofiong, which, however, was really an Efik trading town, and higher up, Unwana, which was a back-water and unfit for a base for inland work. Tentative efforts had been made from time to time to secure a footing elsewhere, but had come to nothing, and the policy of the Mission had been to continue up-river as being the line of least resistance. Her conviction was that extension, for the present at least, should take place not up the river, where the stations were cut off from the base during the dry season, but laterally across the country between the Cross River and the Niger. There were, she saw, three strategetic factors which dominated the situation—the Enyong Creek giving admission to the new territory, Itu at its mouth, and Arochuku, the religious and political centre of the Ibos. The central position of Itu impressed her; it commanded the three contiguous regions and peoples—the Ibo, Ibibio, and Efik, and her plan was to seize and hold it as a base, then one of the towns of Arochuku as the threshold of Iboland, and, if possible, Bende. Her views did not commend themselves to all her colleagues in Calabar, but how wise, how far-seeing, how statesmanlike was her policy the later history of the Mission proves.

She felt she could do nothing until help was obtained for Akpap. Fortunately there was one lady missionary in Calabar who had the courage to prefer Okoyong to quieter stations-Miss Wright of the Girls' Institute, who asked the local Committee to send her there as assistant to Miss Slessor; and although the Committee approved, the matter was referred to the Women's Committee at home. As there seemed no prospect of anything being done, she began to move quietly along her own lines. Her school lads were now old enough and educated enough to be used as advance agents, and her hope lay in these. In January 1903 she left Akpap with two boys, Esien and Effiom, and one of her girls, Mana, and canoed to Itu, and planted them there to teach school and hold services. Esien took the chief part in the latter, whilst Effiom led the singing. Mana's work was the teaching of the girls. A few weeks later she found that the results had exceeded all her dreams. The chief said he was too old to change his ways, but the younger ones could learn the new ideas—anyway God had made him, and so was bound to look after him whatever sins he committed. But the children were eager to learn, and made apt scholars, and the people crowded to the services until there was no more room for them. She went up again and selected a site on the top of the hill with a magnificent view and built a school, speeding the work with her own hands, and set the willing people to construct a church, with two rooms for herself at the end. When one of her fellow-missionaries, Dr. Rattray, heard of this he wrote: "Bravo! Uganda was evangelised by this means, and the teachers there could only read the gospels and could not write or count; the Mission understood its business to be to spread the Gospel, and all who could read taught others and spread the news. Perhaps we educate the people too much, and make them think that education is religion."

When in February she heard that the Roman Catholics were intending to settle at Bende her heart was heavy. "The thought that all that is holiest in the Church, should have been shed to create an opening for that corrupt body makes me ill. And not even a station opened or the hope of one! Oh, if I were able to go or send even a few of my bairns just to take hold. The country is far from being at rest, but if the Roman Catholics can go so can I.... There is a great future for Nigeria; if only I were young again and had money!"

She wrote to Dr. Adam, a Government friend in Bende, a soldier of the Church as well as a servant of the King, and he supplied her with all the information she needed. Bende, he said, was not the place it was supposed to be; the population numbered from two to four thousand; it was not likely to become a trading centre; whilst the overland transport was a disadvantage. The journey was by launch to Itu, by steel canoe up the Enyong Creek, thence by foot or hammock to Arochuku and Bende. He stated that Bishop Johnston of the Church Missionary Society was already in Bende prospecting.

When she received his letter she said to herself, "Shall I go?" She did not wish to compromise the mission in any way, and proposed to go about the matter quietly, at her own expense. She would travel if necessary in a hammock, as she was not so sure of herself as of old, and would find rest at wayside huts, and she would take Iye to act as interpreter where the women did not know Efik. "I would do what I like, and would come back to my work rested and refreshed. But—I want God to send me."

What was influencing her also was the conviction that the end had come for her at Akpap. Again she had the consciousness that it was time for the station to be taken over by an ordained missionary, who would build up a congregation. "I shall not say that I shall leave my home without a pang, but I know that I can do work which new folk cannot do, and my days of service are closing in, and I cannot build up a church in the way a minister can." She believed that in the special conditions of West Africa women were better than men for beginning work in the interior. And she still retained her faith in the home-trained domesticated type—girls who had brothers and sisters and had learned to give and take and find duty in doing common things, rather than those turned out by the training schools, who were, she thought, apt to be too artificial and full of theories. Her ideal of a man missionary was Dr. Rattray, who was a good carpenter and shoemaker and general handy-man,—"far better accomplishments than a college education for the African field." She did not, of course, depreciate culture, so long as practical qualities of heart and hand went with it.

The proposal regarding Miss Wright going to Akpap having been agreed to, she began to look forward to her advent as an event that would determine the future. Seldom has one been so eagerly watched for; for months it was nothing but "When Miss Wright comes," "Wait till Miss Wright comes," so on. For days before she appeared the household were in excited mood, every morning fresh flowers were placed in her bedroom, the boys and girls kept themselves dressed and ready to receive her. When she did arrive it made all the difference that was hoped. She was a capable, unselfish, plucky girl; she knew the language, and was experienced in the ways of the people. Very quietly she slipped into the method of the house, taking the school and dispensary off "Ma's" hands, and looking after the babies with the same pitying sympathy. The girls became quite at home with her, in the long nights she would sing to them, recalling the times in the bush when Mr. Ovens used to entertain them. "She is a right sisterly helpmate," wrote Mary, "and a real help and comfort in every way. Things go as smoothly as on a summer's day, and I don't know how I got on alone. It seems too good to be true."

CHAPTER III
On To Arochuku

On a morning of June 1908 she left Akpap for Itu, tramping the forest path to Ikunetu in order to pick up the Government launch on its weekly journey to the garrisons up-river. The Government, as usual, gave her every facility for carrying on her new work, granted her free passages, took charge of her packages and letters, placed their Rest Houses at her disposal, and told her to ask for whatever she wanted. She did not care to trouble them unduly, but was very grateful for their consideration. On arriving at Ikunetu she went into the teacher's house to rest, charging the boys to call her as soon as they sighted the launch. They did not notice it until it was too late for her to signal, and it passed onwards and out of sight. But she was not put out; her faith was always strong in the guiding hand of God; and she turned and tramped back the same long road. When she reached the Mission House tired and weary, she assured Miss Wright that all was well—God had not meant her to travel that day, and she must have been kept back for some purpose.

Next week she set out again, and when she joined the launch at Ikunetu, Colonel Montanaro, the Commander of the Forces, was on board on his way up to Arochuku. In the course of their conversation he gave her a pressing invitation to go there, and to accept his escort. She was almost startled by what seemed so direct a leading. But she was not prepared for a longer journey; she had no change of clothing or supply of food. She thought and prayed over the matter all the way. "Here is the challenge to enter that region of unbroken gloom and despair," she mused. "If it is not entered now, the Roman Catholics will come in, and the key position to the whole territory will be taken out of our hands, and only the coast tribes be left to the Mission. If I go now we shall be the first in the field, and it will not be discourteous to the Roman Catholics—as it would be if we came in afterwards." Before the end of the journey she consented to go.

When she arrived at Arochuku she found herself in the old slave centre of the Aros, a densely populated district, some 80,000 people living within a radius of a few square miles. It was a strange experience to walk over these roads that had been trodden for centuries by countless feet on their way to the pens of the coast and the horrors of the "middle passage," and latterly to the Efik slave-market, and to gaze on the spot where the secret iniquities of the Long Juju had taken place; stranger still to receive a welcome from the men who had been responsible for these evils. The chiefs and traders, many of whom she knew, were delighted with her courage and touched by her self-sacrifice, and promised to do all they could to assist her work. Making arrangements to come up later and start a school, she left, profoundly thankful for the privilege she had been granted, and praying that the Church at home would have a vision of the grand opportunity opening up before it.

The officials of the Church, of course, knew of the opportunity, but the members at large were not interested. Dr. Robson, as Convener of the Calabar Sub-Committee, pointed out how the situation was practically a crisis—no ground had been broken west of the Cross River, no teachers had been sent to the east. For a quarter of a century the supply of men had not sufficed for the existing needs of the Mission, and extension had been impossible. The givings of the Church for foreign missions had been far below the urgent requirements. Either, he said, the staff and income must be largely increased, or they would have to step aside and invite others to divide the field with them. No adequate response was made to this and similar appeals, and the lonely pioneer was forced onwards upon her solitary path.

A short time afterwards she went back to Arochuku, taking two lads, and a school was opened in the palaver shed of Amasu, one of the towns nearest the Creek, A hundred children crowded into the building along with women and men, and not a few of the old slavers, and the scholars were soon well on in the first book. In one village which she visited she found a young trader who had brought news of the Christ religion from the Niger, and was anxious to introduce a church and teacher. When she left the district again, the people came to the landing-beach and cried after her, "Don't be long in coming back, Ma! If you don't care for us, who will care for us?"

As her canoe was paddled down the creek, she lay back enjoying the beauty of the scene. The water was as smooth as a mirror, and like a mirror reflected the delicate tracery of the overhanging foliage; bright birds sailed hither and thither, gorgeous butterflies flitted about, and brilliant blossoms coloured the banks. She had passed in succession two snakes attempting to cross the stream, and was watching the efforts of a third when a small canoe shot out from behind a clump of bushes and bumped into her craft.

She apologised to the man in it, but standing cap in hand he said, "I meant it, Ma; I have been waiting for you; my master at Akani Obio sent me to waylay you and bring you to his house." Taking a letter from his cap he handed it to her.

The canoe was turned and entered a still creek, a picture of delicate loveliness, with multitudes of lilies and other aquatic plants, which made her feel as if she were moving through an exquisite dream. A shingly beach, evidently a busy trading-place, was reached, and there stood a young man and young woman, handsome and well-dressed, who assisted her to land. They led her into a good house and into a pretty room with concrete floor, a European bedstead, clean and dainty, with mosquito curtains and all the appointments that indicated people of taste. The man was Onoyom Iya Nya, a born statesman, the only one in the district who had not been disarmed by the Government, and the one who had been chosen President of the Native Court, and was shaping well as a wise and enlightened ruler.

It was a moving story that Mary heard from his lips, while his wife stood by and listened. It went back to 1875 when he was a boy. One day a white man appeared in the Creek, and all the people decamped and hid. He, alone, stayed on the beach, and in response to a request from the white man, offered to lead him to the chief's house. During the palaver that ensued he lingered by, an absorbed listener. When the white man left he was tried by the heads of the town and severely punished for having acted as guide. The stranger was the Rev. Dr. Robb, one of the ablest missionaries in the Mission, then stationed at Ikorofiong.

The boy never forgot the incident. But he grew up a heathen, and went to the cannibal feasts at Arochuku. When his father died, ten little girls were slaughtered, and five of the bodies were placed beneath the corpse, and five above, that they might occupy the position of wives in the spirit world. He married, but misfortune seemed to dog him. His house was burned down, and then his child died. Seeking for the man who had wrought these things by witchcraft, in order to murder him, he met a native who had once been a Mission teacher in Calabar, but who had fallen into evil ways and was now homeless and a drunkard.

"How do you know," the latter said, "that it is not the God of the white man that is angry with you? He is all-powerful."

"Where can I find this God!" the chief queried.

"I am not worthy to say, but go to the white Ma at Itu, and she will tell you."

"I will go," was the reply.

He took a canoe and watched for Mary on the Creek, but missed her. In his impatience he engaged the old teacher, who had still his Bible, to come and read *Iko Abasi* to him. Again he sent for "Ma," but she had gone on to Arochuku. Then he kept a man on the look-out in the Creek, and it was he who had intercepted her.

"And now," he said, "will you show me what to do?"

As he told the story several big, fattened ladies had come in, and a number of children and dependants. She prayed with them, sent for the teacher's Bible, and talked with them long and earnestly. The chief's wife made her a cup of tea, and she left, promising to come later and see what she could do to develop a station.

The detour had made her late, and the canoe ran into a sudden storm of wind and rain, but her heart was jubilant, and kept singing and praying all the way to Itu. For God was good, and He was leading her, and that was perfect happiness.

CHAPTER IV
A SLAVE-GIRL'S TRIUMPH

The problem was how to follow up so promising a beginning. It occupied her thoughts day and night, but she came to the conclusion that she could not conscientiously leave Miss Wright alone at Akpap. The station was too isolated for her, and if she became ill it might be weeks before any one knew. An alternative was to remain herself at Akpap, and allow Miss Wright to go to Itu, where she would be in touch with the Mission, and could canoe down to Calabar if anything went wrong. The plan she liked best was to hand the station over to a minister, so that both she and Miss Wright could establish themselves at Itu and work the Creek between them. As the months went by and she paid flying visits to the infant causes at Itu and Amasu, she became more and more convinced of the magnificent opportunity lying to the Church's hand in these regions. At Itu the congregation had grown to one of over three hundred intelligent and well-dressed people meeting in a church built by themselves. In August at Amasu she found a school of sixty-eight on a wet day, and of these thirty-eight could read the first book. That they had been brought under discipline was shown by the fact that as she entered all rose silently and simultaneously, as if they had been years instead of weeks at school.

The same month witnessed an event which gave her unbounded happiness. Jean, and Mana the slave-girl, Iye the twin-mother of Susie, Akom the first-fruit of Ekenge, and Esien the teacher at Itu, were baptized, and sat down at the communion-table. Many others were there, and joined in spirit in the celebration, but owing to difficult native complications could not take the step, and Mary never cared to force matters. Esien's mother had been very unwilling for her son to come under Christian influence, and now she was not only present, but actually sat beside two twin-mothers. Akom's face was transfigured. Jean's adopted child, Dan, was also baptized on the occasion, and it was a great and solemn joy to Mary to see her oldest bairn give him to God, and promise to bring him up in His fear.

In October she was at Itu watching the building of the house for herself and teacher, and nothing delighted her more than the way in which the women worked along with the men. "I wish Crockett had been here to gather the shafts and sparks of wit and satire that flew with as much zest as ever obtained in a Galloway byre or market fairin'. It is such a treat to me, for no intercourse is permitted between the sexes in Okoyong, except that of the family, and then it is strained and unnatural, but here they were daffin' and lauchin' as in Scotland. How wholesome are God's own laws of freedom and simplicity." The house was to, have six rooms—three for herself, one for Miss Wright or other lady missionary, one for Mana, and one for Esien and Effiom. "I'm afraid that is too much for you," she said, thinking of the mats which were not easy to obtain. "It's not too much, Ma; nothing can be too much. We will do it." One woman came and insisted on washing her feet in hot water. She had to give in, and as she sat down the woman said, "Ma, I've been so frightened you would take our teacher away because we are so unworthy. I think I could not live again in darkness. I pray all the time. I lay my basket down and just pray on the road."

This woman sometimes prayed in the meetings, and electrified the audience, and she had begun to have devotions in her own home, though her husband laughed at her. There were many others of the same type, and it was a black slave-girl who had been the one behind it all. Mana taught and nursed and trained them, quietly and modestly, as a mother might. It was an inspiration to Mary to see her; as she looked upon such results she cried, "Oh! if only the Church knew. If only it would back us up." To her friends she wrote, "Prayer can do anything; let us try its power."

Returning to Akpap with two of the girls and some small children, she was caught in a tornado and made her way over the six miles of bush-road through pelting rain. The darkness was lit up by almost continuous lightning, but they lost their way, and she had at last to commandeer an old native to lead them. Such experiences were now part of her ordinary life again. On her trips up and down the Creek she was constantly drifting into strange situations, and being reduced to sleeping on mud floors, or on straw in the open, drinking tea made in empty milk tins, and subsisting for days on yam and oranges. And always she was treated by the natives with as much gallantry and courtesy as if she were a queen, and always she was singing in her heart psalms of thanksgiving and gratitude.

But she was not able as formerly to resist the effects of such exposure, and was often weary, and her weariness brought nervousness and lack of sleep. At times she was afraid of the unknown future opening out before her, and appalled when she thought of all the details of labour, supplies, and management that were coming upon her shoulders. In the dark she would rise and cry, "Calm me, O God, and keep me calm." Then she would go and look at the sleeping children and comfort herself with the sight. "Surely," she would say, "I have more reason to trust God than childhood has after all the way He has led me."

CHAPTER V
A BUSH FURLOUGH

She at last determined to give up her furlough in Scotland, now drawing near, and spend the time instead in prospecting in the new country. All her hopes and aims were expressed in a definite and formal way in the following document, which she sent to be read at the November meeting of the Committee—now the Mission Council—at Calabar:

I think it is an open secret that for many years the workers here have felt that our methods and modes were very far from adequate to overtake the needs of our immense field, and, as the opportunities multiply and the needs grow more clamant, the question grows in importance and gravity. The fact that only by stated consecutive work can a church be evolved and built up, and a pagan nation be moulded into a Christian people, cannot be gainsaid, and yet there is an essential need for something between, something more mobile and flexible than ordinary congregational work and methods. The scattered broken units into which our African populations are divided, their various *jujus* and *mbiams* and superstitions which segregate even the houses of any common village, make it necessary for us to do more than merely pay an occasional visit, even if that visit results in a church or a school being built.

Many plans suggest themselves. Church members organised into bands of two or three or four to itinerate for a week over local neighbourhoods; native teachers spending a given number of days in each month in the outlying parts of their districts; trading members of the church undertaking service in any humble capacity on up-river trading stations—in these and many other ways the gaps might be bridged and a chain of personal interest and living sympathy link on the raw heathen to the church centres, and the first rays of gospel light be conveyed and communication be opened without the material expense which the opening of new stations involves. For instance, I have spent a Sabbath at Umon, and ever so many Efik traders, men and women, joined in the congregational worship, reading from Bibles and hymn-books which had been locked in their boxes; but either timidity or some other cause kept them silent when there was no one to lead. Could not a beginning be made for those, either by initiating such a service or organising those who were trading at any place so that evening worship or some such simple way of bringing gospel truth before the minds of the heathen could go on continuously? The same holds good of Itu and other places.

For the last decade the nearer reaches of the river on which we ply have occupied a great deal of my thoughts, but from various causes no sort of supervision at all adequate suggested itself. So there has been little definite work accomplished. A few readers at Odot, desultory teaching at Eki and the back of Itu, and Umon, covers it all, I fear.

With Miss Wright's coming, opportunities, not of our personal seeking, have forced themselves on us, and though we have done the best we could with the materials at hand, all seems so little and incomplete that the following proposal or petition or request or whatever you may term it, has been prepared, and that from no mere impulse of the moment but after careful, prayerful consideration. I may say here that Miss Wright is fully in sympathy with it, and it is from both of us.

By the 2nd January 1904 I shall have been out five years, and so my furlough would then be due, but as I have not the slightest intention of going to Britain—I am thankful to say I do not feel any necessity for so doing—I propose to ask leave from the station for six months, during which time I should, in a very easy way, try to keep up an informal system of itinerating between Okoyong and Amasu. Already I have seen a church and a dwelling-house built at Itu, and a school and a couple of rooms at Amasu. I have visited several towns of Enyong in the Creek, and have found good enough accommodation, as there are semi- European houses available and open for a lodging. I shall find my own canoe and crew, and shall stay at any given place any length of time which the circumstances suggests so as not to tax my own strength, and members of my own family shall help in the elementary teaching in the schools. From our home here we should thus superintend the small school at Idot, and start in a small way work at Eki, and reside mostly at Itu as the base, working the Creek where the Enyon towns are on the way to the farther base at Amasu, reside there or itinerate from there among the Aro people in an easy way, and back again by Creek and Itu home.

What I have to ask of you is that in order to do this a lady be sent out to be with Miss Wright. The latter is perfectly capable of attending to the station; the school and dispensary work are already in her hands, and with some one to help her I have not the slightest hesitation in leaving her in charge. Both ladies could co-operate in the travelling as choice or circumstances pointed, and as Miss Wright has had a large share in the formation and equipment of the Itu and Aro stations it would be very natural that she should take such a part in developing them as might suggest itself to her. The three of us, I have no doubt, could dovetail the details of the work so that no part should suffer, nor should any special strain be put on our health. We should like this to take shape by the end of the year, as the people will be more get-at-able in their villages in such a visitation kind of way than in the ordinary church methods during the dry season. All work in towns is slack then, and village and visitation work have their proper value.

In proposing this I know I am going in the very face of what seems to be the only possible way of dividing our stations. My own desire is to have a missionary with his wife and a native teacher take over Okoyong, congregate the educated, and at least nominal Christian part of our community, and build up a church in the ordinary way. He has more than he can undertake to work upon in Okoyong alone, and he has endless scope for extension up between the rivers toward Ugep and Edi-Iba.

It may be out of my province to speak of anything outside my own station, but in as far as I know I am voicing the opinion of the missionaries who are now working up Higher. I may say that if we are to compass the peoples that lie at our hands, such as Itu, Enyong, Umon, and those who may be reached all the year round, we ought to have Itu manned as a proper European station. All and each of these peoples can be reached and worked from Itu. Then as a natural and strategic point in the business conduct of our Mission, Itu is incomparable. It was not without reason that it was the slave mart, and that it became the Government base for all work both for north and flank. The gateway to the Aros and the Ibibios, holding the Enyong, and being just a day's journey from what must ever be our base, namely the seaport of the ocean steamers, having waterway all the year round and a good beach front, it is the natural point, I think, at which our up and down river work should converge.

But I am willing to change, and Miss Wright is willing to change, any plan of ours in order to let any larger undertaking make way if it should be proposed.

This communication was considered, and various proposals made, but the finding of the Council was that they were unable to accept the whole responsibility of the scheme, and that the matter should be forwarded to the Women's Committee in Scotland, and Miss Slessor asked to wait their decision. The question of further development was, however, discussed, and the unanimous opinion was that Itu should be adopted as a medical station in view of extension into the Aro country.

Miss Slessor was not discouraged. She next asked Mr. Wilkie to come and see the nature of the ground for himself, and the possibilities it held; and the result was a New Year trip up the Creek, the party consisting of Mr. and Mrs. Wilkie, Miss Wright, and herself. She was far from well—far more unwell than even Miss Wright was aware of—but she, nevertheless, resolved to go, and was conveyed to Ikunetu in a hammock. At Itu they camped at the church and house, neither of which was yet finished, the doors being temporary erections, and the windows being screened by grass mats. Mrs. Wilkie's camp-bed occupied one end of the church, Miss Wright's the centre, whilst at the other end Miss Slessor's native sofa was placed with mats round it for the children. Mr. Wilkie found a resting-place in one of the native houses in the town. Military operations were still progressing, and there was a camp of soldiers at the foot of the hill, whose presence terrified the people, and they besought the missionaries to remain for their protection until the men moved on, and this they did. Colonel Montanaro, who arrived later, called on the ladies, and had a long talk with Mary, to whom he expressed his delight at the result of his invitation to Arochuku. "These men," she wrote, "are held by invisible but strong bands to what is good, though outsiders do not see it."

On the way up the Creek they were obliged to pass the night at Akani Obio, where Chief Onoyom came down to the beach and escorted them to his house, and gave them all the room they required, two courts lit up by European lamps, and new mats. His fine face and courteous manners made the same impression on the strangers as they had done on Miss Slessor. It was found that the native teacher had been doing his best, but the chief was keen for all the advantages of a station, and was relying upon "Ma's" word to assist him. Next morning they again took to the canoe, but the water became so shallow that they had to land and tramp six miles to Amasu, passing the trenches where the natives sought to ambush the punitive force. New roads were being constructed everywhere, and barracks had been erected on a wind-swept hill in the neighbourhood.

The church was built near the Creek, and was still incomplete. As there was no house they camped in the church as best they could, Mrs. Wilkie sleeping on a mud seat. The district, including the scene of the Long Juju, was inspected, and the people interviewed, and the party returned as they had come. They stopped at several villages, in one of which an old chief brought out a box containing Bibles and a *Pilgrim's Progress* and reading-books. "I had a son," he said, "I was fond of him, and he was anxious to learn book and God palavers, and I bought these books and got some one to teach him, and was looking forward to my boy becoming a great man and teaching the people good ways, but two moons ago he died, and I have no more heart for anything.... I want God," he continued fiercely, "and you won't leave me till I find Him." "Oh, father," replied Mary, "God is here. He is waiting for you." The chief found God, and became a Christian.

CHAPTER VI
BEGINNINGS

Miss Slessor's indomitable spirit never gave in, but her body sometimes did. She had been suffering much these past months from weakening ailments brought on as the result of exposure and lack of nourishing food, and she finally collapsed and was again far down in the dark valley. But kind hands ministered to her and nursed her back to health. "I rose," she said, "a mere wreck of what I was, and that was not much at the best. My hair is silvered enough to please any one now, and I am nervous and easily knocked up, and so rheumatic that I cannot get up or down without pain." She was gladdened by the news that the Mission Council had given her permission to make her proposed tour, and was not troubled by the condition that she must not commit the Mission to extension. The Council thought that in view of her illness she ought rather to go home, and offered to provide for the work at Akpap and care for her children until she returned. But the burden of the Creek lay sore on her mind, and as Miss Wright's furlough was also due, she wished to be near Akpap in case of need. She informed the Council that if she could be relieved she would begin her tour at once. When Miss Wright left she gave more into the hands of Jean, who, she said, was as good as any white servant; her right hand and her left.

When the matter once more came up at the Council it was decided to send up two ladies to Akpap, and she was at last free to carry out her desire. She looked forward to the enterprise with mingled feelings. "It seems strange," she said, "to be starting with a family on a gipsy life in a canoe, but God will take care of us. Whether I shall find His place for me up-river or whether I shall come back to my own people again, I do not know. He knows, and that is enough."

Perhaps the most remarkable feature of this new forward movement was that she was going at her own expense, backed by the private liberality of friends in Scotland, and assisted by native girls and boys, who received nothing from her but their board. She never asked the Mission to defray any of the expenditure which she incurred, and the building was accomplished by herself and household, with the free labour of the people. All that the opening up of the Enyong Creek to the Gospel cost the Mission was her salary—which was now £100 per annum. She spent scarcely anything of this on her own personal wants. "I have no object on earth," she wrote at this time, "but to get my food and raiment, which are of the plainest, and to bring up my bairns." A certain amount was reserved at home by Mr. Logie, who all these years had managed her affairs, and even this she was always encroaching upon. Whenever she saw an appeal in the Press for any good object she would write to him and request him to send a contribution.

There were many matters to be attended to before she left Akpap, and she went down to Duke Town to hand over the business of the native Court, and buy material for the buildings in the Creek. It was the first time for many years that she had been on Mission Hill, and she greatly enjoyed her stay with the Wilkies, in whose home she was able to find quietness and comfort. The old people who knew the early pioneers of the Mission flocked to see her, and her sojourn was one long reception. A "command" invitation also came from the Commissioner, but this she had the temerity to decline, saying that she was not visiting. It is doubtful whether she had the attire fit for the occasion. He, however, came to see her, and was charmed with her personality.

It was on this visit that she brought another of the younger missionaries under her spell—the Rev. J. K. Macgregor, B.D., Principal of the Hope Waddell Institute. After his first meeting he wrote: "A slim figure, of middle height, fine eyes full of power, she is no ordinary woman. It was wonderful to sit and listen to her talking, for she is most fascinating, and besides being a humorist is a mine of information on mission history and Efik custom." Mr. and Mrs. Macgregor grew into intimate friends, and their home, like that of the Wilkies', thereafter became a haven of healing and rest.

She reached her base, Itu, with her family, in July, her health still enfeebled, but her spirit burning like a pure fire, and established herself in a house that was still unfinished. "What a picture it presented," writes a Government doctor who visited her then. "A native hut with a few of the barest necessities of furniture. She was sitting on a chair rocking a tiny baby, while five others were quietly sleeping wrapped up in bits of brown paper and newspapers in other parts of the room. How she managed to look after all these children, and to do the colossal work she did my comprehension." The joy of the people at her advent boundless. Her bairns had done wonders; the congregation numbered 350, all devout, intelligent people. "To-day," she wrote, "as the custom is after the lesson, the bairns each took a part in prayer, and before we rose a boy started 'Come, Holy Spirit, come.' We sang it through on our knees."

But calls came every day from other regions. A deputation from the interior of Ibibio pled, "Give us even a boy!" Another brought a message from a chief in the Creek; "It is not book that I want; it is God!" The chief of Akani Obio again came. "Ma," he said, "we have £3 in hand for a teacher, and some of the boys are finished with the books Mr. Wilkie gave us and are at a standstill." And, most pathetic of all, one night, late, while she was reading by the light of a candle, a blaze of light shone through the cracks of the house, and fifteen young men from Okoyong appeared before her to say that the young ladies who had come to Akpap had already gone, and they were left without a "Ma." She sent them to a shelter for the night, and spent the hours in prayer, "Oh Britain," she exclaimed, "surfeited with privilege! tired of Sabbath and Church, would that you could send over to us what you are throwing away!"

Invited to the Mission Council in November 1904, she went, this being her first attendance for six years, and gave what the minutes call a "graphic and interesting account" of what had been accomplished. In Itu a church and teacher's house had been built; and there were regular Sabbath services and a catechumens' class, with forty candidates, and a day-school was conducted. At Amasu, Arochuku, a good school was built, and ground had been given by the chiefs. There were also the beginnings of congregations and buildings at four points in the Creek, at Okpo, Akani Obio, Odot, and Asang. The work, she said, had not yet reached a stage when she could conscientiously leave it; but she hoped before departing to see established such a native, self-supporting agency under the control of the Mission as would guarantee a continuance of the enterprise. The Council received her report with thankfulness, and gave her permission to continue for other six months on the same condition as before—that no expense to the Mission should be involved in what she undertook.

Many months of strenuous upbuilding followed, constantly interrupted by petty illnesses of a depressing kind. The house at Itu was completed, she herself laying down a cement floor, and Jean whitewashing the walls. Cement underfoot for many reasons was preferred, one being that it was impervious to ants. If these pests obtained hold of a house it was difficult to drive them out, and many a night her entire family was up waging battle with them. In connection with her supplies of cement she was once picked up at Ikunetu by some of her colleagues, who remarked on the number of trunks which accompanied her. "You are surely richer than usual in household gear," they said. "Household gear!" she echoed; "these are filled with cement—I had nothing else to bring it in!" Once in Scotland a lady asked her if she had had any lessons in making cement. "No," she replied; "I just stir it like porridge; turn it out, smooth it with a stick, and all the time keep praying, 'Lord, here's the cement if to Thy glory, set it,' and it has never once gone wrong."

A picture of the days at this time is supplied by Miss Welsh: "We visited the women in their homes—we had evening prayers in such yards as the owners were willing to allow them. From morning till night 'Ma' was busy—often far into the night. One brought a story of an unjust divorce, another was sick; one brought a primer for a reading-lesson, another was accused of debt and wished 'Ma' to vouch for his innocence; another had, he declared, been cheated in a land case. All found a ready listener, a friendly adviser and helper, though not all found their protestations of innocence believed in, and none went away without hearing of the salvation God had prepared for them."

The Okoyong people continued to come to her with their troubles. "They seem to think," she says, "that no one can settle their affairs but this old lady." Rescues of twin-children were also going on all this time. She could not now rush off, as she used to do, when the news arrived, but she sent Jean flying to the spot, and the infants would be seized and the excited people held in check until she came on the scene. "One more woman spoilt," she would say, "and another home broken up."

Nothing gave her greater joy than the rapid development going on at Akani Obio. Chief Onoyom had never swerved from his determination to Christianise his people, and, although knowing practically nothing of the white man's religion, had already started to build a church, using for the purpose £800 which he had saved. At first he planned a native building, but reflecting that if he were constructing a house for himself it would be of iron, he felt he could not do less for God. He therefore decided to put up as fine a structure as he could, with walls of iron and cement floor and a bell-tower. To make the seats and pulpit he had the courage to use a magnificent tree which was regarded as the principal juju of the town. The story goes that the people declared the juju would never permit it to be cut down. "God is stronger than juju," said Onoyom, and went out with a following to attack it. They did not succeed the first day, and the people were jubilant. Next morning they returned and knelt down and prayed that God would show Himself stronger than juju, and then, hacking at the trunk with increased vigour, they soon brought it to earth. That the people might have no excuse for absenting themselves from the services during the wet season, Onoyom also erected a bridge over the Creek for their use.

To the dedication of the building came a reverent, well-dressed assembly. The chief himself was attired in a black suit, with black silk necktie and soft felt hat. He provided food for the entire gathering, but would not allow anything stronger than palm wine to be drunk. Very shyly he came up to "Ma" and offered her a handful of money, asking her to buy provisions for herself, as he did not know what kind she liked.

Two short years before, the place and people had been known only to traders.

Up in Arochuku similar progress was being made. Her first long stay there, spent in a hut without furniture—with not even a chair to sit on—was a happy and strenuous one. She was busily engaged in erecting a schoolhouse with two rooms at the back. "Little did I dream," she wrote, "that I would mud walls and hang doors again. But the Creek is at the back door, and we have bathing in the sunshine, and it is a delightful holiday." The earlier meetings were held in the open; the chiefs sat on improvised seats, the principal women, clothed and unclothed, squatted on skins or mats on the ground, lads and children stood about, the townspeople kept well back amongst the protecting foliage. In the centre, in the shade of a giant tree, was a table covered with a fine white cloth, and upon it a Bible and a native primer. Here she stood to conduct the service, so strange to the savage people. As she began, there was a stir at the side and a big chief, one of the principal traders to Okoyong in former days, moved into the circle, along with his head wife. He was followed by another and his children, and then others appeared, until she had a great audience. She could scarcely command her voice. To gain time she asked a chief to begin with prayer in the Ibo tongue. All knelt. A hymn followed; there was not the least semblance of a tune, all joining in anyhow, but sweeter music she never heard. The ten commandments were translated, sentence by sentence, by a chief, as were also the lessons and the address. Another hymn was sung, then came a prayer by an old man, and another by a woman, and the meeting closed with all repeating the Lord's Prayer.

It was the same at other towns and villages along the Creek. Churches or schools were going up and congregations being formed. The notable thing was that women were taking a prominent part in the meetings; this, no doubt, was due to the fact that the pioneer missionary was a woman. And the cry from all the districts was for women and not men—"A White Ma to teach our women book and washing and machine."

In July Mr. Macgregor was able to visit the infant stations, and was greatly impressed. To him the journey up Creek was a new experience. As the canoe pushed its way through the water-lilies the Institute boys sang

Scottish Psalms to the tunes *Invocation* and *St. George's* much to Mary's delight. "It's a long time since I heard these," she exclaimed. "It puts me in a fine key for Sabbath." At Asang she translated Mr. Macgregor's sermon to a gathering of 300 people. "Her interpretation," he says, "was most dramatic; she gave the address far more force in Efik than it had in English. It was magnificent. And how the people listened!" He had the opportunity here of seeing how deftly she handled a "bad" native. "Don't come to God's house." she ended; "God has no need of the likes of you with your deceit and craft. He can get on quite well without you—though you can't get on without God. Ay, you have that lesson to learn yet."

At Arochuku it happened to be Egbo day, and the place was astir with naked people, who came and stared at them as they ate. One man, who was dressed in a hat, a loincloth, and a walking-stick, sat in a corner and received a lecture from "Ma," which lasted the whole meal. They explored the district, saw the tree where criminals were hanged after terrible torture, the old juju-house with its quaint carving and relics of sacrifices, the new palaver-shed of beaten mud, and the great slave- road into the interior. At one spot she stopped and exclaimed, "That was the road to the devil." It was the path to the Long Juju of bloody memory. They returned by the new road through the *Ikot Mbiam*, the accursed bush into which the sick and dying slaves were flung when their days of useful service were over. At first the people would not use this road; but now the land was laid out in farms and cultivations, a tribute to the influence of British rule.

On the voyage down there were frequent showers in the Creek, and Mary sat with a waterproof over her head and shoulders, a strange figure, but with a face glowing with spirit. When the end was in sight she proposed that they should sing the Doxology, and, none offering to accompany her, she sang it herself-twice....

In the quiet of the tropic nights she read the books and magazines and papers which friends sent her, and in this way kept abreast of world affairs. Her favourite journals were *The British Weekly*, *The Christian*, *The Life of Faith*, and *The Westminster Gazette*. Her *Record* she read from cover to cover. It was with painful interest that she followed at this time the developments of the great Church crisis in the homeland. "It tears my heart," she wrote, "to see our beloved Church dragged in and through the mire of public opinion." But she had faith that good would issue out of it all. A keen politician, she thirsted for election telegrams during periods of parliamentary transition. But in all times of public unrest and excitement she fell back on the thought that God was on His throne and all was well.

CHAPTER VII
MOVING INLAND

Ibo or Ibibio—which was it to be? Both regions were calling to her, and both attracted her. As the result of an arrangement with the Church Missionary Society the administrative districts adjoining the Cross River were recognised as the sphere of the United Free Church Mission. "Now that this is settled," she wrote, "I shall try to take a firmer hold in Arochuku. The church there is almost finished. My heart bleeds for the people, but the Spirit has not yet suffered me to go." The dark masses behind her at Itu drew her sympathies even more, simply because they were lower in the scale of humanity. "It is a huge country, and if I go in I can only touch an infinitesimal part of it. But it would be criminal to monopolise the rights of occupation and not be able to occupy."

Her line of advance was practically determined by the Government. Even with military operations still going on a marvellous change was being effected in the condition of Ibibio. The country was being rapidly opened up, roads were being pushed forward, and courts established; the stir and the promise of new life was pulsating from end to end of the land. To her hut at Itu came Government and trade experts, consulting her on all manner of subjects, and obtaining information which no other one could supply. The natives, on the other hand, came to her enquiring as to the meaning of the white man's movements, and she was able to reassure them and keep their confidence unshaken in the beneficial character of the changes.

She made rapid reconnaissances inland, and these set her planning extension. Even the officials urged her to enter. They pointed to the road. "Get a bicycle, Ma," they said, "and come as far as you can—we will soon have a motor car service for you," Motors in Ibibio? The idea to her was incredible, but in a few months it was realised. "Come on to Ikot Okpene," wrote the officer at that distant centre—"the road is going right through, and you will be the first here." She thought of these men and their privations and their enthusiasm for Empire. "Oh," she said, "if we would do as much for Christ!" She, at any rate, would not be found lagging, and in the middle of the year 1905 she sallied forth, taking with her a boy of twelve years named Etim, who read English well, and, at a place called Ikotobong, some five and a half miles inland, she formed a school and the nucleus of a congregation. "I trust," she said, "that it will be the first of a chain of stations stretching across the country. The old chief is pleased. He told me that the future, the mystery of things, was too much for him, and that he would welcome the light. The people are to give Etim food, and I will give him 5s. a month for his mother out of my store."

The lad proved an excellent teacher and disciplinarian, and gathered a school of half a hundred children about him. Soon she was again in the thick of building operations, and for a time was too busy even to write. Slowly but surely Ikotobong became another centre of order and light. The officials who ran in upon her from time to time said it was like coming on a bit of Britain, and the Governor who called one day declared that the place was already too civilised for her.

Much to her joy there was a forward movement also on the part of the Church. The Mission Council had not put aside its decision to make Itu a medical base, and had been pressing the matter upon the Foreign Mission Committee in Scotland, which also recognised the value of her pioneer work and the necessity of following it up and placing it upon a proper basis. It was finally agreed to carry out the suggestion. Dr. Robertson from Creek Town was transferred to Itu to take oversight of the work on the Creek, a new mission house and a hospital were planned, and a motor launch for the Creek journeys was decided on. For the launch the students of New College, Edinburgh, made themselves responsible, and they succeeded in raising a sum of nearly £400 for the purpose. The hospital and dispensary and their equipment were provided by Mr. A. Kemp, a member of Braid United Free Church, Edinburgh, an admirer of Miss Slessor's work, and at his suggestion it was called the Mary Slessor Mission Hospital. When the news came to her she wrote: "It seems like a fairy tale. I don't know what to say. I can just look up into the blue sky and say, 'Even so, Father; in good and ill, let me live and be worthy of it all.' It is a grand gift, and I am so glad for my people."

Thus relieved of Itu she established herself at Ikotobong. But she was again eager to press forwards, and wished to plant a station some fifteen miles farther on. It was a pace faster than the Church could go. It had neither the workers nor the means to cope with all the opportunities she was creating. It is a striking picture this, of the restless little woman ever forging her way into the wilderness and dragging a great Church behind her.

She had been amused at the idea of riding a bicycle, but she would have tried to fly if she could thereby have advanced the cause of Christ, and when Mr. Charles Partridge, the District Commissioner of Ikot Ekpene, presented her with a new machine of the latest pattern, direct from England, she at once started to learn. "Fancy," she wrote, "an old woman like me on a cycle! The new road makes it easy to ride, and I'm running up and down and taking a new bit in a village two miles off. It has done me all the good in the world, and I will soon be able to overtake more work. I wonder what the Andersons and the Goldies and the Edgerleys will say when they see that we can cycle twenty miles in the bush!" The Commissioner had also brought out a phonograph with him, and she was asked to speak into it. She recited In Efik the story of the Prodigal Son, and when the words came forth again, the natives were electrified, "Does not that open up possibilities," she said, "for carrying the Gospel messages into the bush?"

Her work of patient love and faith on the Creek saw fruit towards the end of the year (1905), when the two churches at Akani Obio and Asang were opened. A special meeting of Presbytery was held in the district, and eight members were present at the ceremonies. At Akani Obio the Rev. John Rankin accepted the key from Chief Onoyom in the name of the Presbytery, and handed it to Miss Slessor, who inserted it in the lock and opened the door. There was an atmosphere of intense devotion, and Mr. Weir preached from the text, "This is none other but the house of God, and this is the gate of heaven." The collection was over £5.

Boarding their canoe again the party proceeded to Asang, and were met by crowds of people. Flags floated everywhere, and they passed under an arch of welcome. When the new native church, larger even than that at Akani Obio, came into sight, surrounded by well-dressed men and women and children, words failed the visitors from Calabar. Again Mary opened the door, and again the building was unable to hold the audience. Mr. Rankin preached from "To you is the word of this salvation sent." The collection was watched with astonishment by the visitors. It was piled up before the minister on the table, and bundle after bundle of rods followed one another, coming from those outside as well as those inside, until the amount reached £20—a remarkable sum from a people who were still heathen, but who were eager to know and learn about God and the right way of life. The visitors looked at one another. "It is wonderful," they said. "Surely it is of God." "Ma" was pleased but not surprised; she knew how the people were crying for the light, and how willing they were to give and serve. After the meeting the people would not depart, and she and Mr. Weir addressed them outside. On the party returning to Akani Obio an evening service was held, "and," wrote one of them, "the night closed down on as happy a group of missionaries as one could imagine," "It was grand," said another; "the best apologetic for Christianity I ever saw."

Some weeks later the church at Okpo, where Jean had been teaching the women and girls, was opened in the view of hundreds of the people, who contributed a collection of £7.

Not all the natives regarded these strange doings with equanimity. At Akani Obio some of the chiefs were so alarmed that they left the town in the belief that misfortune would come upon them on account of the church. But when they saw the people throwing away their charms and flocking to the services and no harm befalling them, they returned. They were very angry when Onoyom put away his wives—he made ample provision for them—and took back as his one consort a twin-mother whom he had discarded. By and by came a fine baby boy to be the light of his home. Akani Obio became a prohibition town, and on Sundays a white flag was flown to indicate that no trading was allowed on God's day.

CHAPTER VIII
THE PROBLEM OF THE WOMEN

One of the most baffling of West African problems is the problem of the women. There is no place for them outside the harem; they are dependent on the social system of the country, and helpless when cast adrift from it; they have no proper status in the community, being simply the creatures of man to be exploited and degraded—his labourer, his drudge, the carrier of his kernels and oil, the boiler of his nuts. A girl-child, if not betrothed by her guardian, lacks the protection of the law. She can, if not attached to some man, be insulted or injured with impunity. There was no subject which had given Mary so much thought, and she had long come to the conclusion that it was the economic question which lay at the root of the evil. It seemed clear that until they were capable of supporting themselves, and subsisting independently of men, they would continue in their servility and degradation, a prey to the worst practices of the bush, and a strong conservative force against the introduction of higher and purer methods of existence. Enlightened women frankly told Miss Slessor that they despaired of ever becoming free from the toils of tradition and custom, and that there seemed no better destiny for them than the life of the harem and the ways of sin. It was a serious outlook for those who became Christians,—about whom she was most concerned,—and she could not leave the matter alone. Her active mind was always moving amongst the conditions around her, considering them, seeing beyond them, and suggesting lines of improvement and advance; and in this case she saw that she would have to show how women could be rendered independent of the ties of a House, In Calabar Christian women supported themselves by dressmaking, and much of their work was sent up-country, and she did not wish to take the bread out of their mouths. Gradually there came to her the idea of establishing a home in some populous country centre, where she could place her girls and any twin-mothers, waifs, or strays, or any Christian unable to find a livelihood outside the harem, and where they could support themselves by farm and industrial work. A girls' school could also be attached to it. Two principles were laid down as essential for such an institution: it must be based on the land, and it must be self-supporting—she did not believe in homes maintained from without. All native women understood something of cultivation and the raising of small stock, and their efforts could be chiefly engaged in that direction, as well as in washing and laundrying, baking, basket-making, weaving, shoemaking, and so forth. Machinery of a simple character run by water-power could be added when necessary.

In view of the uncertainty of her own future, and the opening up of the country, she wisely held back from deciding on a site until she knew more about the routes of the Government roads and the possible developments of districts. She wanted virgin land and good water-power, but she also desired what was still more important—a ready and sufficient market for the products. In her journeys into the interior of Ibibio she was constantly prospecting with the home in mind, and once a chief who thought he had found a suitable site took her into a region of more utter solitude than she had ever experienced in all her wanderings, where a path had to be cut for her through the matted vegetation. Not one of her guides would open his lips; while they feared the wild beasts and reptiles, they feared still more the spirits of the forest, and they remained silent in case speech might betray them to these invisible presences.

Being a European she could not, according to the law of the land, buy ground, but she proposed to acquire it in the name of Jean and the other girls, and then give the Mission a perpetual interest in it. In a report of her work on the Creek, which Miss Adam induced her to write at this time, in the shape of a personal letter to herself, and which appeared in the *Record*, and was characterised by masterly breadth of outlook and clear insight into the conditions of the country, she made a reference to the project, saying: "The expenditure of money is not in question—I am guarded against that by the express command of the Committee. I shall only expend my own, or what my personal friends give me."

CHAPTER IX
A CHRISTMAS PARTY

With the few white men in the district she was very friendly. They were chiefly on the Government staff, and included the surveyors on the new road. Most of them were public-school men, and some, she thought, were almost too fine for the work. "Life," she said, "is infinitely harder for these men than for the missionary. But they never complain. They work very cheerfully in depressing surroundings, living in squalid huts, and undergoing many privations, doing their bit for civilisation and the Empire. And they are all somebody's bairns." She won them by her sympathy, entering into their lives, appreciating their difficulties and temptations, and acting towards them as a wise mother would. Her age, she said, gave her a chance others in the Mission had not, and she sought in the most tactful way to lead them to a consideration of the highest things.

Christmastide as a rule came and went in the bush without notice, except for a strange tightening of the heart, and a renewal of old memories. But this year, 1905, the spirit of the day seemed to fall upon these lonely white folk, and they forgathered at Ikotobong, and spent it in something like the home fashion. In a lowly shed, which had no front wall, and where the seats were of mud, no fewer than eight men—officials, engineers, and traders from far and near—sat down to dinner. "They could have gone elsewhere," wrote "Ma," "but they came and held an innocently happy day with an old woman, whose day for entertaining and pleasing is over."

There was no lack of Christmas fare. An officer of high standing had received his usual plum-pudding from home, but as he was leaving on furlough, he sent it to "Ma"; a cake had come from Miss Wright, "the dear lassie at Okoyong," and shortbread had arrived from Scotland, But there was not a drop of intoxicating drink on the table.

After dinner the old home songs and hymns full of memories and associations were sung, often tremulously, for each had loved ones of whom he thought. Jean, who had secured a canoe and come from Okpo, and the other children, were present, and they sang an Efik hymn; and although Mary was the only Scot present the proceedings were rounded off with

"Auld Long Syne." "I just lay back and enjoyed it all," she wrote, "It is fifteen years since I spent a Christmas like it. Wasn't it good of my Father to give me such a treat? I was the happiest woman in the Mission that night! If I could only win these men for Christ— that would be the best reward for their kindness." Next day they sent her a Christmas card on a huge sheet of surveying-paper, with their names in the centre.

Miss Wright, along with Miss Amess, a new colleague, arrived on the 80th on a visit, and three of the Public Works officials spent the evening with them. Mary began to talk as if it were the last night of the year. "Oh," said one of the men, "we have another day in which to repent, Ma." "Have we?" she replied. "I thought it was the last night— and I've been confessing my sins of the past year! I'll have to do it all over again." These officials asked the ladies to dine with them on New Year's night, the form of invitation being—

"The Disgraces three desire the company of the Graces three to dinner this evening at seven o'clock. Lanterns and hammocks at 10 P.M. R.S.V.P."

In reply "Ma" wrote some humorous verses. The dinner was given in the same native shed as before. As the table-boy passed the soup, one of the men made as if to begin. "Ma," who was sitting beside him, put her hand on his and said, "No, you don't, my boy, until the blessing is asked," and then she said grace. After dinner the bairns, who had been sitting at the door in the light of a big fire, were brought in, and prayers were conducted by Mary. On that occasion, when Miss Amess was bidding her "Good-bye," she said to her, "Lassie, keep up your pluck."

These men were very much afraid of the least appearance of cant, but they would do anything for "Ma"; and when, a few days later, in order to give an object-lesson to the natives, she proposed an English service, they agreed, and one of them read the lessons, and another led the singing. A short time before white men were unknown to the district.

CHAPTER X
MUTINOUS

She was, under official ruling, to return to Akpap in April 1906, and she was now reminded of the fact. She was in great distress, and inclined to be mutinous. "There is an impelling power behind me, and I dare not look backward," she said. "Even if it cost me my connection with the Church of my heart's love, I feel I must go forward." And again, "I am not enthusiastic over Church methods. I would not mind cutting the rope and going adrift with my bairns, and I can earn our bite and something more." She had thoughts of taking a post under Government, or, with the help of her girls, opening a store. In a letter to the Rev. William Stevenson, the Secretary of the Women's Foreign Mission Committee, she pointed out how her settlement at Itu had justified itself, and referred to the rapid development of the country:—

In all this how plainly God has been leading me. I had not a thought of such things in my lifetime, nor, indeed, in the next generation, and yet my steps have been led, apart from any plan of mine, right to the line of God's planning for the country. First Itu, then the Creek, then back from Aro, where I had set my heart, to a solitary wilderness of the most forbidding description, where the silence of the bush had never been broken, and here before three months are past there are miles of road, and miles and miles more all surveyed and being worked upon by gangs of men from everywhere, and free labour is being created and accepted as quickly as even a novelist could imagine. And the minutes says "I am to return to Akpap in April!" Okoyong and its people are very dear to me. No place on earth now is quite as dear, but to leave these hordes of untamed, unwashed, unlovely savages and withdraw the little sunlight that has begun to flicker out over its darkness! I dare not think of it. Whether the Church permits it or not, I feel I must stay here and even go on farther as the roads are made. I cannot walk now, nor dare I do anything to trifle with my health, which is very queer now and then, but if the roads are all the easy gradient of those already made I can get four wheels made and set a box on them, and the children can draw me about.... With such facts pressing on me at every point you will understand my saying *I dare not go back*. I shall rather take the risk of finding my own chop if the Mission do not see their way to go on. But if they see their way to meet the new needs and requirements, I shall do all in my power to further them without extra expense to the Church.

"This," she characteristically added, "is not for publication; it is for digestion."

There had never, of course, been any intention on the part of the Church to draw back from the task of evangelising the new regions. But the various bodies responsible for the work were stewards of the money contributed for foreign missions, and they had to proceed in this particular part of the field according to their resources. Both men and means were limited, and had to be adjusted to the needs, not in an impulsive and haphazard way, but with the utmost care and forethought. All connected with the Mission were as eager for extension as she was, but they desired it to be undertaken on thorough and business-like lines. The difference between them and her was one of method; she, all afire with energy and enthusiasm, would have gone on in faith; they, more prudent and calculating, wished to be sure of each step before they advanced another.

To her great relief she was permitted to have her way. When it was seen that she was bent on pressing forward, it was decided to set her free from ordinary trammels and allow her to act in future as a pioneer missionary. It was a remarkable position, one not without its difficulties and dangers, and one naturally that could not become common. But Mary Slessor was an exceptional woman, and it was to the honour of the Church that it at last realised the line of her genius, and in spite of being sometimes at variance with her policy, permitted her to follow her Master in her own fashion.

Her faith in the people and their own ability to support the work was proved more than once. It was a plucky thing for these men and women to become Christians, since it meant the entire recasting of their lives. Yet this is what was now being often witnessed. One event at Akani Obio was to her a "foretaste of heaven" — the baptism of the chief and his slave-wife and baby, a score of her people, and sixteen young boys and girls, including one of the lads who had assisted to paddle the canoe on the day when the Creek was first entered. She was ill, and was carried to and from the town in sharp pain and much discomfort, but she forgot her body in the rare pleasure she experienced at the sight of so many giving themselves to Christ. She had to hide her face on the communion-table. "Over forty sat down in the afternoon to remember our Lord's death 'till He come.' It cannot go back this work of His. Akani Obio is now linked on to Calvary." She thought of those rejoicing above. "I am sure our Lord will never keep it from my mother."

The news from Arochuku was also cheering, although the messages told of persecution of the Infant Church by the chiefs, who threatened to expel the teachers if they spoiled the old fashions. "And what did you say to that?" she enquired. "We replied, 'You can put us out of our country, but you cannot put us away from God.'" "And the women?" "They said they would die for Jesus Christ." She was anxious to visit Arochuku again, but there had been exceptional rains, and the Creek had risen beyond its usual height and flooded the villages. Akani Obio suffered greatly, the church being inundated. The chief was downcast, and in his simplicity of faith thought God was punishing him, and searched his heart to find the cause, until "Ma" comforted him. He determined to rebuild the church on higher ground, and this intention he carried out later. About a mile further up the Creek he chose a good site, and erected a new town called Obufa Obio, the first to be laid out on a regular plan. The main street is about forty yards wide, and in the middle of it is the chief's house, with the church close by. The side streets are about ten yards wide. All the houses have lamps hanging in front, and these are lit in the evenings, The boys have a large football field to themselves. Chief Onoyom, who is one of the elders of session, continues to exercise a powerful influence for good throughout the Creek.

One incident of the floods greatly saddened Mary. A native family were sleeping in their hut, but above the waters. The mother woke suddenly at the sound of something splashing about below. Thinking it was some wild animal, she seized a machete and hacked at it. Her husband also obtained his sword and joined in. When lights came, the mangled form of the baby, who had fallen from the bed, was seen in the red water. Distracted at having murdered her child, the mother threw herself into the Creek and was drowned.

So convinced was Mary of the importance of Arochuku, and so anxious to have a recognised station there, that she offered to build a house free of expense to the Mission, if two agents could be sent up. This brought the whole matter of extension to a definite issue, and a forward movement was unanimously agreed on by the Council—the ladies being specially anxious for this—any developments to take place by the way of the Enyong Creek. A committee was appointed to visit Arochuku and to confer with Mary. Two ladies were actually appointed by the Council, one being Miss Martha Peacock, who was afterwards to be so closely allied with her. When these matters came before the Foreign Mission Committee in Scotland, a resolution was passed, which it is well to give in full:

1. That they recognise the general principle, that, in all ordinary circumstances the Women's Foreign Mission should not make the first advance into new territory, but follow the lead of the Foreign Mission Committee, the function of the former being to supply the necessary complement to the work of the latter.

2. That, however, in view of (*a*) the earnest desire of the people of the district in question to receive Christian teaching, and their willingness to help in providing it; (*b*) the fact that the region has been claimed by the United Free Church as within the sphere of its operations, and has had that claim acknowledged by the Church Missionary Society; (*c*) the steps which have already been taken by Miss Slessor, and what she is further prepared to do: they regard it as not only highly desirable, but the duty of the Church to occupy the region in question as soon as it is possible.

3. That in view, on the other hand, of the present condition of their funds, which are overtaxed by the already existing work, the Committee deeply regret that it is beyond their means to add two new members to the staff, as the Council requests, and that, therefore, the sending of two new agents to Arochuku must be meantime delayed.

4. That the Committee, however, approve of the acceptance by the Mission Council of Miss Slessor's generous offer to build the house, but recommend the Council to consider whether the execution of the work should not be delayed till there is a nearer prospect of new agents being supplied.

They further return thanks to Miss Slessor for her generosity, and record their warm appreciation of her brave pioneer work; and they express the earnest hope that the Church, by larger liberality, may soon enable them to make the advance which has been so well prepared.

Meanwhile the Rev. John Rankln had been given a roving commission in order to ascertain the best location for the future station, and he came back from a tour in Ibo and Ibibio and fired the Council with the tale of what he had seen, and the wonderful possibilities of this great and populous region.

"Close to Arochuku within a circle, the diameter of which is less than three miles, there are," he said, "nineteen large towns. I visited sixteen of these, each of which is larger than Creek Town, The people are a stalwart race, far in advance of Efik. The majority are very anxious for help. A section is strongly opposed, even to the point of persecution of those who are under the influence of Miss Slessor, and others have already begun to try to live in 'God's fashion.' This opposition seems to be one of the most hopeful signs, as proving that there will be at least no indifference. The head chief of all the Aros, who was the chief formerly in control of the 'long juju' is one of those most favourable. He has already announced to the other chiefs his intention to rule in God's ways. He has been the most keen in asking the missionary to come. A new church will be built, and he offers to build a house for any missionary who will come."

With something like enthusiasm the Committee set apart Mr. Rankin himself to take up the work at Arochuku, and accepted the responsibility of sending him at once....

Thus Arochuku, like Itu, passed into the control of the Foreign Mission Committee, and became one of their stations and the centre of further developments, and thus Miss Slessor's long period of anxiety regarding its position and future was at an end.

CHAPTER XI
ON THE BENCH

Recognising that "Ma" had an influence with the natives, which it was impossible to abrogate, the Government decided to invest her with the powers of a magistrate.

The native courts of Nigeria consist of a number of leading chiefs in each district, who take turns to try cases between native and native. The District Commissioner is *ex-officio* president of those within his sphere, and each court is composed of a permanent vice-president and three chiefs.

Before leaving Itu she was asked informally whether she would consent to take the superintendence of Court affairs in the district, as she had done in Okoyong, but on a recognised basis. If she agreed, the Court would be transferred to Ikotobong to suit her convenience and safeguard her strength. She was pleased that the Government thought her worthy of the position, and was favourable to the idea. Already she was by common consent the chief arbiter in all disputes, and wielded unique power, but she thought that if she were also the official agent of the Government she might increase the range of her usefulness. Her aim was to help the poor and the oppressed, and specially to protect her own downtrodden sex and secure their rights, and to educate the people up to the Christian standard of conduct; and such an appointment would give her additional advantage and authority. "It will be a good chance," she said, "to preach the Gospel, and to create confidence and inspire hope in these poor wretches, who fear white and black man alike; while it will neither hamper my work nor restrict my liberty." On stating that she would do the work she was told that a salary was attached to the post, but she declared that nothing would induce her to accept it, "I'm born and bred, and am in every fibre of my being, a voluntary."

The formal offer came in May 1905, in the shape of this letter:

1. I am directed by His Excellency the High Commissioner to enquire whether you would accept office as a Member of Itu Native Court with the status of permanent Vice-President. His Excellency is desirous of securing

the advantage of your experience and intimate knowledge of native affairs and sympathetic interest in the welfare of the villagers, and understands that you would not be averse to place your service at the disposal of the Government.

2. It is proposed to assign you a nominal salary of one pound a year, and to hand you the balance—forty-seven pounds per annum—for use in forwarding your Mission work.

3. It is proposed to transfer Itu Court to Ikotobong.

She thanked the Government for the honour and for the confidence reposed in her, and said she was willing to give her services for the good of the people in any way, but she declined to accept any remuneration.

She took over the books in October, acting then and often afterwards, as clerk, and carrying through all the tedious clerical duties. It was strange and terrible, but to her not unfamiliar work. She came face to face with the worst side of a low-down savage people, and dealt with the queerest of queer cases. One of the first was a murder charge in which a woman was involved. Women were indeed at the bottom of almost every mischief and palaver in the country. With marriage was mixed up poisoning, sacrifice, exactions, oaths, debts, and cruelty unspeakable. Mary was often sick with the loathing of it all. "God help these poor helpless women!" she wrote. "What a crowd of people I have had to-day, and how debased! They are just like brutes in regard to women. I have had a murder, an eséré case, a suicide, a man for branding his slave- wife all over her face and body; a man with a gun who has shot four persons—it is all horrible!"

Here are three specimen charges, and the results, in her own writing:—

FOR IMPRISONMENT

O. I. Found guilty of brawling in market and taking by force 8 rods from a woman's basket. One month's hard labour.

P. B. Chasing a girl into the bush with intent to injure. One month's hard labour.

U. A. (a) Seizing a woman in the market. (b) Chaining her for 14 days by neck and wrists. Throwing *mbiam* with intent to kill should she reveal it to white man. Sentenced to six months' hard labour, and to be sent back on expiry of sentence to pay costs.

She had the right of inflicting punishment up to six months' imprisonment, but often, instead of administering the law, she administered justice by giving the prisoner a blow on the side of the head!

The oath taken was usually the heathen mbiam. For this were needed a skull and a vile concoction in a bottle, that was kept outside the Court House on account of the smell. After a witness had promised to speak the truth, one of the members of the Court would take some of the stuff and draw it across his tongue and over his face, and touch his legs and arms. It was believed that if he spoke falsely he would die. After Miss Slessor took up her duties, a heathen native, who had clearly borne false witness, dropped down dead on leaving the Court, with the result that *mbiam* was in high repute for a time in the district.

Although three local chiefs sat by her side on the "bench," and the jury behind her, she ruled supreme. "I have seen her get up," says a Government official of that time, "and box the ears of a chief because he continued to interrupt after being warned to be quiet. The act caused the greatest amusement to the other chiefs." They often writhed under her new edicts regarding women, but they always acquiesced in her judgment. For not providing water for twin-mothers, she fined a town £3. Miss Amess tells of a poor woman wishing a divorce from her scamp of a husband. The "Court" evidently thought she had sufficient cause, and there and then granted the request, and asked her colleague to witness the act. The woman was triumphant, feeling very important at having two white people on her side, while the man stood trembling, as "Ma" expressed her candid opinion of him. In the Government report for 1907 it was stated that a number of summonses had been issued by the District Commissioner against husbands of twin-bearing women for desertion and support, and in every case the husbands agreed to take the women back, the sequel being that other women in the same plight were also received again into their families. "The result," says the report, "is a sign of the civilising influence worked through the Court by that admirable lady, Miss Slessor."

Some of her methods were not of the accepted judicial character. She would try a batch of men for an offence, lecture them, and then impose a fine. Finding they had no money she would take them up to the house and give them work to earn the amount, and feed them well. Needless to say they went back to their homes her devoted admirers. Her excuse for such irregular procedure was, that while they were working she could talk to them, and exercise an influence that might prove abiding in their lives. This was the motive animating all her actions in the Court. "When 'Ma' Slessor presided," it was said, "her Master was beside her, and His spirit guided her."

The Court was popular, for the natives had their tales heard at first hand, and not through an interpreter. "Ma's" complete mastery of their tongue, customs, habits, and very nature, gave her, of course, an exceptional advantage. One District Commissioner spent three days in trying a single case, hearing innumerable witnesses, without coming within sight of the truth. In despair he sought her aid, and she settled the whole dispute to the satisfaction of every one by asking two simple questions. It was impossible for any native to deceive her. A Government doctor had occasion to interview a chief through an interpreter. She was standing by. As the chief spoke she suddenly broke in, and the man simply crumpled up before her. The doctor afterwards asked her what the chief had done. "He told a lie, and I reprimanded him—but I cannot understand how he could possibly expect me not to know." Again and again she reverted to the matter. "To think he could have expected to deceive *me!*" Another official tells how a tall, well-built, muscular chief cowered before her. "Having no knowledge of the language, I could not tell what it was all about, but plainly the man looked as if his very soul had been laid bare, and as though he wished the earth would open and swallow him. She combined most happily kindliness and severity, and indeed I cannot imagine any native trying to take advantage of her kindness and of her great-hearted love for the people. This is the more remarkable to any one with intimate personal acquaintance with the native, and of his readiness to regard kindness as weakness or softness, and his endeavour to exploit it to the utmost."

All this Court business added to her toil, as a constant stream of people came to her at the Mission House in connection with their cases. She did not, however, see them all. It became her practice to sit in a room writing at her desk or reading, and send the girls to obtain the salient features of the story. They knew how to question, and what facts to take to her, and she sent them back with directions as to what should be done. When she was ill and feeble she extended this practice to other palavers. People still came from great distances to secure her ruling on some knotty dispute, and having had their statements conveyed to her, she would either give the reply through the girls, or speak out of the open window, and the deputation would depart satisfied, and act on her advice. Her correspondence also increased in volume, and she received many a curious communication. The natives would sometimes be puzzled how to address her, and to make absolutely sure they would send their letters to "Madam, Mr., Miss, Slessor."

CHAPTER XII
A VISITOR'S NOTES

A pleasant glimpse of her at this time is given in some notes by Miss Amess. On Miss Wright going home—she shortly afterwards married Dr. Rattray of the Mission staff, both subsequently settling in England— Miss Amess was not permitted to stay alone in Okoyong, and she asked to be associated with Miss Slessor at Ikotobong. It was a happy arrangement for the latter. "What a relief it is," she wrote, "to have some one to lean on and share the responsibility of the bairns. Miss Amess is so sane and capable and helpful, and is always on the watch to do what is to be done—a dear consecrated lassie." Miss Amess says:

When I went to Calabar I heard a great deal about Miss Slessor, and naturally I wished to see her. She had been so courageous that I imagined she must be somewhat masculine, with a very commanding appearance, but I was pleasantly disappointed when I found she was a true woman, with a heart full of motherly affection. Her welcome was the heartiest I received. Her originality, brightness, and almost girlish spirit fascinated me. One could not be long in her company without enjoying a right hearty laugh. As her semi-native house was just finished, and she always did with the minimum of furniture and culinary articles, the Council authorised me to take a filter, dishes, and cooking utensils from Akpap, and I had also provision cases and personal luggage. I was not sure of what "Ma" would say about sixteen loads arriving, because there were no wardrobes or presses, and one had just to live in one's boxes. When "Ma" saw the filter she said, "Ye maun a' hae yer filters noo-a-days. Filters werna created; they were an after-thocht." She quite approved of my having it all the same.

Mail day was always a red-letter day. We only got letters fortnightly then. She was always interested in my home news and told me hers, so that we had generally a very happy hour together. Then the papers would be read and their contents discussed. To be with her was an education. She had such a complete grasp of all that was going on in the world. One day after studying Efik for two hours she said to me, "Lassie, you have had enough of that to-day, go away and read a novel for a short time."

She was very childlike with her bairns and dearly loved them. One night I had to share her bed, and during the night felt her clapping me on the shoulder. I think she had been so used with black babies that this was the force of habit, for she was amused when I told her of it in the morning.

There was no routine with "Ma." One never knew what she would be doing. One hour she might be having a political discussion with a District Commissioner, the next supervising the building of a house, and later on judging native palavers. Late one evening I heard a good deal of talking and also the sound of working. I went in to see what was doing and there was "Ma" making cement and the bairns spreading it on the floor with their hands in candle light. The whole scene at so late an hour was too much for my gravity.

When at prayers with her children she would sometimes play a tambourine at the singing, and if the bairns were half asleep it struck their curly heads instead of her elbow.

Her outstanding characteristic was her great sympathy, which enabled her to get into touch with the highest and the lowest. Once while cycling together we met the Provincial Commissioner. After salutations and some conversation with him she finished up by saying, "Good-bye, and see and be a guid laddie!"

While out walking one Sabbath we came across several booths where the natives who were making the Government road were living. She began chatting with them, and then told them the Parable of the Lost Sheep. She told everything in a graphic way, and with a perfect knowledge of the vernacular, and they followed her with reverence and intense interest all through. To most of them, if not to all, that would be the first time they had heard of a God of Love.

She had really two personalities. In the morning one would hear evildoers getting hotly lectured for their "fashions," and in the evening when all was quiet she lifted one up to the very heights regarding the things of the Kingdom. She always had a wonderful vision of what the power of the Gospel could make of the most degraded, though bound by the strongest chains of superstition and heathenism. One might enter her house feeling pessimistic, but one always left it an optimist.

CHAPTER XIII
A REST-HOME

A touch of romance seemed to be connected with all her work. The next idea she sought to develop was a Rest-House or week-end, holiday, or convalescent home, where the ladies of the Mission, when out of spirits, or run down in health, could reside and recuperate without the fear of being a trouble or expense to others. In a tropical country, where a change and rest is so often essential to white workers, such a quiet accessible resort would, she thought, prove a blessing. But there was no money for the purpose. One day, however, she received a cheque for £20. Years before, in Okoyong, Dr. Dutton of the Tropical School of Medicine had stayed with her for scientific study. He went on to the Congo, and there succumbed. On going over his papers, his family found her letters, and in recognition of her kindness and interest, sent her a gift of £20. Thinking of a way of spending the money which would have pleased her friend, she determined to apply it to the building of her Rest-House.

The site for such a resort required to be near the Creek, and she discovered one on high land at Use between Ikotobong and Itu, and two miles from the landing-beach. The road here winds round hills from which beautiful views are obtained. On this side one sees far into Ibo beyond Arochuku, on that the vision is of Itu and the country behind it, while on the west the palm-covered plain rises into the highlands of Ikot Ekpene. It is one of the fairest of landscapes, but is the haunt of leopards and other wild beasts, and after rain the roadway is often covered with the marks of their feet.

The ground was cleared, and building operations begun, the plan worked out being a small semi-European cottage and native yard. Other cottages would follow. Before long, however, the feeling grew that Ikotobong should be taken over by the Women's Foreign Mission Committee, and she foresaw that Use would require to be her own headquarters.

Towards the end of the year Miss E, M'Kinney, one of the lady agents, called at Use, and found her living in a single room, and sleeping on a mattress placed upon a sheet of corrugated iron. As the visitor had to leave early in the morning, and there were no clocks in the hut, "Ma" adopted the novel device of tying a rooster to her bed. The plan succeeded; at first cock-crow the sleepers were aroused from their slumbers.

It was not so much a rest-house for others that was needed, as a rest for herself. She was gradually coming to the end of her strength. Throughout the year 1906 she suffered from diarrhoea, boils, and other weakening complaints, and the Government doctor at last frankly told her that if she wished to live and work another day, she must go home at once. Her answer to his fiat was to rally in a wonderful way. "It looks," she said, "as if God has forbidden my going. Does this appear as if He could not do without me? Oh, dear me, poor old lady, how little you can do! But I can at least keep a door open." It was, however, only a respite. By the beginning of 1907 she could not walk half-a-dozen steps, her limbs refused to move, and she needed to be carried about. It was obvious, even to herself, that she must go home. Home! the very word brought tears to her eyes. The passion for the old land and "kent" faces, and the graves of her beloved, grew with her failing power. A home picture made her heart leap and long. "Oh, the dear homeland," she cried, "shall I really be there and worship in its churches again! How I long for a wee look at a winter landscape, to feel the cold wind, and see the frost in the cart-ruts, to hear the ring of shoes on the hard frozen ground, to see the glare of the shops, and the hurrying scurrying crowd, to take a back seat in a church, and hear without a care of my own the congregation singing, and hear how they preach and pray and rest their souls in the hush and solemnity."

She arranged to leave in May, and set about putting her household affairs in order. The safeguarding of the children gave her much solicitude. For Jean and the older girls she trembled. "They must be left in charge of the babies, with only God to protect them." Dan, now six years old, she took with her as a help to fetch and carry. Her departure and journey were made wonderfully easy by the kindness of Government officials, who vied with each other in taking care of her and making her comfortable. One of her friends, Mr. Gray, packed for her, stored her furniture, conveyed her to Duke Town, and asked his sister in Edinburgh to meet her. Mr. Middleton, of Lagos, wrote to say he was going home, and would wait for her in order to "convoy her safely through all the foreign countries between Lagos and the other side of the Tweed." "Now there," she wrote to the Wilkies—"Doth Job serve God for nought?" Very grateful she was for all the attention. "God must repay these men," she said, "for I cannot. He will not forget they did it to a child of His, unworthy though she is." After the voyage she wrote: "Mr. Middleton has faithfully and very tenderly carried out all his promises. Had I been his mother, he could not have been more attentive or kind."

CHAPTER XIV
SCOTLAND: THE LAST FAREWELL

A telegram to Mrs. M'Crindle at Joppa informed her that her friend had arrived at Liverpool and was on the way to Edinburgh. She met the train, and saw an old wrinkled lady huddled in a corner of a carriage. Could that be Miss Slessor? With a pitying hand she helped her out and conveyed her, with Dan, to the comfort of her home.

But soon letters, postcards, invitations, parcels began flowing in. "This correspondence," she wrote, "is overwhelming. I cannot keep pace with it." There was no end to the kindness which people showered upon her. Gifts of flowers, clothes, and money for herself and her work, and toys for Dan were her daily portion. "It is a wonderful service this," she said, "which makes the heart leap to do His will, and it is all unknown to the nearest neighbour or the dearest friend, but it keeps the Kingdom of Heaven coming every day anew on the earth." One £5 was slipped into her hand for her bairns. "My bairns don't require it," she replied, "and won't get it either, but it is put aside, till I see the Board, as the nest-egg of my Home for Girls and Women in Calabar. If I can get them to give the woman or women, I shall give half of my salary to help hers, and will give the house and find the servants, and I can find the passage money from personal friends. Pray that the Board may dare to go on in faith, and take up this work."

Between spells of colds and fevers she visited friends. At Bowden again she had the exquisite experience of enjoying utter rest and happiness. A pleasant stay was at Stanley, with the family of Miss Amess, who was also at home, and with whom she rose early in the morning and went out cycling. She cycled also with Miss Logie at Newport, but was very timid on the road. If she saw a dog in front she would dismount, and remount after she had passed it. She went over to Dundee and roamed through her former haunts with an old factory companion, looking wistfully at the scenes of her girlhood.

"I have been gladdened," she wrote to an English friend, "at finding many of those I taught in young days walking in the fear and love of God, and many are heads of families who are a strength and ornament to the

Church of Christ. About thirty-five or thirty-eight years ago three ladies and myself began to work in a dreadful district-one became a district nurse, one worked among the fallen women and the prisons of our cities, and one has been at home working quietly—and we all met in good health and had such a day together. We went up the old roads and talked of all God had done for us and for the people, and again dedicated ourselves to Him. It was probably the last time we shall meet down here, but we were glad in the hope of eternity."

She had not been in Scotland since the Union of the Churches, and one of her first duties was to call upon Mr. Stevenson, the Secretary of the Women's Foreign Mission Committee, and his assistant, Miss Crawford. She had a high sense of the value of the work going on at headquarters, and always maintained that the task of organising at home was much harder than service in the field. But she had a natural aversion to officialdom, and anticipated the interviews with dread. She pictured two cold, unsympathetic individuals—a conception afterwards recalled with amusement. What the reality was may be gathered from a letter she wrote later to Mr. Stevenson: "I have never felt much at home with our new conditions, and feared the result of the Union in its detail, though I most heartily approved of it in theory and fact. No! I shall not be afraid of you. Both Miss Crawford and yourself have been a revelation to me, and I am ashamed of my former fancies and fears, and I shall ever think of, and pray for the secretaries with a very warm and thankful heart."

There was an element of humour in her meeting with Miss Crawford. The two women, somewhat nervous, stood on opposite sides of the office door. She, without, was afraid to enter, shrinking from the task of facing the unknown personage within—a woman who had been in India and written a book, and was sure to be masculine and hard! She, within, of gentle face and soft speech, leant timidly on her desk, nerving herself for the coming shock, for the famous pioneer missionary was sure to be "difficult" and aggressive. When Mary entered they glanced at one another, looked into each other's eyes, and with a sigh of relief smiled and straightway fell in love. When Mary gave her affection she gave it with a passionate abandon, and Miss Crawford was taken into the inmost sanctuary of her heart. "You have been one of God's most precious gifts to me on this furlough," she said later. In her humility Miss Crawford spoke about not being worthy to tie her shoe. "Dear daughter of the King," exclaimed the missionary, "why do you say that? If you knew me as God does! Never say that kind of thing again!"

The ordeal of meeting the Women's Foreign Mission Committee was also a disillusionment. Her friend, Dr. Robson, was in the chair, and his opening prayer was an inspiration, and lifted the proceedings to the highest level. Nothing could have been kinder than her reception, which delighted her greatly. "There was such a sympathetic hearing for Calabar, especially from the old Free Church section, who are as eager for the Mission as the old United Presbyterians." A conference was held with her in regard to the position of Ikotobong, and her heart was gladdened by the decision to take over the station and place two lady missionaries there, Miss Peacock and Miss Reid. At another conference with a sub-committee she discussed the matter of the Settlement, gave an outline of her plans, and intimated that already two ladies had offered £100 each to start the enterprise, while other sums were also on hand. The sub-committee was much impressed with the sense of both the necessity and promise of the scheme, and recommended the Women's Committee to express general approval of it, and earnest sympathy with the end in view, and to authorise her to take the necessary steps on her return for the selection of a suitable site, the preparation of plans, and estimates of the cost of the ground, buildings, and agents, in order that the whole scheme might be submitted through the Mission Council, at the earliest practicable date, for sanction. The general Committee unanimously and cordially adopted this recommendation.

It was expected that she would address many meetings throughout the country during her furlough to interest people in her work and projects, but she astonished every one by intimating that she was leaving for Calabar in October, although she had only been a few months at home. In her eyes friends saw a look of sorrow, and said to one another that the burden of the work was lying upon her heart. But few knew the secret of her sadness. To some who remonstrated she said, "My heart yearns for my bairns—they are more to me than myself." The truth was that a story about Jean had been set afloat by a native and had reached her in letters, and she could hardly contain herself until she had found out the meaning of it. At all costs she must get back. Even her pilgrimage to the graves of her dear ones in Devon must be given up.

Much against her will and pleading she was tied down to give at least three addresses in the great towns, but with her whole being unhinged by the shadow that overhung her, she had little mind for public speaking. Her old nervousness in the face of an audience returned with tenfold force. "I am trembling for the meetings," she wrote, "but surely God will help me. It is His own cause." And again, "I am suffering tortures of fear, and yet why is it that I cannot rest in Him? If He sends me work, surely He will help me to deliver His message, and to do it for His glory. He never failed me before. If He be glorified that is all, whether I be considered able or not."

She never prepared a set speech, and when she was going up to the Edinburgh meeting with Mrs. M'Crindle, she turned to her and said, "What am I to say?" "Just open your lips and let God speak," replied her friend. She was greatly pleased with the answer, and on that occasion she never spoke better. Dr. Robson presided, and Mrs. Duncan M'Laren, in bidding her farewell on behalf of the audience, said, "There are times when it needs God-given vision to see the guiding hand. We feel that our friend has this heavenly vision, and that she has not been disobedient to it. We all feel humbled when we hear what she and her brave colleagues have done. In God's keeping we may safely leave her."

At the meeting in Glasgow the feeling was even more tense and emotional, and a hush came over the audience as the plain little woman made her appeal, and told them that in all probability she would never again be back. At the benediction she stood, a pathetic figure, her head drooping, her whole attitude one of utter weariness.

On the eve of her departure she was staying with friends. At night they went into her room and found her weeping quietly in bed. They tried to comfort her, and she said half-whimsically that she had been overcome by the feeling that she was homeless and without kith and kin la her own country. "I'm a poor solitary with only memories." "But you have troops of friends—you have us all—we all love you." "Yes, I ken, and I am grateful," she replied, "but"—wistfully—"it's just that I've none of my ain folk to say good-bye to."

She was very tired when she left, "I'm hardly myself in this country," she said. "It has too many things, and it is always in such a hurry. I lose my head." Again kind hands eased her way, and settled her on the steamer. Dan was inconsolable, and wept to be taken back to Joppa.

The voyage gave her a new lease of life. The quietness and peace and meditation, the warm sunshine and the breezes, the loveliness of the sky and sea, rested and healed her. This, despite the conduct of some wild passengers bound for the gold-mines. One day she rose and left the table by way of protest, but in the end they bade her a kindly good- bye, and listened to her advice. At Lagos the Governor sent off his aide-de-camp with greetings, and a case of milk for the children. Mr. Grey also appeared and escorted her to Calabar. "Am I not a privileged and happy woman?" she wrote to his sister.

The same note of gratitude filled a letter which she wrote on board to Dr. Robson, asking him to put a few lines in the *Record* thanking every one for their kindness, as it was impossible to answer all the letters she had received. The letter itself was inserted, and we give the concluding paragraph:

To all who have received me into their homes, and given me a share of what are the most sacred things of earth, I give heartfelt thanks. What the Bethany house must have been to our Lord, no one can better appreciate than the missionary coming home to a strange place, homeless. I thank all those who have rested me, and nursed me back to health and strength, and who have nerved me for future service by the sweet ministries and hallowing influences of their home life. To the members of the Mission Board for their courtesy, their confidence, and sympathetic helpfulness, I owe much gratitude. And not only for services which can be tabulated, but for the whole atmosphere of sympathy which has surrounded me; for the hand-clasps which have spoken volumes; for the looks of love which have beamed from eyes soft with feeling; for the prayer which has upheld and guided in days gone by, and on which I count for strength in days to come; for all I pray that God may say to each giving, sympathetic heart, "Inasmuch as ye did it to one of the least of these my brethren, ye did it unto Me."

She was praying all the while for her bairn. On her arrival, as fast as boat would take her, she sped up to Use. The chiefs and people came crowding to welcome her, bringing lavish gifts of food-yams and salt and fish and fowl. There were even fifty yams, and a goat from the back of Okoyong. Dan with his English clothes was the centre of admiration, and grave greybeards sat and listened to the ticking of his watch, and played with his toy train....

To her unspeakable relief she found the story about Jean to be a native lie. She was too grateful to be angry.

CHAPTER XV
GROWING WEATHER

The short furlough in Scotland, broken by so much movement and excitement, had done little permanent good. She was tired when she began her work, and there came a long series of "up and down" days which handicapped her activity, yet she continued her duties with a resolution that was unquenched and unquenchable. "Things are humdrum," she wrote, "just like this growing weather of ours, rainy and cloudy, with a blink here and there. We know the brightness would scorch and destroy if it were constant; still the bursts of glory that come between the clouds are a rich provision for our frail and sensitive lives." Her conception of achievement was a little out of the common. One day she sat in court for eight hours; other two hours were spent with the clerk making out warrants; afterwards she had to find tasks to employ some labour; then she went out at dusk and attended a birth case all night, returning at dawn. Whole days were occupied with palavers, many of the people coming such long distances that she had to provide sleeping accommodation for them. Old chiefs would pay her visits and stay for hours. "It is a great tax," she remarked, "but it pays even if it tires." Sundays were her busiest days; she went far afield preaching, and had usually from six to twelve meetings in villages and by the wayside. Often on these excursions she came across natives who had made the journey to Okoyong to consult her in the old days. The situation was now reversed, for people from Okoyong came to her. One day after a ten hours' sitting in Court she went home to find about fifty natives from the hinterland of that district waiting with their usual tributes of food and a peck of troubles for her to straighten out. It was after midnight before there was quiet and sleep for her. Her heart went out to these great-limbed, straight-nosed, sons of the aboriginal forest, and she determined to cross the river and visit them. She spent three days fixing up all their domestic and social affairs, and making a few proclamations, and diligently sowing the seeds of the Gospel. When she left she had with her four boys and a girl as wild and undisciplined as mountain goats, who were added to her household to undergo the process of taming, training, and educating ere they were sent back.

In what she called her spare time she was engaged in the endless task of repairing and extending her forlorn little shanties. There was always something on hand, and she worked as hard as the children, nailing up corrugated iron, sawing boards, cementing floors, or cutting bush. Jean, the ever-willing and cheerful, was practically in charge of the house, keeping the babies, looking after their mothers, and teaching the little ones in the school. Up to this period she had never received more than her board, and "Ma" felt it was time to acknowledge her services, and she therefore began to pay her 1s. per week.

Now and again in her letters there came the ominous words, "I'm tired, tired." On the last night of the year she was sitting up writing. "I'm tired," she said, "and have a few things to do. My mother went home eighteen years ago on the passage of the old year, so it is rather lonely to-night with so many memories. The bairns are all asleep. But He hath not failed, and He is all-sufficient." She was often so wearied that she could not sit up straight. She was too exhausted to take off her clothes and brush her hair until she had obtained what she called her "first rest." Then she rose and finished her undressing. She would begin a letter and not be able to finish it. The ladies nearest her, Miss Peacock and Miss Reid at Ikotobong, redoubled their attentions. Miss Reid she said was "a bonnie lassie, tenderly kind to me." What Miss Peacock was to her no one but herself knew. She was a keen judge of character, though generous, almost extravagant in her appreciation of those she loved, and Miss Peacock has justified her estimate and her praise. "Sterling as a Christian, splendid as a woman, whole-hearted as a missionary, capable as a teacher, she is one after my own heart," she wrote. "She is very good and kind to me, and a tower of strength. I am proud of her and the great work she is doing." Miss Peacock began the habit about this time of cycling down on Saturday afternoons and spending a few hours with her, and Mary looked forward to these visits with the greatest zest.

The friends at home were also ceaseless in their kindness. They scrutinised every letter she sent, and were frequently able to read between the lines and anticipate and supply her needs, — much to her surprise. "Have I been grumbling?" she would enquire. "You make me ashamed. I am better off than thousands who give their money to support me." A carpet arrived. "And oh," she writes, "what a difference it has made to our comfort. You have no idea of the transformation! The mud and cement were transformed at once into something as artistic as the 'boards' of the bungalow, and the coziness was simply beyond belief. It did not look a bit hot, and it was so soothing to the bare feet, and I need not say it was a wonder to the natives, who can't understand a white man stepping on a cloth — and such a cloth!" On another occasion a bed was sent out to her, and she wrote: "I've been jumping my tired body up and down on it just to get the beautiful swing, and to feel that I am lying level. I'm tired and I'm happy and I'm half-ashamed at my own luxury." And next morning, "What a lovely sleep I've had!"

The Macgregors made their first visit to Use in 1908, and on arrival found "Ma" sitting with a morsel of infant in her lap. She was dressed in a print overall with low neck; it was tied at the middle with a sash, and she was without stockings or shoes. On the Sunday she set out early on foot on her customary round, carrying two roasted corn-cobs as her day's rations, whilst Mr. Macgregor took the service at Ikotobong. He was tired after his one effort, but when he returned in the evening he discovered her preaching at Use Church-her tenth meeting for the day, and her tour had not been so extensive as usual. At six o'clock next morning people had already arrived with palavers. One woman wanted a husband. "Ma" looked at her with those shrewd eyes that read people through and through, and then began in Scots, "It's bad eneuch being a marriage registrar, without being a matrimonial agent forby. *Eke mi'o!* Mr. Macgregor, send up any o' your laddies that's wanting wives." Then she went into Efik that made the woman wince, and pointed out that she had come to the wrong place.

She watched with interest the progress of the Creek stations, although they were out of her hands. There were now at Okpo forty members in full communion, and the contributions for the year amounted to £48: 3: 3. At Akani Obio, where there were forty-five members in full communion, the total contributions amounted to £98: 11: 4. And at Asang, where there were one hundred and fifteen members, the contributions amounted to £146: 68. At those three stations the total expenses were fully met, and there was a large surplus. Where four years ago there was no church member and no offering, there were now two hundred members, and contributions amounting in all to £287.

So the Kingdom of her Lord grew.

CHAPTER XVI"
"THE PITY OF IT"

One experience of 1908, when she was down at Duke Town attending the Council meetings, is worth noting. Though she liked the bush better she was always interested in watching the movements there. "It is a great cheer to me," she said, "to meet all the young folks, and to be with them in their enthusiasm and optimism, and this vast hive of industry, the Hope Waddell Institution, with its swarm of young men and boys, gives me the highest hopes for the future of the Church and the nation now in their infancy. Mr. Macgregor is a perfect Principal, sane, self- restrained, and tactful, but I would not be in his place for millions." The town was a very different place from that which she first saw in 1876. It was now a flourishing seaport, with many fine streets and buildings. The swamp had been drained. There was a fully-equipped native hospital, and a magnificent church in the centre of the town, and the Europeans enjoyed most of the conveniences and even the luxuries of civilisation.

On this occasion an invitation came from the High Commissioner to dine at Government House, and meet a certain woman writer of books. She would not hear of it. She had no clothes for such a function, and she did not wish to be lionised. The Macgregors, with whom she was staying, advised her to go; they thought it would do her good. She consented at last, but when she left in a hammock, which had been specially sent for her, there was the light of battle in her eyes. Mr. Macgregor knew that look and laughed; there was no doubt she was going to enjoy herself; she had still the heart of a school-girl, and greatly loved a prank. When she returned, her face was full of mischief. "Ay," she said, "I met your lady writer, and I made her greet four times and she gied me half a sovereign for my bairns!"

Under the title of "But yet the pity of it," the authoress gave an account of the meeting in the *Morning Post*, in a way which excited laughter and derision in the Calabar bush. It was in the pathetic strain:

"I am not given to admiring missionary enterprise," she wrote. "The enthusiasm which seems to so many magnificent seems to me but a meddling in other people's business; the money that is poured out, so much bread and light and air and happiness filched from the smitten children at home.

"But this missionary conquered me if she did not convert me.

"She was a woman close on sixty, with a heavily-lined face, and a skin from which the freshness and bloom had long, long ago departed; but there was fire in her old eyes still, tired though they looked; there was sweetness and firmness about her lined mouth. Heaven knows who had dressed her. She wore a skimpy tweed skirt and a cheap nun's veiling blouse, and on her iron-grey hair was perched rakishly a forlorn broken picture-hat of faded green, chiffon with a knot of bright red ribbon to give the bizarre touch of colour she had learned to admire among her surroundings.

"'Ye'll excuse my hands,' she said, and she held them out.

"They were hardened and roughened by work, work in the past, and they were just now bleeding from work finished but now; the skin of the palms was gone, the nails were worn to the quick; that they were painful there could be no doubt, but she only apologised for their appearance."

"Ma" is thus made to tell the incident of the witness dying suddenly after attending the court at Ikotobong:

"'If you put *mbiam* on a man and he swears falsely he dies. Oh, he does. I ken it. I've seen it mysel'. There was a man brought up before me in the court and he was charged wi' stealing some plantains. He said he had naught to do with them, so I put *mbiam* on him, an' still he said he had naught to do wi' them, so I sent him down to Calabar. An' see now. As he was going he stopped the policeman an' laid himself down, because he was sick. An' he died. He died there. I put *mbiam* on him, an' he knew he had stolen them and died.'

"There was pity in her face for the man she had killed with his own lie, but only pity, no regret."

So well was she succeeding with her mystification that she went on to talk of the hard lot of women and "the puir bairns," and then comes the conclusion:

"'My time's been wasted. The puir bairns. They'd be better dead.'

"Her scarred hands fumbled with her dress, her tired eyes looked out into the blazing tropical sunshine, her lips quivered as she summed up her life's work. 'Failed, failed,' she cried. All that she had hoped, all that she had prayed for, nothing for herself had she ever sought except the power to help these children, and she felt that she had not helped them. They would be better dead....

"But the Commissioner did not think she had failed. Is the victory always to the strong?

"'She has influence and weight,' he said 'she can go where no white man dare go. She can sway the people when we cannot sway them. Because of her they are not so hard on the twins and their mothers as they used to be. No, she has not failed.'"

And so with a reference to Thermopylae, and the Coliseum and Smithfield, the lady litterateur places her in the ranks of the immortal martyrs of the world.

CHAPTER XVII
THE SETTLEMENT BEGUN

This was one of the waiting periods in Mary Slessor's life, which tried her patience and affected her spirits. The mist had fallen upon her path, and the direction was dim and uncertain. She had received what she thought was a call from a distant region up-country, but if she settled far away, what would become of her home for women and girls? She had no clear leading, and she wished the way to be made so plain that there could be no possibility of mistake. Friends were sending her money, and the Government were urging her to start the Settlement, and promising to take all the products that were grown. "The District Commissioner was here to-day," she wrote. "He wonders how he can help me, has had orders from the Governor to assist me in any way, but the Pillar does not move. I have building material lying here, and have a £10 note from a friend at home for any material I want, but there is no leading towards anything yet…. I am longing for an outlet, but I can't move without guidance." She would not hurry—the matter was not in her hands. God, she was assured, was "softly, softly," working towards a natural solution, and as she was only His instrument, she could afford to wait His time.

One night the mist on the path lifted a little, and next day she walked over the land at Use, and there and then fixed the site for the undertaking. There was ample room for all the cultivations that would be required, and plenty of material for building and fencing, and good surface water. Already she had three cottages built, including the one she occupied, and these would make a beginning. She at once set about obtaining legal possession, and with the permission and help of Government she secured the land in the name of the girls. The Council agreed with her that it was most advisable to develop industries which the people had not yet undertaken, such as basket-making, the weaving of cocoanut fibre, and cane and bamboo work. When asked if she would agree to remain at Use for one year to establish the Settlement and put it in working order with the assistance of one or two agents, she would not commit herself. She rather shrank from the idea of a large institution; it ought, in her view, to begin in a simple and natural way by bringing in a few people, instructing them, and then getting them to teach others. And there were other regions calling to her. When reminded that a large sum of money was on hand for the project, she said it was not all intended for this special purpose; much of it was for extension; and she pointed to the needs of the region up the Cross River, stating that she was willing to have the funds used for providing agents there.

Nothing more definite was decided, and meanwhile she went on quietly with the beginnings of things. She planted fruit trees sent up by the Government,—mangoes, guavas, pawpaws, bananas, plantains, avocado pears, as well as pineapples, and other produce, and began to think of rubber and cocoa. She also started to accumulate stock, though the leopards were a constant menace. She had even a cow, which she bought from a man to prevent him going to prison for debt—and often wished she had not, for it caused infinite trouble, and the natives went in terror of it. Although it had a pail attached to it by a rope, it was often lost, and the whole town were out at nights searching for it. It would run away with the whole household hanging on, and so little respect did it pay to dignitaries, that on one occasion it ran off with the Mother of the Mission and the Principal of the Hope Waddell Institute, who had been pressed into the humble service of leading it home. "Ma Slessor's coo" became quite famous in the Mission.

It was characteristic of her that she did not want her name to be put to anything, and she thought the Settlement should be called after Mrs. Anderson or Mrs. Goldie, who did so much for women and girls.

CHAPTER XVIII
A SCOTTISH GUEST

During the year 1909 she continued to fight a battle with ill-health. She was compelled to give up much of her outdoor work, for an oppressive sense of heart-weakness made her afraid to cross deep streams and climb the hills. Sometimes she used her cycle, but only when she could obtain one of the girls or lads to run alongside and assist her up the ascents. Boils, an old enemy, tortured her again; she was covered with them from head to foot, and was one mass of pain. "Only sleeping draughts," she said, "keep me from going off my head." As the months went on she became feeble almost to fainting point, and had given up hope of betterment. A note of sadness crept into her letters. "I cannot write," she told a friend at home, "but there is no change in the heart's affection, except that it grows stronger and perhaps a little more wistful as the days go by and life gets more uncertain." She was anxious to recover sufficiently before March, to do honour to two deputies who had been appointed by the home Church to visit the Mission, and who were expected then, and if possible to return to Scotland with them. But she scarcely anticipated holding out so long. Jean, unfortunately, was not with her. It had been discovered that she had long been suffering in silence from an internal complaint, and the medical men now advised an operation. "Ma" was opposed to this, and left her for a time at Duke Town for a change and treatment, which did her much good.

It was sheer will-power that gained her a little strength to face the ordeal of the official visit. She determined to make no change whatever in the course of her daily life, and she was afraid the deputies might not find things to their liking and be disappointed. They were the Rev. James Adamson, M.A., B.Sc., of Bonnington, Leith, and the Rev. John Lindsay, M.A., Bathgate, who was accompanied by Mrs. Lindsay. They entered the Creek one market day, when it was crowded with canoes, and the landing-beach—one for the missionaries had just been constructed at Okopedi—was swarming with people, amongst whom the arrival of the strangers caused the greatest excitement. On bicycles the party proceeded uphill to Use. Mr. Adamson went on ahead, and at a spot where a few rough steps were cut in the steep bank he saw a boy standing, He called out, "Ma Slessor?" The boy signed to Mm to come—it was a short cut to the house. Clambering up the bank and making his way through the bush, Mr. Adamson came upon a little native hut. Miss Slessor advanced to meet him. "Come awa in, laddie, oot o' the heat," was her greeting. When the Lindsays arrived it was also her chief concern to get them into the shade. Mr. Adamson was her guest, whilst the Lindsays went on to Ikotobong. His room—an erection built out from the house—had mud walls and a mat roof, and was furnished with a camp-bed, a box for dressing-table and another for a washstand, and for company he had abundance of spiders and beetles and lizards. He proved a delightful guest. "He is a dear laddie," wrote Mary; "all the bairns are in love with him, and so am I!"

While he was with her a woman came to the yard with twins. She had been driven out of her house and town, and had come several miles to "Ma" for shelter. Her husband and her father were with her—which denoted some advance—and the three were crouched on the ground, a picture of misery. The twins were lying in a basket and had not been touched. Mr. Adamson helped "Ma" to attend to them, and she felt as proud of him as of a son when she saw him sitting down beside the weeping mother and gently trying to comfort her. She gave the parents some food and a hut to sleep in, and made the man promise to stay until the morning. Neither would, however, look at the twins, and they were given over to the girls.

A service was held at which Mr. Lindsay was also present, and about a hundred people attended. "Take our compliments to the people of your country," the latter said to the deputies, "and tell them that our need is great, and that we are in darkness and waiting for the light." What astonished the natives was to see the white visitors standing up courteously when spoken to by black men.

From the meeting the party cycled to the little wattle-and-thatch Court House at Ikotobong, Miss Slessor being pushed by Dan up the hills. She took her seat at the table in the simplest possible attire. Before her was a tin of toffee, her only refreshment, with the exception of a cup of tea, during a long sitting. The jury, composed of the older and more responsible men in the various villages, occupied a raised platform behind. In front was a bamboo railing, which formed the dock; at the side another railing marked the witness-box. Several cases were heard, the witnesses giving their evidence with volubility and abundant gesture, and the judge, jury, and clerk retiring to a little shed at the back to discuss the verdicts. One was that of a man who, under the influence of trade gin, had hacked his wife with a machete, because she had insulted his dignity by accidentally stumbling against him. Such a case always aroused "Ma's" ire, and she wished a severe punishment awarded. The jury were very unwilling. The headman started by laying down as a fundamental principle that men had a perfect right to do whatever they liked with their wives; otherwise they would become unmanageable. But in deference to the white woman's peculiar views they would go the length of admitting that perhaps the husband had gone a little too far in the use of his instrument. He had not done anything to merit a severe sentence, but in view of the prejudices of the "Court," they would send him to prison for a short term.

Suddenly the "toot" of the Government motor-car was heard, and in a moment jury, witnesses, prisoners, and policemen rushed out of the building to catch a glimpse of the "new steamer" that ran on the road. Then back they drifted, and the proceedings went on.

Mr. Adamson appreciated the service which Miss Slessor was accomplishing by her work in the Court. She told him she did not care for it; "the moral atmosphere of a native court is so bad," she declared, "that I would never go near one were it not that I want the people to get justice." But he saw the exceptional opportunity she possessed of dispensing gospel as well as law. "As a rule," he says, "her decision is accompanied by some sound words of Christian counsel." He left Use with a profound admiration both for herself and Miss Peacock. "Words," he wrote in the *Record*, "cannot describe the value of the work that is being done by these heroic women."

There was no improvement in her health as the months went on, and another severe illness caused by blood-poisoning shattered her nerves. The Wilkies spared no labour or love to heal and strengthen her. "Once more," she wrote, "I believe I owe my life to them."

She felt that the time had come to relinquish her court work, and accordingly in November she sent in her resignation. The Commissioner of the Eastern Province wrote in reply:

DEAR MISS SLESSOR—I have been informed of your decision to resign the Vice-Presidentship of the Ikotobong Native Court by the District Commissioner, Ikot Ekpene, which I note with great regret, and take this opportunity of thanking you for the assistance you have in the past given the Government, and of expressing my deep appreciation of the services you have rendered to the country during the period you have held the office which you have now relinquished.—Believe me, Yours very sincerely,

W. FOSBERY.

She slipped out of the work very quietly, and was glad to be free of a tie which hindered her from moving onward on her King's more pressing business.

CHAPTER XIX
A MOTOR CAR ROMANCE

The Government motor car, which now ran up and down the road into the interior, was the cause of several changes in the household of Use. In charge of it at first was a white chauffeur, who, curiously enough, was a member of Wellington Street Church in Glasgow, which now supported Miss Slessor, and with him was a native assistant, a young well- educated Anglican, who came from Lagos. When the car made its appearance Dan was so fascinated with it that he could scarcely keep off the road, and he now struck up an acquaintance with the native driver, which brought him many a rapturous hour. "Ma," who did not then know the lad, was in terror for the safety of his body and his morals, and so despatched him as a pupil to the Institute at Duke Town to be under the care of Mr. Macgregor. But David, the driver, had done more than capture Dan; he had captured the heart of one of the girls—Mary. Annie was already happily married, and she and her husband were preparing to join the Church; but Mary was not disposed to follow her example, although she had two suitors, one in Okoyong, and one in Ibibio. "Why can't I stay at home with you?" she said to "Ma." "I don't want to go anywhere." But the Lagos lad succeeded where others had failed, and "Ma," giving her consent, they were married, before the District Commissioner in Court. David went back to his work, and his wife to the Mission House, for "Ma" would not allow him to take her home until the Church ceremony had been performed. Mr. Cruickshank appeared one day before he was expected, and before the wedding-gown was quite ready, but a note was sent to David, and he cycled down in his black suit. Miss Annie M'Minn, then at Ikotobong, came and dressed the bride, the children put on white frocks, and there was a quaint and picturesque wedding.

There was also, of course, a breakfast. It was given in the verandah of the hut. David was early on the scene arranging tables and forms, and Miss Peacock and Miss M'Minn laid and decorated them, a conspicuous object being a bunch of heather from Scotland. Jean and the bride cooked the breakfast. By 11 o'clock the company had assembled. At the head sat an aged Mohammedan in white robes and turban, a friend of David's family. A number of his co-religionists had come to the district, and some even attended "Ma's" services. This particular man greatly admired her. "Only God can make you such a mother and helper to everybody," he had said at his first interview, and on leaving he had taken her hand and bent over and kissed it, and with tears in his eyes invoked a blessing upon her. Few expressions of respect from white men had touched her more, though she was half-afraid her feeling was scarcely orthodox. Then came the bride and bridegroom and "Ma's" clerk. At the next table sat another of David's friends—an interpreter—and a lad from the bride's house, headman on the road Department; David's next-door neighbours, a man and his wife; and eight headmen over the road labourers. Outside were the school children, who were fed by Jean with Calabar chop, sweets, and biscuits.

After the breakfast the Mohammedan came indoors to Miss Slessor and made a speech. "I knew David's mother before he was born," he said, "and I praise God he was led here for a wife." David came forward, "Mother," he said, "you won't let us go without prayer?" and down he knelt, and she committed the couple to God, A pie and cake, which the Ikotobong ladies had baked, were presented, along with a motor cap, silk handkerchief, ribbon, and scissors. One of "Ma's" presents was a sewing-machine. Then she walked down to see them off, supported in her weakness by the Mohammedan, When the pair arrived at their home, the latter stood on the doorstep praying for them as they entered on their new life. It was only a bamboo shanty run up by the Government, but it was a home, and not, like all others, a room in a compound, and family worship was conducted in it in English. Good news came from it as time went on. The bride was sometimes seen driving in the motor car. "She was here this morning," writes the house-mother, "full of importance as she passed to market. She had biscuits for the children, a new water- jar and a bunch of fine bananas for me, and the whole house were round her full of questions and fun, and you would think she had become a heroine, just because she was married two months ago. She is very happy and proud of her husband." "Ma" watched over her with jealous care, and when in due time a baby arrived, she was as delighted as if it had been of her own blood.

CHAPTER XX
STRUCK DOWN

The hot, dry season was always a trial to Miss Slessor; it shrivelled her up, and reduced her energy, and she panted for the cooling rains. This year it affected her more than ever. The harmattan was like an Edinburgh "haar," though it was not cold except between midnight and daybreak; the air was thick with fine sand dust, and often she could not see three yards away. She longed for a "wee blink of home," and a home Sabbath. "But though the tears are coming at the thought, you are not to think for one moment that I would take the offer if it were given me! A thousand times no! I feel too grateful to God for His wonderful condescension in letting me have the privilege of ministering to those around me here."

How the interest of the spiritual aspects of her work submerged the afflictions of her body was seen when the first baptismal service and communion at Use took place. With her dread of the spectacular she did not make the event known, but the little native church was crowded, men and women squatting on the floor, and the mothers with babies on the verandah. Mr. Cruickshank conducted the service. Mary took a "creepie" stool—her mother's footstool of old—and sat down by the young communicants to help them and show them what to do. "David," she wrote, "had bought a bottle of wine for his wedding, but of course it was never opened, and he said to me, 'Keep it, Ma, it may be useful yet.' So it was drawn for our first communion well-watered. The glass sugar- dish on a teaplate was the baptismal font, but it was all transfigured and glorified by the Light which never shone on hill or lake or even on human face, and some of us saw the King in His beauty—and not far off. Bear with me in my joy; this sounds small in comparison with home events, but it is only a very short time since this place was dark and degraded and drunken and besotted."

The glow and exaltation of the service lingered with her for weeks, and her letters are full of sprightliness and wit. She told of a visit from Lady Egerton—"a true woman"—and of the Christmas gift from their Excellencies—a case of milk; and of the present of a new cycle sent from England from "her old chief" Mr. Partridge, to replace the old one which he thought must be worn out by this time. The wonders of aviation were engrossing the world then, and she merrily imagined a descent upon her some afternoon of her friends from Scotland, and discussed the capabilities of her tea-caddy.

Well on into the next year she was busy with regular station work, teaching, training, preaching, building up the congregation, and acting as Mother to her people and to many more. Then in the midst of her strenuous activity she was suddenly and swiftly struck down by what she termed "one of the funniest illnesses" she ever had. The children were alarmed, and sent word to David. He informed the white officers, and they rushed in a motor car down to Use and removed her to Itu, where she was nursed back to life by Mrs. Robertson. "I shall never forget the kindness and the tenderness and the skill which have encompassed me, and I shall ever remember Dr. Robertson and his devoted wife, and ask God to remember them for their goodness. Dr. Robertson brought me out of the valley of the shadows and when I was convalescent he lifted me up in his strong arms and took me to see the church and garden and anywhere I wished, just as he might have done to his own mother." Her friends in Calabar also did everything they could for her, the Hon. Mr. Bedwell, the Provincial Commissioner, sending up ice and English chicken and other delicacies in a special launch.

The little daughter of the missionaries was a source of great delight to her who loved all children. She was a very winsome girl, and had won the hearts of the natives, who regarded her with not a little awe. She was the only white child they had seen, and were not sure whether she was not a spirit. "Ma" and she had good times together, playing and make-believing. "Maimie and I," she wrote, "have been having the dolls out for a drive, and we have just given them their bread and milk and put them to bed!"

When she was convalescent the Macgregors insisted on her coming down to Duke Town for a change, and the Government placed the fast and comfortable *Maple Leaf* at their disposal. She protested, saying she could not put herself on a brother and sister whose lives were so strenuous, but they would take no refusal. They turned their dining- room into a bedroom for her convenience, and here she talked and read the newspapers and the latest new books and her Bible, and wrote long letters to her friends. "I am doing nothing but eating," she told her children, "and am growing fat and shedding my buttons all over the place." But underneath all her gaiety and high spirits she felt profoundly grateful for the wonderful goodness and mercy God had made to pass before her, and the perfect peace He had given her. "Here I am," she said, "being spoiled anew in an atmosphere not merely of tender love, but of literary and cultured Christian grace and winsomeness, and it has been as perfect a fortnight as ever I spent." She had literally to run away from the kind attentions of the Government officials and doctors, and a swift Government launch again conveyed her up-river. Jean, who had long since returned, had bravely held the fort for the five Sabbaths she had been absent, and David and his wife had been there to protect her, and the work, therefore, had been kept going.

After each breakdown she seemed to feel that she must make up for lost time, and she planned an advance towards Ikot Ekpene, being anxious to secure that point and the intervening area for her church. On her bicycle she made a series of pioneer trips into the bush, here and there selecting sites for schools, interviewing chiefs about twin- mothers, and generally preparing the way for further operations. About twelve miles' distant, or half-way to Ikot Ekpene, where there was a camp, she met some forty chiefs and arranged for ground for a school and the beginning of the work, and for a hut for herself at the back of the native prison, where, she thought, she would have some influence over the warders. As she was never able to establish this station, its history may be rounded off here. Early in the year 1911 she brought the matter before the Calabar Council, which agreed to build a house at Ibiacu out of the extension fund, and later she went in a hammock to complete the arrangement, accompanied by Miss Welsh, who, as "Ma" phrased it, "fitted into bush life like a glove," and who occupied and developed the station. This young missionary lives alone, looks after the children, has a clever pen and clever hands, and Is following very much on the lines of the great "Ma." To the chagrin of the latter, Ikot Ekpene was taken over by the Primitive Methodist Mission before she could secure it, but she consoled herself with the thought that it did not matter who did the Master's works so long as it done....

Then her path, which had been so long hidden, cleared, and she saw it stretching out plain and straight before her.

FIFTH PHASE

1910-January 1915. Age 62-66.

ONWARD STILL

"It is a dark and difficult land, and I am old and weak—but happy."

CHAPTER I
IN HEATHEN DEEPS

The new sphere to which Miss Slessor felt she was called, had been occupying her attention for some time. During one of the minor military expeditions into the interior, the troops were suddenly attacked by a tribe who fled at the first experience of disciplined firing. A lad who had been used by the soldiers was persuaded by some of their number to conduct them to the great White Mother for her advice and help. When they appeared at Use, she and they talked long and earnestly, and they returned consoled and hopeful. Some time afterwards the guide came down on his own account, bringing a few other lads with him. Her influence was such that they wished to become God-men, and they returned to begin the first Christian movement in one of the most degraded regions of Nigeria.

She knew nothing of the place save that it was away up in the north-west, on one of the higher reaches of the Enyong Creek, and a two days' journey for her by water. The lads lived at a town called Ikpe, an old slave centre, that had been in league with Aro, and the focus of the trade of a wide and populous area. It was a "closed" market, no Calabar trader being allowed to enter.

On her return from Scotland the young men again appeared, saying that there were forty others ready to become Christians, begging her to come up, and offering to send down a canoe. She disliked all water journeys, and even on the quiet creek was usually in a state of inward trepidation. But nothing could separate her from her duty, and she responded to the call. For eight hours she was paddled along the beautiful windings of the

Creek; then a huge hippopotamus was encountered, and frightened her into landing for the night on the Ibibio side, where she put up in a wretched hut reeking with filth and mosquitoes. Here the Chief was reaching out for the Gospel, holding prayers in his house, and trying to keep Sabbath, though not a soul could read, and the people were laughing at him. As the Creek made a bend she left the canoe and trudged through the bush to Ikpe. She found the town larger and more prosperous than she had anticipated, with four different races mingling in the market, but the darkness was terrible, and the wickedness shameless, even the children being foul-mouthed and abandoned. The younger and more progressive men gave her a warm welcome, but the older chiefs were sulky—"Poor old heathen souls," she remarked, "they have good reason to be, with all they have to hope from tumbling down about their ears." The would-be Christians had begun to erect a small church, with two rooms for her at the end. That they were in earnest was proved by their attitude. She had eager and reverent audiences, and once, on going unexpectedly into a yard, she found two lads on their knees praying to the white man's God.

She made a survey of the district, and came to the conclusion that Ikpe was another strategic point, the key to several different tribes, which it would be well to secure for the Church, and she made up her mind to come and live in the two rooms, and work inland and backwards towards Arochuku. There was the Settlement to consider, but that, she thought, she could manage to carry on along with the occupation of Ikpe.

Her bright and eager spirit did not reckon with the frailties of the body. When she returned, she entered on a long period of weakness. Now and again deputations came down to her. Once a score of young men appeared, and before stating their business said, "Let us pray." She made another visit, saw the beginnings of the church at Ikpe, and another at Nkanga on the Creek bank, three miles below Ikpe, and, what affected her more, heard rumours of a possible occupation by the Roman Catholics. "I must come," she said to herself.

On one journey she was accompanied by Miss Peacock, who rose still more highly in her regard on account of the resolute way in which she braved the awful smells in the villages. On another, Mr. and Mrs. Macgregor shared the hardships of the trip with her. When these two arrived at the landing-beach for Use, a note was put into their hands from "Ma," to the effect that she had not been able to obtain a canoe, and they had better come to the house until she saw what the Lord meant by it. They remained at Use some days, "Ma" suffering from fever, but refusing to postpone the trip, saying that if she had faith she would be able to go. They were to start early one morning, but her guests sought to keep her in sleep until it was too late. They succeeded until 1 A.M., when she awoke, gave directions about packing, and rose. "What do you think of her?" they asked of Jean. "She is often like that, and gets better on the road," she replied, which was true. As "Ma" herself said, "I begin every day, almost every journey in pain, and in such tiredness that I am sure I can't go on, and whenever I begin, the strength comes, and it increases."

The party left at 3.15 in the moonlight, and soon afterwards were in a canoe. For hours they paddled, past men with two-pronged fish-spears fishing, by long stretches of water-lilies of dazzling whiteness, by farms where the fresh green corn was beginning to sprout, by extensive reaches of jungle where brilliant birds flitted, and parrots chattered, and monkeys swung from branch to branch by a bridge of hands. They stopped for lunch, and Mr. Macgregor was interested in watching her methods with the people. A chief wished to see the Principal, and said he was anxious to place two more boys with him in the Institute. She told Mr. Macgregor to say he would see him after they had eaten. The business-like Principal thought this a waste of time, but she held that he must not cheapen himself—if he made food of more importance than the education of their boys they would think him dignified and respect him. And she was right.

By and by they came to a tortuous channel as narrow as a mill-dam, and it was with difficulty that the canoe was punted through. They swept on under trees, hung with orchids, where dragon-flies flashed in and out of the sunlight. This was the country of the hippos, and the banks were scored by their massive feet; it was also, as they found to their cost, the haunt of ibots, a fly with a poisonous bite. After passing over a series of shallows they reached Ikpe beach towards dark, and camped in the unfinished church, "Ma" in the "vestry," and the Macgregors inside the building.

Mr. Macgregor had seen much of Nigeria, but he had never witnessed such degradation as he found existing here. The girls went without any clothing, except a string of beads, and the married women wore only a narrow strip of cloth. He had again a lesson in native manners. Paying ceremonial visits to the chiefs, they sat and looked at the ground, and yawned repeatedly, and after a time left. To him the yawning seemed rude, but "Ma" said it was the correct thing, and when the chiefs returned the calls he knew that, as usual, she was right.

One of the questions that the chiefs asked was, "Is this the man you have brought to stay and teach us?" "Ma" turned to the Principal with a wry face. "Well," she said in English, "I like that. They'll need to be content wi' something less than a B.D. for a wee while—till they get started at any rate." She informed them who Mr. Macgregor was, and the great work he was doing in Calabar, and that in the goodness of his heart he had come up to see the position of things in the town.

"Ma"—incredulously—"do you mean that this is not the man who is to come and lead us out of darkness?"

"No, he is not the man-yet."

"Ma"—reproachfully—"you always say wait. We have waited two years, and again you come to us and say wait. When are you coming to us?"

There was nothing for it but to put them off once more. But she improved the occasion by extolling the Institute, with the result that when they left, two boys were taken to the canoe and consigned to Mr. Macgregor's care, one decently clad in a singlet and loin-cloth, and the other with only a single bead hanging at the throat.

Mr. Macgregor went exploring on his own account, and came across a Government Rest House perched on the brow of a cliff, with a magnificent view over the plain. Here he noticed that the people were particularly opposed to white men. One of the villages "Ma" had labelled "dangerous," and he learnt that when the Court messengers appeared, they were promptly seized, beaten, and cast out. This, it is interesting to note, came to be the scene of "Ma's" last exploits. He rejoined the ladies at Nkanga, where the little native church had been completed. They held the opening service. The Principal had no jacket; his shirt was torn, his boots bore traces of the streams and mud through which he had passed. Miss Slessor wore the lightest of garments. It was one of the strangest opening ceremonies in the history of Missions, but they worshipped God from the heart, and "Ma" seemed lifted out of herself, and to be inspired, as she told the people what the church there in their midst meant, and the way they should use it for their highest good.

The Macgregors left her at Arochuku, and she continued down-creek. She had been upheld by her indomitable spirit throughout the journey, but now collapsed, and was so ill that she had to spend the night in the canoe. In the darkness she was awakened by one of the babies crying, but was so weak that she could not move. The girls were sound asleep, and could not hear her. Exerting her willpower, she rolled over to the child, whose head had become wedged between a box and the footboard of the canoe, and was being slowly killed. In the early dawn the journey was resumed to Okopedi beach, and thence she crawled over the weary miles to Use.

CHAPTER II
"REAL LIFE"

"I must go. I am in honour bound to go." It was her constant cry. She heard that services were being held regularly at Ikpe on Sundays and week-days, and yet no one knew more than the merest rudiments of Christian truth; none could read. A teacher had gone from Asang, but he was himself only at the stage of the first standard in the schools, and could impart but the crudest instruction. They were groping for the light, and worshipping what to most of them was still the Unknown God, and yet were already able to withstand persecution. The pathos of the situation broke her down. "Why," she cried, "cannot the Church send two ladies there? Why don't they use the money on hand for the purpose? If the wherewithal should fail at the end of two years, let them take my salary, I shall only be too glad to live on native food with my bairns."

Once more she went up, and once more she stood ashamed before their reproaches. She could not hold out any longer. "I am coming," she said decisively. She was not well—she was never well now—she had bad nights, was always "tired out," "too tired for anything," yet she went forward to the new life with unshakeable fortitude. In a short time she was back with fifty sheets of corrugated iron and other material for the house. "I am committed now," she wrote. "No more idleness for me. I am entering in the dark as to how and where and when. How I am to manage I do not know, but my mind is at perfect peace about it, and I am not afraid. God will carry it through. The Pillar leads."

She did not care much for the situation that had been granted; it was low-lying, and she was anxious to conserve her health for the work's sake, but she had faith that she would be taken care of. Palm trees bordered the site on three sides, and amidst these the monkeys loved to romp. "These palms," she said, "are my first joy in the morning when the dawn comes up, pearly grey in the mist and fine rain, fresh and cool and beautiful." She lived in two rooms at the back of the church, with a bit of ground fenced off for kitchen, and her furniture consisted of a camp-bed and a few dishes. But she was chiefly out of doors, for she had as many as two hundred and fifty people engaged in cutting bush, levelling, and stumping. Despite the discomfort and worry incidental to such conditions, she was quite happy. The natives as a whole were hostile to white people; they wanted neither them nor their religion; but there was nothing martial or predatory about "Ma," and her very helplessness protected her. And there was that in her blood which made her face the conflict with zest; it always braced her to meet the dark forces of hell, and conquer them with the simple power of the Gospel.

Her fearlessness was as marked as ever. One Sunday, during service, there was an uproar in the market. She went out and found a mob fighting with sticks and swords, a woman bleeding, and her husband wounded and at bay. She seized the man's wrist and compelled quiet, and soon settled the matter by palaver. On another occasion the Government sent native agents with police escort to vaccinate the people, as small-pox was rife. They resented the white man's "juju," and there was much excitement. The conduct of the agents enraged the crowd, guns appeared, and bloodshed was imminent, when an appeal was made to "Ma." She succeeded in calming the rising passions, and in reassuring the people as to the purpose of the inoculation. "This poor frail woman," she said, "is the broken reed on which they lean. Isn't it strange? I'm glad anyhow that I'm of use in protecting the helpless." The people said if she would perform the operation they would agree, and she sent to Bende for lymph, and was busy for days. It was a difficult task, the people were suspicious, and she had to banter and joke and coax when she herself was at fainting point. Apart from this she doctored men and women for the worst diseases, nursed the sickly babies, and generally acted her old part of a "mother in Israel."

"It is a real life I am living now," she wrote, "not all preaching and holding meetings, but rather a life and an atmosphere which the people can touch and live in and be made willing to believe in when the higher truths are brought before them. In many things it is a most prosaic life, dirt and dust and noise and silliness and sin in every form, but full, too, of the kindliness and homeliness and dependence of children who are not averse to be disciplined and taught, and who understand and love just as we do. The excitements and surprises and novel situations would not, however, need to be continuous, as they wear and fray the body, and fret the spirit and rob one of sleep and restfulness of soul."

Use was still her headquarters, and she often traversed the long stretch of Creek, though the journey always left her terribly exhausted. On one occasion, when she had arrived at Use racked with pain, she was asked how she could ever endure it. "Oh," she said, "I just had to take as big a dose of laudanum as I dared, and wrap myself up in a blanket, and lie in the bottom of the canoe all the time, and managed fine." She often met adventures by the way. Once, after thirteen hours in the canoe, she arrived at Okopedi beach late in the evening, along with Maggie and Whitie and a big boy baby. Stowing the baggage in the beach house they started in the dark for Use, "Ma" carrying a box with five fowls and some odds and ends, and Maggie, who was ill, the baby. When they reached the house they found they had no matches and were afraid of snakes, but she was so tired that she lay down as she was on a bed piled high with clothes, the others on the floor, the baby crying itself to sleep. At cock-crow fire was obtained from the village, and a cup of tea made her herself again, and ready for the inevitable palavers. Again, she went up to Ikpe with supplies by night; the water had risen, she had to lie flat to escape the overhanging branches, and finally the canoe ran into a submerged tree and three of the paddle boys were pitched into the water. Not long afterwards she left Ikpe at 6.30 A.M., was in the canoe all night, and reached the landing-beach at 5.30 on Christmas morning with the usual motherless baby.

On this occasion she received a message, "Ekereki said I was to tell you that his mother is asleep"—referring to the death of one of the first members of the congregation, a gentle and superior woman for whom she had a great regard. The wording of the message made her realise how soon the Gospel had the power of changing even the language of a people. Some time previously Annie's two-year-old boy had died, and the question of a Christian burial-place had been considered by the congregation. Heathen adults were buried in the house and the children under the doorstep. It seemed cruel to leave bodies out in the cold earth, but of their own volition the members secured a piece of ground and laid the child there; and now this woman was placed by his side, the first adult to obtain a Christian burial in that part of Ibibio.

On New Year's eve she was down with fever, and was very weak, but, she wrote, "My heart is singing all the time to Him Whose love and tender mercy crown all the days." In the middle of the night she was obliged to rise. "My 'first-feet' were driver ants, thousands and thousands of them, pouring in on every side, and dropping from the roof. We had two hours' hard work to clear them out."

CHAPTER III
THE AUTOCRATIC DOCTOR

Returning from Ikpe on one occasion in 1911, she found that a tornado had played havoc with the Use house, and immediately set to, and with her own hands repaired it. The strain was too great for her enfeebled frame, and symptoms of heart weakness developed. She had nights of high fever and delirium, and yet so great was her power of will, that she would rise next day and teach and work, while on Sundays she took the services, although she was unable to stand. "I had a grand day," she would say, "notwithstanding intense weakness."

Dr. Robertson of Itu had gone home on furlough, and there came to take his place, Dr. Hitchcock, a young, eager, clear-headed man, as masterful in his quiet way as "Ma." He had proposed going to China in the service of the Church, but agreed meanwhile to put in a year at Itu. She watched him for a time with growing admiration, and saw the curiosity of the natives turn rapidly to confidence, then to appreciation, then to blind devotion and worship. When she looked at the great crowds flocking day after day to the dispensary and hospital, she thought of the scene of old when the poor and the halt and the maimed gathered round Christ. "A rare man," she said, "a rare Christian, a rare doctor. A physician for soul and body. I am beginning to love him like a son." And like a son he treated her. Although he had scarcely a minute to spare from his work, he ran up every second day to Use to study her. He believed that she was not being nourished. That there were grounds for his suspicions her own diary records. There was money for her in Duke Town, she had often cheques lying beside her, but it was not always easy to obtain ready cash, and sometimes she ran short. On June 14 she wrote:

Market Morning.—Have only 3d. in cash in the house; sent it with 2 Ikpats (the first Efik schoolbook) and New Testament to buy food, and sold all 3 books for 6d. Got 5 small yams, oil, and shrimps, with pepper and a few small fresh fish.

It was on the following morning as early as six o'clock that the doctor called to examine her again. His decision was that she was not to go to Ikpe, she was not to cycle, she was to lie down as much as possible. She laughed, and on the Sunday went to church and conducted two services; but she almost collapsed, and when the doctor came next day he ordered her to take to her bed, and not go to any more meetings until she obtained his permission. Mary had at last met her equal in resolution. "He is very strict," she confessed, "but he is a dear man. Thank God for him."

A trip to Ikpe which she had planned for the Macgregors had to be cancelled, and they decided to go to Use instead, and aid and abet the doctor in his care of her. She got up to receive them, and then wrote, "The doctor has sent me back to bed under a more stringent rule than ever. Very stern. I dare not rise." "You must eat meat twice a day," the doctor said. "I'm not a meat eater, doctor," she rejoined. His reply was to send over a fowl from Itu with instructions as to its cooking. "Why did you send that fowl, doctor?" she asked next day, "Because it could not come itself," was all the satisfaction she got. It was not the first fowl that came from Itu—the next came cooked— while the Macgregors telegraphed to Duke Town for their entire stock. "What a trouble you dear folk take," she sighed.

"You will have to go to Duke Town for a change," suggested the doctor one day. "Na, na," she replied; "I've all my plans laid, and I cannot draw a salary and not do what I can." "You have done so well in the past," remarked Mr. Macgregor, "that you need not have any qualms about that." "I've been paid for all I've done," was her retort. But the doctor insisted, and the very thought of leaving the station and the household work unattended to, put her in a fever. "Of course," she said, "to the doctor my health is the only thing, but I can't get rest for body while my mind is torn about things. He is vexed, and I am vexed at vexing him."

Not satisfied with the progress she was making, the doctor transferred her to Use, where she was under his constant observation. "Life is hardly worth living," she complained, "but I'm doing what I can to help him to help me, so that I can be fit again for another spell of work." That was her one desire, to be well enough to go back to the bush. A messenger from Ikpe came down to find out when she was returning. "Seven weeks," was the doctor's firm reply. "I may run up sooner than that," was hers. "I'm quite well, if he would only believe it."

But it was well on towards the end of the year before she was, in her own words, out of the clutches of the "dearest and cleverest and most autocratic Mission doctor that ever lived." She literally ran away, and was up at Ikpe at once, exultant at having the privilege of ministering again to the needs of the people. There was a throng at the beach to welcome her. She was soon as busy as she had ever been, though she was usually carried now to and from church and other meetings. Jean she placed at Nkanga as teacher and evangelist, the people giving her 1s. per week and her food, and "Ma" providing her clothes. It was astonishing to her to see how she had developed. An insatiable reader, she would place a book open anywhere in order that she might obtain a glimpse of the words in passing, reminding "Ma" of her own device in the Dundee weaving-shed. Her knowledge of the Bible was so thorough and correct that the latter considered her the best Efik teacher she knew. Soon she gathered about her some two hundred men and women from the upper Enyong farms, who were greatly pleased with her preaching. She came over to Ikpe for Christmas, the first the household had spent in that savage land, and there was a service in the church, which was decorated with palms and wreaths of ferns. Mary told the story of Bethlehem, and the scholar lads, of their own accord, marched through the town singing hymns.... About this time Miss Slessor rendered important service to the Mission by her testimony before an Imperial Government Commission, which had been sent out to Investigate the effects of the import, sale, and consumption of alcoholic liquor in Southern Nigeria. She provided very convincing evidence of the demoralisation caused through drink, but with keen intuition she felt that little would come of the "palaver," and she was right.

CHAPTER IV
GOD'S WONDERFUL PALAVER

Her attitude to money was as unconventional as her attitude to most things. It had no place in her interests; she never thought of it except as a means of helping her to carry out her projects. "How I wish we could do without it!" she often used to say. "I have no head for it, or for business." Her salary she counted as Church money, and never spent a penny of it on herself except for bare living, and until the last years the girls received nothing but food and their clothes, "You say," she wrote to one giver, "that you would like me to spend the money on my personal comfort. Dear friend, I need nothing. My every want is met and supplied without my asking." Her belief was thus expressed: "What is money to God? The difficult thing is to make men and women. Money lies all about us in the world, and He can turn it on to our path as easily as He sends a shower of rain." Her faith was justified in a marvellous way, for throughout all these years and onwards to the end she obtained all she needed, and that was not little. She required funds for extension, for building, for furniture, for teachers' wages, for medicines, for the schooling of her children, and many other purposes, and yet she was never in want. Nothing came from her people, for she would not accept collections at first, not wishing to give them the impression that the Gospel was in any way connected with money. It came from friends, known and unknown, at home and abroad, who were interested in her and in her brave and lonely struggle. There was scarcely a mail that did not bring her a cheque or bank-draft or Post-Office order. "It often happens," she said once, "that when the purse is empty, immediately comes a new instalment. God is superbly kind in the matter of money. I do not know how to thank Him. It is just wonderful how we ever fail in our trust for a moment." On one occasion, when she was a little anxious, she cried, "Shame on you, Mary Slessor, after all you know of Him!"

Her attitude towards all this giving was one of curious detachment. She looked upon herself as an instrument carrying out the wishes of the people at home who supplied the means, and she gave them the honour of what was accomplished. Their gifts justified her going forward in the work; each fresh £10 note she took as a sign to advance another stage, so that, in one sense, she felt her Church was backing up her efforts. As she regarded herself as being owned by the Church, all the money she received was devoted exclusively to its service; even donations from outside sources she would not use for personal needs. One day she received a letter from the Governor conveying to her, with the "deep thanks of the Government," a gift of £25 to herself, in recognition of her work. The letter she valued more than the money, which she would only accept as a contribution towards her home for women. All the sums were handed over to Mr. Wilkie or Mr. Macgregor, who banked them at Duke Town, and they formed a general fund upon which she drew when necessary. She looked upon this fund as belonging to the Mission Council, to be used for extension purposes either up the Cross River or the Enyong Creek, or for the Home for Women and Girls when the scheme matured, and she never sought to have control of it. Mr. Wilkie was always afraid that she was not just to herself, and she had sometimes to restrain him from sending more than she required. It was the same later when Mr. Hart, C.A., had charge of the accounts. This explains why, on more than one occasion, she was reduced to borrowing or selling books in order to obtain food for herself and her household. There was money in abundance at Duke Town, but she would not ask it for private necessities. Sometimes also she was so remote from civilisation that she was unable to cash a cheque or draft in time to meet her wants.

Many a hidden romance lay behind these gifts that came to her—the romance of love and sacrifice and devotion to Christ. One day there arrived a sum of £50, accompanied by a charming letter. Long she looked at both with wonder and tears. Her thoughts went back to the Edinburgh days, when she was a girl, on the eve of leaving for Calabar. One of her friends then was a Biblewoman, who was very good to her. Always on her furloughs she had gone to see her in the humble home in which she lay an invalid, or as Mary expressed it, "lingering at the gate of the city." She thought she must now be dependent upon others, for she was old and frail. And yet here she had sent out £50 to help on her work.

If there was romance in the giving, there was pathos in the spending. Acknowledging sums she was bidden expend upon herself, she would go into detail as to her purchases—a new Efik Bible to replace her old tattered copy, the hire of three boys to carry her over the streams, seed coco yams for the girls' plots, a basin and ewer for her guest- room—"I can't," she said, "ask visitors to wash in a pail,"—a lamp, and so on. She sought to explain and extenuate the spending of every penny. "Is that extravagant?" "Is that too selfish?" she anxiously asked. After enumerating a number of things which she intended to buy for Ikpe house, she said, "Does that seem too prosaic? But it will clarify your views of Mission work, and make them more practical and real, for, you see, the missionary cannot go about like Adam and Eve, and the natives must be taught cleanliness and order, and be civilised as well as Christianised."

Her own small financial affairs had been in the hands of her old friend Mr. Logic, Dundee, whose death in 1910 sent her into silence and darkness for weeks. He had been like a father to her; to him, indeed, she chiefly owed the realisation of her dream to be a missionary. She did not know for a time how she stood, and as her purse was nearly empty, she was growing anxious, when a small amount arrived from a friend, to whom she wrote: "I have been praying for a fortnight for money to come from somewhere, as I have been living on 7s. given to the children by a merchant here who is a great friend of our household. So your gift is a direct answer to prayer. *'Before they call I will answer.'*" She applied to Mr. Slight, another tried friend, who had been Treasurer of the United Presbyterian Church, and took a warm personal interest in all the missionaries, and after the Union was the accountant of the United Free Church. He made matters simple and clear to her understanding and set her fears at rest—she had no debts of any kind save debts of gratitude. Mr. Slight's death in 1912 again made her feel orphaned. "I had no idea how much I leant on him till he was removed, and it seems now that my last link with the old Church has snapped. What he has done for me through a score of years I can never acknowledge warmly enough." In later years her affairs at home were managed by Miss Adam.

Congregations continued to send her boxes of goods, whilst her own friends were unceasing in their thought for her. "I should never mention a want," she told them, "because you just take it up and bear the burden yourselves, and it makes me ashamed. Here are all my needs in clothing for the children and myself anticipated, and here are luxuries of food and good things, and all steeped and folded in the most delicate and tender sympathy and love. Surely no one has so many mercies as I have." She saw few pretty things, and had never the opportunity of looking into a shop window, so that the arrival of these boxes was an occasion of much pleasurable excitement to her and to the girls. Her only trouble was that she could not hand on some of the food to others; "When you have a good thing, or read a good thing, or see a humorous thing, and can't share it, it is worse than having to bear a trial alone." She was particularly grateful for a box of Christmas goods that came in 1911. She had been much upset by the local food, and she ate nothing but shortbread and bun for a week, and that made her better!

The people about her, too, were kind. Women would bring her presents of produce; one, for instance, gave her fifteen large yams and a half-crown bag of rice, and a large quantity of shrimps. "You are a stranger in these markets," she said, "and the children may be hungry."

CHAPTER V
WEAK BUT STRONG

She met with a severe disappointment early in 1912. The Calabar Council was willing to send two ladies to Ikpe, but thought it right to obtain a medical report on the site which had been given for the house. This was unfavourable; the Creek overflowed its banks for four hundred paces on one side and thirty on the other, and the surroundings of the house would be muddy and damp. She would not, however, acquiesce in the judgment thus passed, and remained on, and prosecuted the work as usual. The Council was very anxious for her to take a furlough, and her friends, personal and official, in Scotland were also urging her to come for a rest. She had now never an hour of real health or strength, and was growing deaf, and felt like "a spluttering candle," and she began to think it would be the wisest thing to do. As the idea took definite shape in her mind, she looked forward with zest to the renewal of old friendships. "We shall have our fill of talk and the silences which are the music of friendship." The East Coast of Scotland was now barred to her by medical opinion, but she had visions of the lonely hills of the south, and of Yarrow, and all that Border country where she had spent so many happy days, and would go there, away from the crowds and the rush.

Discerning a note of pity in the letters from Scotland, she bade her friends not to waste their sympathy upon her. "I am just surrounded with love," she wrote. It was to the children she referred. "I wake up in the early dusk of the dawn and call them, and before I can see to take my Bible, the hot cup of tea is there, and a kiddie to kiss me 'Good-morning' and ask, 'Ma, did you sleep?'" It was not wonderful that she loved those black girls. They had been with her from their birth. She had nursed them and brought them up and taught them all they knew, and they had been faithful to her with the faithfulness which is one of the most remarkable traits in the African nature. Mary could never abide the superior folk who referred slightingly to them because of their black skin, and she was too proud to justify her feelings towards them. Alice, the "princess," had now grown into a fine womanly girl, quiet and steady and thoughtful. One night in the dark she crept to "Ma's" side and shyly told her that some months before she had given her heart to Christ. It was a moment of rare joy. As neither Alice nor Maggie was betrothed-though often sought after-and they had no legal protector against insult, she decided to send them for training to the Edgerley Memorial School, where they would be under the influence and care of Miss Young, another capable agent whom she had led to become a missionary and with whom she had a very close and tender friendship. She regarded her as an ideal worker, for she had been thoroughly trained in domestic science. "I would have liked that sort of training better than the Normal training I got at Moray House," she said.

Meanwhile, as she was forbidden to cycle, her thoughts harked back to her old plan of a "box on wheels." She had never been reconciled to a hammock. "I feel a brute in it, it seems so selfish to be lying there, while four boys sweat like beasts of burden. To push a little carriage is like skilled labour and no degradation." She, therefore, wrote to Miss Adam, whom she called the "joint-pastor" of her people, to send out a catalogue of "these things." Miss Adam was, however, unwell, and the ladles of Wellington Street Church, Glasgow, hearing of the request, promptly despatched what was called a Cape cart, a kind of basket-chair, capable of being wheeled by two boys or girls. The gift sent her whole being thrilling with gratitude, as well as with shame for being so unworthy of so much kindness, but her comfort was that it was for God's work, and she took it as from Him.

The vehicle proved a success, but the success proved the undoing of her furlough. "Instead of going home as I had planned, in order to get strength for a wider range of work, I shall stay on and enjoy the privilege of going over ground impossible for my poor limbs." On one of the first drives she had, she went in search of a site for a new and larger church which she had determined to build., and was gathering material for, at Use, and then she planned to go to Ikpe via Ikot Ekpene by the new Government road, opening up out-stations wherever she could get a village to listen to the message. Her aim, indeed, was nothing less than to plant the whole Ibibio territory with a network of schools and churches. She seemed to grow more wonderful the older and frailer she became.

The spurt lasted for a time, but again the terrible weakness troubled her, and she had to conduct household affairs from a couch. School work was carried through on the verandah, and when she spoke in the church she was borne there and back. She came to see that only a real change would do her permanent good, and that it would be true economy to take a trip home, even for the sake of the voyage, which, much as she feared the sea, always invigorated her. What made her hesitate now was the depleted condition of the Mission. "We were never so short-handed before," she said, "and I can do what others cannot do, what, indeed, medical opinion would not allow them to try. No one meddles with me, and I can slip along and do my work with less expenditure of strength than any," Had there been some one to fill her place she would have gone, but she was very reluctant to shut the doors of the stations for so long a period. How she regarded the idea may be gathered from a letter to a friend who had given her some domestic news:—

These little glimpses, like pictures, of home and the old country, of family ties and love, make me long for just one long summer day in the midst, if only as an onlooker, and for the touch of loving hands and a bit of family worship in our own tongue, and maybe a Sabbath service thrown in with a psalm and an old-fashioned tune, and then I should feel ready for a long spell of work. But I should fret if it were to take me from this, my own real life and home and bairns. This life is full, the other lies at the back quiescent, and is a precious possession to muse on during the night or in the long evening hours when I'm too tired to sleep and the light is not good enough to read or sew, or mostly when I'm not well and the doldrums come very near. But I should choose this life if I had to begin again; only I should try to live it to better purpose.

Another respite or two carried her into the middle of the year, when her opportunity of a furlough was lost. She said she would have to hold on now for another winter—or go up higher. In September she completed thirty-six years as a missionary, and took humorous stock of herself: "I'm lame and feeble and foolish; the wrinkles are wonderful-no concertina is so wonderfully folded and convulated. I'm a wee, wee wifie, verra little buikit—but I grip on well, none the less." "Ay," said an old doctor friend to her, "you are a strong woman, 'Ma.' You ought to have been dead by ordinary rule long ago—any one else would."

CHAPTER VI
HER FIRST HOLIDAY

Anxiety as to her health deepened both in Calabar and Scotland, and pressure was brought upon her to take a rest. One of her lady friends on the Women's Foreign Mission Committee, Miss Cook, appreciated her fear of the home winter, and wrote asking her to take a holiday to the Canary Islands, and begged the kindness at her hands of being allowed to pay the expense. "I believe," she said, "in taking care of the Lord's servant. I am afraid you do not fully realise how valuable you are to us all, the Church at home, and the Church In Nigeria." The offer, so delicately put, brought tears to Mary's eyes, and it made her wonder whether after all she was safeguarding her health enough in the interests of the Church. As soon as the matter became a duty, she gave it careful consideration, resolving to abstain from going up to Ikpe, and to go down to Duke Town instead, where she would consult the Wilkies and the Macgregors. But she would not dream of the cost of any change being borne by Miss Cook, and she asked Miss Adam to find out if her funds would allow of her taking a trip. There was no difficulty regarding clothing. Among the Mission boxes she had received was one full of warm material, and she surmised that God was on the side of a holiday.

Her friends at Calabar did not hesitate a moment; they wanted her off at once. She went to consult her old friend, Dr. Adam, the senior medical officer, that "burning and shining light," as she called him, who first showed her through the Hospital, where she spoke with loving entreaty to every patient she passed, and left many in tears. After a thorough examination, he earnestly besought her to take the next boat to Grand Canary. Still she shrank from the prospect. It was a selfish thing to do; there were others more in need of a holiday than she, it was a piece of extravagance, it would involve closing up the stations. And yet might it not be meant? Might it not be of the nature of a good investment? Might she not be able for better work? Might it not do away with the necessity for a furlough in the following year? She decided to go.

It was arranged that Jean should accompany her, and that she should put up at the Hotel Santa Catalina, Las Palmas. Letters from Government officials were sent to smooth the way there for her. Miss Young and others prepared her outfit, and made her, as she said, "wise-like and decent," — she, the while, holding daily receptions, for she was now regarded as one of the West African sights, and every one came to call upon her. Mr. Wilkie managed the financial side, and gave the cash-box to the Captain. When she transhipped at Forcados. it was handed to the other Captain, and he on arrival at the Islands passed it on to the manager of the hotel. On board she was carried up and down to meals, and received the utmost kindness from officers and passengers alike. The Captain said he was prouder to have shaken hands with her than if she had been King George. The season at Grand Canary had not begun, and there were very few visitors at the hotel. Those who were there saw a frail nervous old lady, followed by a black girl who was too shy to raise her eyes. "We were certainly a frightened pair," Mary afterwards confessed. But the management attended to her as if she were a princess. "What love is wrapped round me!" she wrote. "All are kind,— the manager's family, the doctor's family, and the visitors. It is simply wonderful. I can't say anything else."

The first days were spent in the grounds, drinking in the pure air, watching the changing sea and sky, and admiring the brilliant vegetation. The English flowers, roses and geraniums and Michaelmas daisies and mignonette, were a continual joy, whilst the crimson clouds piled above the sapphire sea often made her think of the "city of pure gold." Later, she was able to ascend the hill at the back, and "there" she says, "I sat and knitted and crocheted and sewed and worked through the Bible all the day long, fanned by the sea-breeze and warmed by the sun, and the good housekeeper sent up lunch and tea to save my walking, and in the silence and beauty and peace I communed with God. He is so near and so dear. Oh, if I only get another day in which to work! I hope it will be more full of earnestness and blessing than the past."

It was her first real holiday, but she felt it had been worth waiting a lifetime for. There was something infinitely pathetic in her ecstasy of enjoyment and the gratitude for the simple pleasures that came to her. Only one thread of anxiety ran through her days, the thought of the appalling expense she was incurring, for she had made up her mind that the cost was to be paid out of her own slender funds.

A lady in the hotel, with whom she formed an intimate and lasting friendship, and who saw much of her, gives this impression of her character:

She made many friends, her loving sympathy, her simplicity, her keen interest in all around her, her sense of humour and love of fun endearing her to all. The entire negation of self which she evinced was remarkable, as well as her childlike faith and devotion to her Master and to His service. A lady was heard to say, "Well, after talking to Miss Slessor I am converted to foreign missions," Her mind was ever upon her work and her children, and she used often to say she was idling, there was so much to be done, and so little time in which to do it. Of all the people I have met she impressed me the most as the perfect embodiment of the Christian life,

Jean waited upon her mother-mistress with a patient and thoughtful devotion which was a wonder to those who saw it. She wore her Calabar frock and bandana, and had she not been a very sane person, her head would have been turned, for she was a favourite with every one, and was given as many ribbons as would serve her all her life. But she was as shy the day she left as when she arrived.

The departure came in the middle of the night. A general and his aide- de-camp and a merchant each offered to convoy her to the ship, and pleaded that they had conveyances, but the manager of the hotel would not hear of it, saw her himself safely into her cabin, and placed the cash-box once more into the Captain's hands. It was the same steamer by which she had travelled to the Islands, so that she felt at home. On board also was Dr. Hitchcock, on his way out again to take up work at Uburu, a large market town in the far north amongst a strangely interesting tribe. How she envied him, young and strong and enthusiastic, entering on such glorious pioneer work! At Accra the Governor of the Gold Coast, a stranger to her, sent off to the steamer a bouquet of flowers, with an expression of his homage and best wishes for a renewal of her health.

When she arrived at Duke Town Dr. Adam again examined her, assisted by Professor Leiper of the London School of Tropical Medicine, and the verdict was: "Good for many years-if you only take care."

She was given written directions as to the care of her health, and these she regarded with a rueful face. "Life will hardly be worth living now," she said. "But for the work's sake I must obey. God wants us to be efficient, and we cannot be so except by living decently and taking care of the wonderful body He has given us."

She turned up her Bible and found the verse she had marked as a "promise" before leaving: "*But if the Spirit of Him that raised up Jesus from the dead dwell in you, He that raised up Christ from the dead shall also quicken your mortal bodies by the spirit that dwelleth in you.*" She saw now that this meant something besides the Resurrection, for the voyage, the climate, the food, and the rest had worked in her a miracle, and she realised more than ever what prayer and faith could do for the body as well as for the spirit. There was a lesson in it, too, she thought, for the Church. She had had a month at sea, and a month in the Islands, with the best of care and food, and no furlough had ever done her more good. She felt that a visit to Scotland would not have rested her so much. There was the bustle and excitement and movement and speaking-of all the bugbears of a furlough, she said, speaking at meetings was the chief. If only the hard deputy work at home could be eliminated from the missionaries' programme, they would have a happier and a better time. But here the personal equation obscured her judgment. For to abandon the system would be to do away with the intimate touch and association by which interest in the Mission Field is so largely maintained. To many missionaries, also, the duty of telling to the congregations up and down the country the story of their work is one of the chief pleasures of their furlough.

Laden with chemical foods, medicines, and advice, she returned to Use to find that the entire cost of the trip had been defrayed by Miss Cook, who wrote: "I am only sorry that I did not beg you to stay longer in order to reap more benefit. Come home next year; we all want to see you."

CHAPTER VII
INJURED

But a furlough home was far from her thoughts. She rejoiced in her new strength, and set herself with grim determination to redeem the time. She was now doing double work, carrying on all the activities of the settled station at Use, and establishing her pioneer centre at Ikpe. During the next two years she travelled between the two points, sometimes using the canoe, but more often now the Government motor car, which ran round by Ikot Ekpene and dropped her at the terminus, five miles from Ikpe. David was the driver, and she had thus always the opportunity of seeing Mary, his wife, who lived at Ikot Ekpene.

At Use the work had gone on as usual; there had been no backsliding, and the services and classes had been kept up by the people themselves; and she proceeded with the building of the new church, which was erected under her superintendence and without any outside help. When she was at Ikpe she placed Annie's husband—they were both now members of the Church—in charge, and he conducted the services, but Miss Peacock, whom Mary styled her "Bishop," gave general supervision.

On one of her early journeys up to Ikpe she met with a slight accident, a pellet of mud striking one of her eyes. The people were alarmed at the result, and would have gone off at once to the District Commissioner had she not restrained them. Some native workmen passing his station later mentioned the incident, and within a few minutes the officer had a mounted messenger speeding along the tract to Ikpe, with an urgent order to the people to get her conveyed in the Cape cart to the nearest point on the road, where he would have a motor car waiting. Next morning, although it was market day, the members of the church left everything and took her to the spot indicated. Here were the District Commissioner and a doctor, with eye-shade and medicine and every comfort, and with the utmost despatch she was taken round the Government road to Use. The hurt was followed by erysipelas, and she was blind for a fortnight and suffered acute pain and heavy fever; but very shame at being ill after so fine a holiday made her get up although the eye was swollen and "sulky," and she was soon in the midst of her work at Ikpe as if nothing had happened.

Building, cementing, painting, varnishing, teaching, healing, and preaching filled in the days. A visitor found her once at 10 A.M. finishing school in a shed. She continued it in the afternoon. Then she visited the yards of the people, and they crowded round her and brought her gifts of food. Later she leant against a fallen tree trunk and talked to one and another. In the gathering dusk she sat on a small stool and attended to the sick and dressed their sores. After dinner some men and lads arrived carrying lamps, and she held her catechumens' class—a very earnest and prayerful gathering.

The burden of the untouched region around her vexed her mind. Sometimes she was depressed about it all, and said she would need to fill her letters with nonsense, for "it would not bear writing." Time and again she sought to impress her friends with the needs of the situation: "The last time I was at school I counted eight hundred women and girls running past in eager competition to secure the best places at the fishing-grounds where the men had been working all the morning, and these are but a fraction of our womankind. But what can I do with supervision of the school and church and dispensary and household?" She did not pretend that she worked her station properly, and she pointed out how necessary settled, steady, persevering teaching was. "These infant churches," she said, "need so much to be instructed. The adults are illiterate, and the young need systematic teaching of the Bible. They are an emotional people, and are fain to keep to speaking and singing and long prayers, and the sterner practical side of Christianity is set aside. They are children in everything that matters, and when we have led them to Christ we are apt to forget how much more they need in order to make a strong, upright, ethical character on which to build a nation. Then we need a literature, and this, too, is the work of the Church. What ails it? *Is it not forgetting that God can't give His best till we have given ours?*"

With all its bustle it was a very lonely and isolated life she led. There was no mail delivery, and she had to depend mainly on the kindness of Government officials to forward her correspondence. "I have been here seven weeks," she wrote on one occasion, "without one scrap from the outside—letter or paper—nothing to read but the old advertisement sheets of papers lining the press and the boxes. If you wish for the names of hotels or boarding-houses In any part of Europe— send to me. I have them all on my tongue's end." It was a red-letter day when a stray white visitor entered the district, for there would be tea and a talk, and a bundle of newspapers would be left—one never forgets another in this way in the bush. She was amused to receive a note from Scotland asking her to hand on a message to Dr. Hitchcock at Uburu. "Do you know?" she replied, "you are nearer him than I am—the quickest way for me to send it is via Britain!"

Life was not without its menace from wild beasts, the forest being full of them, and the doors had always to be closed and fastened at night to keep them out. Snakes were prevalent, and prowled about the building, and many a fight Jean and the others had with the intruders.

CHAPTER VIII
FRIENDSHIPS WITH OFFICIALS

Throughout these years, as always, "Ma" Slessor's relations with the Government officials were of the most friendly nature, It was remarkable that although she was essentially feminine and religious, and although she was engaged in Mission work, she attracted men of all types of character. Much of this power was due to her intense sympathy, which enabled her to get close to minds that would otherwise have been shut to her. What she wrote of another applies to herself:

What a strange thing is sympathy! Undefinable, untranslatable, and yet the most real thing and the greatest power in human life! How strangely our souls leap out to some other soul without our choosing or knowing the why. The man or woman who has this subtle gift of sympathy and magnetism of soul possesses the most precious thing on earth. Hence it is rare. So few could be trusted with such a delicate, sensitive, Godlike power and hold it unsullied that God seems to be hampered for want of means for its expression. Is that the reason that He made His Son a "Man of Sorrows and acquainted with grief"?

Most of these men had no interest in missions, and some did not believe in them. "The more I see of mission work in West Africa the less I like it," said one frankly to her. "Give me the genuine bushman, who respects his ancestral deities and his chief and himself.... But if all missionaries were like you!" None of these men belonged to her own Church; three of her favourites were Roman Catholics. Her introductions to some were of the most informal character. One day a stranger appeared and found her busy on the roof of the house. "Well," she said, eyeing him critically, "what do you want?" He stood, hat in hand. "Please, Ma'am," he replied meekly, "I'm your new District Commissioner—but I can't help it!" She was delighted, and took him into the inner circle at once. As frequent changes took place in the staff, the number whose acquaintance she made gradually increased, until she became known and talked of in all the colonies on the West Coast and even in other parts of the world.

The official view of her work and character differed little from any other. Says one who knew her long and well:

I suppose that a pluckier woman has rarely existed. Her life-work she carried out with immeasurable courage and capacity. Her strength of character was extraordinary, and her life was one of absolute unselfishness. She commanded the respect and confidence of all parties, and for years I would have personally trusted to her judgment on native matters in preference to all others. Shrewd, quick-witted, sympathetic, yet down on any one who presumed, she would with wonderful patience hear all sides equally. Her judgment was prompt, sometimes severe, but always just. She would speak much of her work to those who, she knew, took an interest in it, but very rarely of herself.

Another writes:

My first impression of her was that she was a lady of great strength of mind and sound common sense. Also that for one who had lived so many years in the bush wilds she was very well read and up-to-date on all subjects.

Mr. T. D. Maxwell, who knew her in Okoyong days and to the end, says:

I am sure that her own Church never had a more loyal adherent, but her outlook on this life—and the next—was never narrow. Her religion was above religions—certainly above religious differences, I have often heard her speak of the faiths and rituals of others, but never without the deepest interest and sympathy. She was young to the end; young in her enthusiasm, her sympathy, her boundless energy, her never-failing sense of humour, her gift of repartee, her ability always to strike the apt—even the corrosive—epithet. A visit to her was, to use one of her own phrases, "like a breath o' caller air to a weary body"—and in West Africa that means incomparably more than it can at Home.

It was a peculiarly affectionate relation that existed between her and many of those men whom she regarded as "the strength and the glory of Britain." A witty member of the Mission once said they were given over to "Mariolatry"—an allusion to her first name. They never were near without visiting her, and often made long journeys for the privilege of a talk. They were delighted with her sense of humour, and teased her as well as lionised her. Half the fun of a visit to her was taking her unawares, and they often threatened to bring their cameras and "snapshot" her on sight, "Ma," they would write before calling, "get your shoes on, we are coming to tea!"

They wrote her about their work and ambitions and worries as if she were a mother or sister, and discussed the political and racial problems of the country as if she were a colleague, always with a delicate deference to her experience and knowledge, sometimes veiled in light banter. "I am at your feet, Ma," said one, "and your wisdom is that of Solomon." They often twitted her about being able to twist them round her little finger: "You break our hearts, and get your own way shockingly." On one occasion she received a grave and formal Government typewritten communication about land, which ended in this way:

> I have the honour to be,
> Madam,
>
> *and affectionate*
> Your obedient servant.

When they left the Colony they kept up the friendship. Many were bad correspondents, yet from the remotest parts of the world they wrote letters, as long as her own, full of kind enquiries about her work and the bairns, and begging for a reply.

On her part she wrote them racy and informative letters; and she also got into touch with their mothers, sisters, and wives at home, who welcomed her news of the absent ones, and were good to her in turn. One lady she delighted by praising her husband. "Naturally," the lady replied, "I agree with you, and you are welcome to court and woo him as much as you like!" A high official brought out his wife, and she wrote Mary from a desire to make her husband's friends hers also. She ended in the usual way, but he added, "She sends her kindest regards—*I* send my love!" The nature of some of the friendships formed at home through officials may be surmised from an order she gave for a silver gift, value £5, to be sent to the first-born child of one of her "chums." It went to the mother, and the inscription was "From one whom his father has helped."

Very notable was the kindness shown by the Government to her as woman and missionary. Instructions were issued that she was to be allowed to use any and every conveyance belonging to them in the Colony, on any road or river, and that every help was to be afforded to her. Workmen were lent to her to execute repairs on her houses. Individual members sought opportunities to be kind to her. She was taken her first motor- car drive by a Commissioner. The highest officials did not think it beneath them to buy feeding-bottles and forward them on by express messenger. They sent her gifts of books, magazines, and papers—one forwarded *The Times* for years—and at Christmas there would come plum puddings, crackers, and sweets. One dark, showery night the Governor of Southern Nigeria, Sir W. Egerton, and several officials appeared at her house to greet her, and left a case of milk, two cakes, and boxes of chocolates and crystallised fruit. "The Governor is a Scotsman," she wrote, "and must be sympathetic to mission work, or else why did he come with his retinue and all to a mud house and see me at that cost to his comfort and time on a wet night?" Lord Egerton was charmed with her. Replying to some remark of his she said, "Hoots, my dear laddie—I mean Sir!"

It was the great anxiety of her official friends that she should not outlive her powers: her influence generally was so great that to them the thought of this was distressing. They were always very solicitous about her health, writing to her frequently to say that she should take life more easily, "Take care of yourself, Ma—as much as you can." "Don't be so ridiculously unselfish." "Learn a little selfishness—it will do you all the good in the world," was the advice showered upon her. When she had the Court work she was often urged to take a month's holiday. On hearing of her intention to go to Ikpe one wrote, "Dear Lady, I hate the idea of your going so far into the bush. Don't go. There are plenty of men willing and eager to be of service to you, but away up there you are far away from help or care." Another warned her against the people; "But," he added, "we know you will go in spite of it—and conquer!"

Latterly they became more importunate. "Do be careful," one wrote. "Do take quinine and sleep under a net and drink filtered water." Her custom of going hatless into the blazing sunshine was long a sore point, and when they failed to persuade her of the danger, they resorted to scheming. "We know why you do it," they said artfully. "You know you have pretty hair and like to display it uncovered, imagining that it gets its golden glint from the sun. Oh, vanity of vanities! Fancy a nice, quiet missionary being so vain!" Certainly no argument could have sent her more quickly to the milliner's.

CHAPTER IX
POWER THROUGH PRAYER

The power which enabled Mary Slessor to live so intensely, to triumph over physical weakness, and to face the dangers of the African bush, and gave her the magnetic personality that captivated the hearts of white and black alike, was derived from her intimate and constant contact with the Unseen, and the means of that contact were prayer and the Bible.

She had an implicit belief in the reality of prayer, simply because she had tested its efficacy every day of her life, and had never found it to fail. When her old friend, Mr. Smith of Dundee, asked for her testimony to include in his book, *Our Faithful God: Answers to Prayer*, she wrote:

My life is one long daily, hourly, record of answered prayer. For physical health, for mental overstrain, for guidance given marvellously, for errors and dangers averted, for enmity to the Gospel subdued, for food provided at the exact hour needed, for everything that goes to make up life and my poor service, I can testify with a full and often wonder-stricken awe that I believe God answers prayer. I know God answers prayer. I have proved during long decades while alone, as far as man's help and presence are concerned, that God answers prayer. Cavilings, logical or physical, are of no avail to me. It is the very atmosphere in which I live and breathe and have my being, and it makes life glad and free and a million times worth living. I can give no other testimony. I am sitting alone here on a log among a company of natives. My children, whose very lives are a testimony that God answers prayer, are working round me. Natives are crowding past on the bush road to attend palavers, and I am at perfect peace, far from my own countrymen and conditions, because I know God answers prayer. Food is scarce just now. We live from hand to mouth. We have not more than will be our breakfast to-day, but I know we shall be fed, for God answers prayer.

She realised that prayer was hedged round by conditions, and that everything depended upon the nature of the correspondence between earth and heaven. She likened the process to a wireless message, saying, "We can only obtain God's best by fitness of receiving power. Without receivers fitted and kept in order the air may tingle and thrill with the message, but it will not reach my spirit and consciousness." And she knew equally well that all prayer was not worthy of being answered. Those who were disappointed she would ask to look intelligently at first causes as well as regretfully at second causes. To one who said he had prayed without avail, she wrote: "You thought God was to hear and answer you by making everything straight and pleasant—not so are nations or churches or men and women born; not so is character made. God is answering your prayer in His way." And to another who was in similar mood she wrote: "I know what it is to pray long years and never get the answer—I had to pray for my father. But I know my heavenly Father so well that I can leave it with Him for the lower fatherhood." In this as in other things she had to confess that she herself often failed. "I am a poor exponent of faith," she would say. "I ought to have full faith in our Father that He will do everything, but I am ashamed of myself, for I want to 'see,' and that sends faith out of court. I never felt more in sympathy with that old afflicted father before in his prayer, 'Lord, I believe, help Thou my unbelief'—every syllable suits me."

She had absolute faith in intercession, "Prayer," she said, "is the greatest power God has put into our hands for service—praying is harder work than doing, at least I find it so, but the dynamic lies that way to advance the Kingdom." She believed that some of her official friends, the Empire-builders, were kept straight in this way: "The bands that mothers and sisters weave by prayer and precept are the strongest in the world." There was nothing she asked her friends more often at home to do than to pray for the Mission and the workers. "Don't stop praying for us," she pleaded, and her injunctions were sometimes pathetic in their personal application: "Pray that the power of Christ may rest on me, that He may never be disappointed in me or find me disobedient to the heavenly vision when He shows the way, pray that I may make no false moves, but that the spirit will say, 'Go here and go there,'" She was always convinced that it was the prayers of the people in Scotland that carried her on and made the work possible. "It is so customary to put aside those who, like myself, are old-fashioned and unable for the burden and heat of the day; but in my case it is care and love and forbearance all the way through; and all this I trace back to the great amount of prayer which has ever followed me, to the quality more than the quantity of that intercession. Prayer-waves pulsate from Britain all through Calabar." To one who had always prayed for her she also wrote: "I have always said that I have no idea how and why God has carried me over so many funny and hard places, and made these hordes of people submit to me, or why the Government should have given me the privilege of a magistrate among them, except in answer to prayer made at home for me.

It is all beyond my comprehension. The only way I can explain it is on the ground that I have been prayed for more than most. Pray on, dear one-the power lies that way." She also urged prayer for the Mission Committees, Home and Foreign—"We expect them to do so much and to do it so well, and yet we withhold the means by which alone they can do it."

Almost invariably, when acknowledging money, she would beg the donors to follow up their gifts by prayer for workers. "Now," she would say, "let us ask God earnestly and constantly for the greater gift of men and women to fill all these vacant posts."

She used to pray much for her friends in all their circumstances, asking for many things for them that they desired, but eventually her petition came to be, "Lord give them Thy best and it shall suffice them and me."

Her religion was a religion of the heart, and her communion with her Father was of the most natural, most childlike character. No rule or habit guided her. She just spoke to Him as a child to her Father when she needed help and strength, or when her heart was filled with joy and gratitude, at any time, in any place. He was so real to her, so near, that her words were almost of the nature of conversation. There was no formality, no self-conscious or stereotyped diction, only the simplest language from a quiet and humble heart. It is told of her that when in Scotland, after a tiresome journey, she sat down at the tea-table alone, and, lifting her eyes, said, "Thank ye, Faither—ye ken I'm tired," in the most ordinary way, as if she had been addressing her friends. On another occasion, in the country, she lost her spectacles while coming from a meeting in the dark. Snow lay on the ground, and there seemed little hope of recovering them. She could not do without them, and she prayed simply and directly: "O Father, give me back my spectacles." Early next morning the milk-boy saw something glistening in the snow, and she had the spectacles in time to read her Bible. A lady asked her how she obtained such intimacy with God. "Ah, woman," she said, "when I am out there in the bush I have often no other one to speak to but my Father, and I just talk to Him." It was in that way she kept herself in tune with the highest. Sometimes, when there had been laughing and frivolous conversation before a meeting, she lost "grip," and was vexed and restless and dumb. But a little communion with her Father would put matters right. Once, oppressed by a similar mood, she foresaw complete failure, but the minister who presided, as if conscious of her attitude, prayed in such a way as to lift the burden from her heart, and she was given not only a calm spirit but also an eloquent tongue.

How natural it was for her to pray is evidenced by an incident at one of the ladies' committee meetings at Duke Town. Speaking of it she said, "All the ladies were laughing and daffin' over something of a picturesque sort, when it struck me we ought to be praying rather, and I just said so, and at once the whole lot jumped up, and we went into the nearest room and were closeted with our Master for a bit." Sometimes in the Mission House she would call the children to prayer at odd hours, and Jean would remonstrate and say, "Ma, the time is long past." "Jean," she would reply, "the gate of heaven is never shut." She said she wished to teach them that they could pray anywhere and at any time, and not only in the church.

"_We are not really apart," she once wrote to a friend in Scotland, "*for you can touch God direct by prayer, and so can I.*"

CHAPTER X
BIBLE STUDENT

She had always been an earnest and intelligent student of the Bible, and to her it grew more wonderful every day. She believed that the spread of the Book was the simplest and most natural and direct way of preaching the Gospel and keeping it pure. Her own reading of it was mainly accomplished in the early morning. As soon as there was light enough—which was usually about 5.30—she took a fine pen and her Bible and turned to the book she was studying in the Old or New Testament. She underlined the governing words and sentences as she went along in her endeavour to grasp the meaning of the writer and the course of his argument; word by word, sentence by sentence, she patiently followed his thought. Sometimes it would be three days before she completed a chapter, but she would not leave it until she had some kind of idea as to its purpose. She was her own commentator, and on the margin she noted the truths she had learned, the lessons she had received, her opinions about the sentiment expressed, or the character described. If her expositions were not according to the ordinary canons of exegesis, they had the merit of being simple, fresh, and unconventional. Her language was as candid, often as pungent, as her remarks in conversation, its very frankness and force indicating how real to her were the life and conditions she was studying. When one Bible was finished she began another, and repeated the process, for she found that new thoughts came as the years went by. On one occasion we find her interested in a recent translation, reading it to discover whether it gave any clearer construction of the more difficult passages. Such sedulous study had its effect upon her character and life; she was interpenetrated with the spirit of the Book; it gave her direction in all her affairs—in her difficult palavers she would remark, "Let us see what the Bible says on this point "—it inspired her with hope, faith, and, and, and courage. Often after an hour or two of meditation over it she felt no desire for ordinary literature, all other books seeming tame and tasteless after its pages.

Some of the later Bibles she used are in existence, and bear testimony to the thoroughness of her methods. Almost every page is a mass of interlineations and notes. As one turns them over, phrases here and there catch the eye, arresting in thought and epigrammatic in form; such for instance as these:

_God is never behind time.

If you play with temptation do not expect God will deliver you.

A gracious woman has gracious friendships.

No gift or genius or position can keep us safe or free from sin.

Nature is under fixed and fine laws, but it cannot meet the need of man.

We must see and know Christ before we can teach.

Good is good, but it is not enough; it must be God.

The secret of all failure is disobedience,

Unspiritual man cannot stand success.

There is no escape from the reflex action of sin; broken law will have its revenge,

Sin is loss for time and eternity,

The smallest things are as absolutely necessary as the great things.

An arm of flesh never brings power.

Half the world's sorrow comes from the unwisdom of parents.

Obedience brings health,

Blessed the man and woman who is able to serve cheerfully in the second rank—a big test,

What they were weary of was the punishment, not the sin that brought it.

Slavery never pays; the slave is spoiled as a man, and the master not less so.

It were worth while to die, if thereby a soul could be born again._

She was deeply interested in the earlier books, for the reason that the moral and social conditions depicted there were analogous to those she had to deal with in Calabar. Every now and then we come across such remarks as these: "a Calabar palaver," "a chapter of Calabar history," "a picture of Calabar outside the gospel area," "this happens in Okoyong every day." Her own experience helped her to understand the story of these primitive civilisations, and her annotations on this part of the Bible have always the sharpest point. To the sentence, "The Lord watch between me and thee," she appends, "Beautiful sentiment, but a *mbiam* oath of fear." Jacob she terms in one place a "selfish beggar." Of Jael she says, "Not a womanly woman, a sorry story; would God not have showed her a better way if she had asked?" and of part of Deborah's song she remarks, "Fine poetry, poor morality." Her opinion of Jezebel is thus expressed: "A vain, heartless woman; one of the most revolting stories in history, and she might have been such a queen! A good woman is the most beautiful thing on earth, but a bad woman is a source of corruption.... Had only her soul been clean, dogs might have been welcome to her body."

The book of Job was always well studied. She had a great admiration for the "upright, wealthy, greatly-feared, and respected sheikh," and little or none for the "typical philosophers," who came, Calabar fashion, and sought to comfort him in his day of trial. Job was not, in her view, rebellious; "his plaint was a relief to his own spirit, and an appeal for sympathy." On chapter ix. she writes, "The atmosphere is clearing; the clouds are scattering, glimpses of sunshine, of starlight, and beauty; the spirit swings back on its pivot and begins to see God." Farther on, "Right, Job—turn to God I Leave it to Him— the fit of depression will pass when you have sounded the depths, and profit will follow." On chapter xviii. her comment is, "Such is the friendship of the world"; on chapter xx., "How very sure the fool is in his explanations of God's ways"; on chapter xxvii., "The ultimate values of life shall be fixed not by wealth but by character"; on chapter xxviii., "A very mine of gems and precious things—exquisitely lovely thoughts and language. Poetry like this in the earliest ages of the world!" Of Elihu's contentions in chapter xxxiv., "A good many truths, but served up with bitter herbs, not with love": on chapter xxxvii., "Beautiful poetry, but a very bleak and barren picture of God; hard, arbitrary, selfish, self-centred, striking terror into His works, and compelling obedience and service. Nature cannot reveal Him, Elihu!" On the next chapter, "The God of nature turns the picture, and behold it is no more destruction and blind force, but beneficence and gracious design and beauty,"—and so on to the end, when we read, "The voice of humanity demands some such judgment and relief from the mysteries and trials and misrepresentations of this life. The poem rings true to the cry of the spirit of man. Is there a modern drama in any language to come near to this ancient production?"

The New Testament was brooded over and absorbed with a care and thoroughness which must have made every line and every thought familiar to her. St. John was her favourite book. A few specimens of her remarks may be given:

"When the people saw that Jesus was not there ... they took shipping and came ... seeking for Jesus."

"The secret of our failures in winning men; they don't find Him with us."

"*The Pharisees also with the Sadducees came and tempted Him that He would, show them a sign from Heaven.*"

"Man's cry for the moon! What does a sign prove? Is God known by magic?"

"*And the people asked Him saying, What shall we do then? ... 'He that hath two coats let him impart to him that hath none.'*"

"By love serve."

"*And He said unto them, When I sent you without purse and scrip and shoes lacked you anything?*"

"No, Lord, never was lack with Thee!"

"*And her parents were astonished, but He charged them that they should tell no man what He had done.*"

"Life will tell. Speech will end in chatter."

These illustrations, picked out at random, will serve to indicate what an intimate companion she made of her Bible, and with what loving patience and insight she studied it for the illumination and deepening of her spiritual life.

CHAPTER XI
BACK TO THE OLD HAUNTS

Eight years had passed since she had left Akpap, and she had never been back, although she had paid flying visits to the hinterland. Miss Amess, with whom her friendship had grown close, was in charge, being minister, doctor, dispenser, teacher, and mentor to the people, and with her was Miss Ramsay. They had built a new church, which was almost ready, and Miss Amess determined to bring "Ma" over and have the Macgregors to meet her. "Ma" could not resist the temptation to revisit the scenes of her greatest adventures, and went in July 1913, taking the children with her, except Mary, and ordering the others at Calabar, including the two youngest, Whitie and Asuquö, who were also natives of the district, to join her.

Her arrival caused much excitement, and her stay was one long reception. All day the Mission House was like a market; from far and near the people came to *köm* their Mother. She could scarcely be got to come to meals. On the first day when she was called, she said, "These are my meat to-day," and then she told those about her what Christ had said to His disciples after His conversation with the woman of Samaria. Such love as the ladies saw on both sides they had not thought possible between missionary and native. She seemed to remember the names of most of the people, and all the details of their family histories. One after another came forward and talked and revived stories of the old times. But she seemed vexed to see so many who were interested in her, and with no concern for the things of God, and with these she pled earnestly to come to church and give themselves to the Saviour. Two notable figures were Mana, and the mother of Susie, Iye.

The children were a source of astonishment to all. These healthy, happy, handsome young people, the babies that had been cast away or despised—it was wonderful! They gazed upon them in a kind of awe. A few of the older and women held aloof from the twins, but not in any offensive way, and the general disposition was to ignore the stain on their birth.

There was a touching meeting with Ma Eme, who could not conceal her affection and joy at seeing her old "Ma" again. Much to Mary's sorrow she was still a heathen, and a very zealous one, as she sacrificed daily to the spirits in the crudest way, with food and blood, in abasement and fear. So strong was superstition rooted in her nature that she would not touch the twins, although she confessed it was marvellous that they had grown up.

The two women, bound by so strange a friendship, talked long about the old days. It was, "Do you remember this?" "Do you remember that?" and then would follow reminiscences of the killing time when they worked hand in hand in secret for the preservation of life. Nothing that "Ma" could say would induce Ma Eme to throw off her allegiance to her African beliefs, and at the end of a long day she left, the same kind, high-bred, mysterious heathen woman that she had always been. She died shortly after. "My dear old friend and almost sister," said Mary, "she made the saving of life so often possible in the early days, It is sad that she did not come out for Christ. She could have been the honoured leader of God's work had she risen to it. I cannot fancy Okoyong without her. She made a foolish choice, and yet God cannot forget all she was to me, and all she helped me to do in those dark and bloody days."

A service was arranged, but the throng who wished to hear "Ma" was so great that it had to be held in the unfinished church, and thus Mary had the joy of being at the first service. Over four hundred well- dressed natives were present, the largest number ever in a church in Okoyong, She thought of the wild old days, and contrasted them with the present scene. "Truly," she said to herself, "one soweth and another reapeth." She spoke for half an hour, giving a strong, inspiring talk on the duties of those who are believers to the world around them.

With her usual thought for others she sat down and wrote to her old comrade, Miss Wright (Mrs. Rattray), in England, giving her the details of her visit, and accounts of the people. "This house," she said, "is full of memories of you, and you are not forgotten." She described with pride and hope the way in which the ladies were conducting the station, and praised them in her usual generous manner. After she left, it seemed to them that they had greater influence among the people than ever.

CHAPTER XII
ROYAL RECOGNITION

The friends who had known her long were noticing that a new softness and graciousness were stealing into her life. She never grew commonplace, and was original as ever, but her character was mellowing, and her love and humility becoming even more marked. "Love will overcome all," was her belief, and love, for her, included all the qualities of the Christian faith— simplicity, kindness, patience, charity, selflessness, confidence, hope. In herself she was conscious of many faults. "I don't half live up to the ideal missionary life," she said, with a sigh. "It is not easier to be a saint here than at home. We are very human, and not goody-goody at all." Often she was deep in the valley of humiliation over hasty words spoken and opportunities of service let slip. But she was saved from depression by her sense of humour. She laughed and dared the devil. Of one who had just come out she wrote: "She is very serious, and will take life and work more in the sense of tasks than of a glad free life ... we want one to laugh, to hitch on to the yoke, and joke over all that we don't like." She also became less uncompromising in her views. "My opinions," she acknowledged, "may not just suit every one, and it is possible other people may be right and I far wrong.... But although we differ amongst ourselves, and some things differentiate our work, we are all in full friendship and sympathy with one another."

It was not possible for self-abnegation to go farther than it did in her case. She was unable to see that she had done anything out of the common. "I have lived my life very quietly and in a very natural and humble way," she would say, and all the credit of her work was given to God. "It isn't Mary Slessor doing anything, but Something outside of her altogether uses her as her small ability allows." She did not say "my plan," or "my scheme"—if she did she checked herself and said, "What God wants me to do." And she always paid generous tribute to her girls, who, she said, did more than she did, though no one counted it to them. She was distressed to receive letters praising her. One who saw her go out from Scotland to her life-work, and had lovingly followed her career ever since, wrote saying that her reward would be a starry crown in the glory land, and her reply was, *"What would I do with starry crowns except to cast them at His feet?"*

Nothing illustrated this feature so notably as an event which occurred shortly after her visit to Akpap. Two years previously a few of her friends in Calabar, official and missionary, had talked over the possibility of securing some public recognition of her unique service. Mr. Macgregor wrote an account of her life-work for the Government, but it was not until Sir Frederick Lugard arrived as Governor-General of the united provinces of Northern and Southern Nigeria that action was taken. He was so struck by the heroic record placed before him that he at once sent home a strong recommendation to the Secretary of State for the Colonies, that Mary's services should be brought to Royal notice. The Secretary of State was equally impressed, and laid the matter before the Chapter-General of the Order of the Hospital of St. John of Jerusalem in England, of which the King is Sovereign Head, and the Duke of Connaught Grand Prior. This was done, and she was selected for admission. When she received the august-looking document asking her to accept the honour, she said to herself, "Now, who has done this? Who am I, and what is my distinction that I should have it?" She was in a quandary how to answer, but eventually complied with the request, thinking that would be the end of it. Shortly afterwards came a letter stating that "her selection had received the sanction and approval of His Most Gracious Majesty King George V." The Chapter-General, it was stated, elected her "with particular satisfaction" to the grade of Honorary Associate. This honour is only conferred on persons professing the Christian faith, who are eminently distinguished for philanthropy, or who have specially devoted their exertions or professional skill in aid of the objects of the Order. The Badge of an Honorary Associate is a Maltese Cross in silver, embellished at the four principal angles with a lion passant guardant and a unicorn passant alternately. It is worn by women on the left shoulder, attached to a black watered riband tied in a bow.

"Ma" kept the matter a secret, even after she had received the diploma, but the silver Badge came through the Colonial Office to the Commissioner at Duke Town, and the honour being made public, her friends schemed to get her down to a formal presentation. It was a difficult problem, but it was solved by a letter being sent stating that the decoration had arrived, that, of course, she would not care to have it given to her surreptitiously, and that her duty was to come to Calabar for it. A telegraph form, ready for dispatch, and bearing the one word "Coming," was enclosed. They knew she would get agitated, and have no peace until the telegram was out of her hands. Their surmise was correct. She sent the message and committed herself to the ordeal.

She was not elated at the prospect of appearing at a Government function; neither was she perturbed, and she went about her duties as usual. Miss Gilmour, one of the new lady agents, tells how on the eve of her departure she gathered the bairns for family worship, and in a simple and beautiful way read to them the story of the Good Shepherd and the sheep that followed. Then, as an illustration, she took the story of Peter's denial of our Lord, and showed that Peter sinned because he followed "afar off." "Eh, bairns," she said, "it's the wee lassie that sits beside her mother at meal times that gets all the nice bittocks. The one who sits far away and sulks disna ken what she misses. Even the pussy gets more than she does. Keep close to Jesus the Good Shepherd all the way."

A Government launch was sent to bring her down, an honour she felt as much as the bestowal of the insignia, and as she walked up to the Macgregors' house—the Wilkies were in Scotland—there were many who were struck by the dignity of her appearance, dressed though she was in an old but clean cotton dress, straw hat, and list shoes. On the Saturday afternoon she went to an "At Home" at the Barracks, where she was lionised in a quiet way. She attended a cricket match—she was an advocate of all games, and believed they were excellent civilising agencies—and also witnessed a sham fight, where the "enemy" dressed themselves up as "savage warriors" and attacked the Barrack Hill. She was much impressed, and kept saying to her old friend the Hon. Horace Bedwell, the Provincial Commissioner, "That's just splendid. Look how the officers lead them." On Sunday she spoke for three-quarters of an hour to the boys in the Institute in Efik, and no boys could have listened more intently. On Monday night she was at Government House at dinner.

The presentation took place in the Goldie Memorial Hall on Wednesday, Mr. Macgregor presiding. All the Europeans who could leave business gathered to do her honour. The boys of the Training Institute and the girls of the Edgerley Memorial School were also in the hall. Had it not been that Mr. Bedwell and Mrs. Bedwell were beside her, and that it was the former who made the presentation, she would have felt more nervous. As it was, she sat with her head buried in her hands. Mr. Bedwell spoke of her unique work and influence, and of her genius for friendship in a way that overcame her. She could not at first find words to reply. She turned to the children, and in Efik told them to be faithful to the Government, for at bottom it was Christian, and, as the silver Badge proved, friendly to missions. Self was thus entirely effaced in her interpretation of the act; she made it appear to be the recognition by the Government of the work of the Mission, and suggested that it might have been awarded to any member of the staff.

Having recovered her courage she spoke in English, saying that she did not understand why she had been chosen for the distinction, when others deserved it more. In a closing passage of simple beauty, she gave

God the honour and praise for all she had been able to accomplish. What had impressed her at the sham fight was that the officer was always in front leading and guiding his men. "If I have done anything in my life it has been easy because the Master has gone before."

Forty Europeans came to tea at the Macgregors', and "Ma" was brilliant and entertaining. On Thursday her hosts convoyed her back to Use. Mrs. Bedwell had presented her with a bouquet of flowers, and she had taken out the roses—of which she was passionately fond—and placed them in water. On her arrival she carefully planted one of the stems, and to her great joy it grew and flourished in front of her hut.

"Don't think," she wrote home, "that there is any difference in my designation. I am Mary Mitchell Slessor, nothing more and none other than the unworthy, unprofitable, but most willing, servant of the King of Kings. May this be an incentive to work, and to be better than ever I have been in the past."

At home the honour was made known chiefly through the *Record* of the Church, in which Mr. Macgregor gave some account of her romantic career. He stipulated that this should be anonymous, for "Ma," he feared, would never forgive him if she knew that he had been connected with it. She gained a repute that was akin to fame. Congratulations from all parts of the world were showered upon her. Sir Frederick Lugard sent his "hearty and sincere congratulations, and his appreciation of this well-earned reward for her life of heroic self- sacrifice." In confusion of heart she escaped to Ikpe. "I shall never look the world in the face again until all this blarney and publicity is over," she said. "I feel so glad that I can hide here quietly where no one knows about newspapers and *Records*, and do my small portion of work out of sight."

For a time she was kept busy replying to the correspondence that the event evoked, and to all she made the same modest reply, that she saw in the honour "God's goodness to the Mission and her fellow-labourers, who were levelling and building and consolidating the work on every side. It is a token that He means to encourage them in the midst of their discouraging circumstances."

CHAPTER XIII
BATTLE FOR A LIFE

Each new kindness shown her was an incentive to harder service. She threw herself again into work with an extraordinary keenness. Dissatisfied with what she was doing at Ikpe, she moved in all directions in her "box on wheels," prospecting for new spheres of usefulness, fording rivers, crossing swamps, climbing hills, pushing through bush, traversing roads that were unsafe and where by the law people had to go in couples, and often putting up at villages six or ten miles distant. She saw crowds of people, and hundreds of women and children in every street, but no light; not even a desire for it, though here and there she found a disciple or two. She met with more opposition from the chiefs than she had done in all her experience. They would not hear of "God fashions," and would not permit teachers to enter their districts or churches to be built; they forbade all meetings for worship. She braced herself, body and mind, for the fight. She spent days in palaver, but they would not give in. She insisted that at least the right of the disciples to meet and worship in their own homes must be recognised. When the chiefs saw her face, set with iron resolution, they were afraid, wavered, and agreed. They then became quite friendly. "We don't object to schools," they admitted. "We want our children to learn to read and write, but we want no interference with our fashions. If houses of God are built, we shall all die, and we are dying fast enough."

"I shall never give you teachers without the Gospel," she declared. "If you don't take the one, you won't have the other. But I'm going to bring both. I shall put up a shed on the roadside, and hold services there whenever I get a chance."

"All right, Ma," they said with something like admiration. "Come yourself, but don't send boys."

And then she remembered. "How can this poor tabernacle do it, even with six lads to push and pull and carry the cart through the streams? But I have opened the way, and that is something."

In Ikpe itself the currents of heathenism ran deep and strong, and she found progress as difficult as in Okoyong. But she solved all the problems in the same fearless way as she had done there. Unlike those in other centres, the women and girls of the town took no interest in the work, and would not come forward, and she knew there was no hope for the community unless she secured their sympathy and attachment to the cause. At first a few girls had ventured to sit by themselves in church. Then some village accident made the chiefs believe that their juju was angry because the girls had forsaken their sacrifices and deserted the heathen plays, and they placed pressure on them to return. Some were flogged and made to pray before a clay-pot with an egg in it, and all were forced out on the moonlight nights to take part in the plays. "If they don't do that," demanded the chiefs, "how can they have children for us?" The girls lost courage and forsook the church, but she did not blame them. "Poor things, they are as timid as hares, and have never had a choice of what to do until I came. But the chiefs—I will be hard on them!"

One day she gathered all those who were faithful to the church laws, and interviewed the chiefs. The spokesman for her party urged that the antagonism that had been shown should cease; he agreed that any one who broke the ordinary laws should be punished, but no girl or young man should be compelled to sacrifice or pray to idols, or be ostracised or fined for fearing God. The words were received with scornful looks and laughs, the chiefs being hardly able to restrain themselves, but they had a wholesome fear of "Ma," and were never outwardly disrespectful in her presence. They looked at her. She kept a severe and solemn face, and they were a little nonplussed.

"Ma, have you heard?" they asked,

"Am I not here?" she replied.

Taking the gift of rods that had been offered, the chiefs retired. When they returned they said: "Ma, we hear. Let the present of rods lie, we accept of it, and we promise that we will respect God's laws, in regard to the joining in our sacrifices; and in regard to the Sabbath, we shall respect it and leave our work; but we will *not* join in the confusions of the church, that we cannot do."

"God will doubtless be immensely pleased and benefited by your wondrous condescension," said she with good-humoured sarcasm, and they laughed heartily and tried to be friendly, but Mary airily told her people to rise and go.

Fearing she was not pleased, the chiefs made to accompany her.

"I'm going round to see a woman in the next street," said Mary pointedly. They stopped dead at once. Here was the "confusion" they referred to, for the woman was a twin-mother.

It was the old weary battle over again,

Her patience and persistence eventually won a victory for the girls. They were allowed to return to church, but the line was drawn at the day-school. The chiefs said girls were meant to work and mother the babies, and not to learn "book." Even the boys who attended, each burdened with an infant to justify the waste of time, were not allowed to bring a baby girl. If the baby of the home was a girl, he looked after her there and his place was vacant. Mary began to think of teaching the girls apart from the boys, when one day several girls marched in; she courted them with all the skill she possessed, and gradually one or two chiefs brought their daughters, who returned with dresses from the Mission box, and that ended the opposition.

But there was no end to the struggle over twins. Time and again she had to send the girls to bring babes to the Mission House, and many a stirring night she had, she sleeping with them in her bed, whilst outside stealthy forms watched for a chance to free the town from the defilement of their presence. The first that survived was a boy. The husband, angry and sullen, was for murdering it and putting the mother into a hole in the swamp. She faced him with the old flash in her eye, and made him take oath not to hurt or kill the child. He even promised to permit it to live, for which magnanimity she bowed ironically to the ground, an act that put his courage at once to flight. She had come to realise that it was not good to take twins from their mother, and she insisted on the child being kept in the home. Jean was sent to stay and sleep with the woman, and as she had, on occasion, as caustic a tongue as "Ma," the man had not a very agreeable time. It was decided later to bring the woman and child to the hut, and there, beneath her verandah, they rigged up a little lean-to, where they were housed, Jean sleeping with them at night and keeping a watchful eye on the mother. "It is really," said "Ma," "far braver and kinder of her to live with that heathen woman with her fretting habits than it is for her to go out in the dark and fight with snakes. Jean has as many faults as myself, but she is a darling, none the less, and a treasure." All going well, they went on Sunday to church and left the mother. When they returned they found she had broken the baby's thigh and given him some poisonous stuff. With care the boy recovered, but they redoubled their precautions, hoping that when the parents saw how handsome and healthy and normal the little fellow was, they would consent to keep him.

"Ma" was due at Use, but she would not leave Ikpe until she had conquered. Another month passed, and she was running out of provisions, including tea. To be without tea was a tremendous deprivation. She thought of the big fragrant package that had been sent out as a gift, and was lying fifty miles away but un-get-at-able, and felt far from saintly as she resorted to the infusion of old leaves. One Sunday evening there was a shout. A canoe had arrived, and in it was a box. With sudden prescience Jean flew for a hammer and chisel and broke it open, and sure enough inside was the tea from Use. Mary marvelled, and with all the young folk round her stood and thanked God, the Lord of the Sabbath, for His goodness. The beverage had never tasted so sweet and invigorating. Though her thrifty Scottish nature rejoiced that she had been able to save a little, she confessed that she would never be a miser where tea was concerned, Whenever she received a package she invariably sent a share to old Mammy Fuller at Duke Town. "Mammy," she told a home friend, "has lived a holy and consecrated life here for fifty years, and is perhaps the best-loved woman in Duke Town. Uncle Tom in the old cabin is a child in the knowledge of God to Mammy. So we all love to share anything with her, and she especially loves a cup of tea."

The parents of the twin were at last persuaded to take the big happy child home and provide for it. Four days later they sent for Jean, who returned, carrying a weak, pinched form that had death written on its face. It succumbed shortly afterwards—and that was the end of "Ma's" strenuous fight and Jean's ten weeks' toil by night and day.

CHAPTER XIV
A VISION OF THE NIGHT

She was down at Use for Christmastide with all her children about her, and was very happy at seeing the consummation of her efforts to build a new church. The opening took place on Christmas Day,

"A bonnie kirk it is," she wrote. "Mr. Cruickshank officiated, and was at his very best. Miss Peacock, my dear comrade and her young helper Miss Cooper—a fine lassie—came and spent the whole day, so we had a grand time, the biggest Christmas I've ever had in Calabar. Three tall flag-poles with trade-cloth flags in the most flaming colours hung over the village from point to point embracing the old and the new churches. The people provided a plain breakfast in their several homes for over eighty of our visitors, who therefore stayed over the forenoon. It made our Christian population look fairly formidable, and certainly very reputable as a force for uplifting and regenerating society. It looks but yesterday that they were a horde of the most unlikely and unresponsive people one could approach, and yet the Gospel has made of them already something to prove that it is the power of God unto salvation to a people and to an individual every and anywhere."

It was to her "one of the reddest of red-letter days," such a day as only comes at rare intervals, and she fell into the snare, as she said, "of being carried away with it," with the result that at night she was down with fever. This kept recurring every alternate night. It was the harmattan season, in which she always wilted like some delicate flower in the sun, and she grew so limp and fragile that she could not sit up. She felt that she would be compelled to go home in the summer with the Macgregors, but the idea frightened her, chiefly because of the stir that had been caused by the honour she had received. "I dare not appear at home after all this publicity," she said. "I simply could not face the music." As she recovered a little she superintended the work of the girls outside, and was amused at the way her advice was now received. "Jean and Annie do not hesitate to set it aside quietly in their superior way; it often works out better than mine, truth to tell— though I say it does so by accident!" This was a different house-mother from the one who ruled years before.

In one of her fever nights, tossing in semi-delirium, she had a vision. She had been following the Chapman-Alexander Mission in Glasgow with keen interest, and in the long watches her excited brain continued to dwell on the meetings. She dreamt, or imagined, that out of gratitude for what had been accomplished, two young Glasgow engineers had taken a six months' holiday, and come out with their motor car to Calabar. They spent their days running up and down the Government Road through Ibibio, singing and giving evangelistic addresses, she interpreting, the girls, who were packed into the cars, doing the catering and cooking, and the Government Rest Houses providing the lodging. "What a night it was!" she wrote. "The bairns were afraid, for I was babbling more than usual, but to me it was as real as if it had all happened. We ran backwards and forwards between Itu and Ikpe, spending alternate Sundays with the Churches, and taking Miss Peacock to her outstations, and visiting Miss Welsh, It was magnificent."

The vision did not pass away; she took it as a sign from God; and out of it in the morning she formulated a scheme which one day she hoped would be realised. "It is strange," she said, "that it has never dawned on us before. Here is the Government making use of the motor car to do its work. Why should not the Church do the same when the roads are here? It would permit one man to do the work of three, it would save strength, and make for efficiency. The reason why I have been able to go farther than my colleagues, is that I have had the privilege of using Government conveyances by land and water; to have a car and a mechanic missionary would be supplying us with a grand opportunity for multiplied service." She expatiated on the matter in letters to her friends at home, and the longer she thought of the idea, the more it fired her imagination. Within a few days she was flying over the ground in the Government car on her way to Ikpe—with many a "ca' canny" to the driver—and her experience brought the conviction that the proposal was a good one. It might be too novel a plan for the Church to take up officially, but she thought wealthy men in Scotland might materialise her vision as a thank-offering.

CHAPTER XV
STORMING THE CITADELS

The Government road went as far as Odoro Ikpe, where a Rest House, used as a shelter by officials on the march or on judging tours, and the one seen by Mr. Macgregor, had been built on the brow of a hill above the township. It was Saturday when she arrived here, and she climbed the ascent, taking over an hour to do it, and was captivated by the situation. It had the widest outlook of any spot she had seen; she seemed to be on the very roof of the world. A vast extent of bush stretched out before her, unbroken save by the white road winding down the hill, and instead of the stifling stillness of the plains, a soft breeze blew and cooled the atmosphere. It was five miles from Ikpe, and the centre of a number of populous towns. For months past she had been praying for an entrance into these closed haunts of heathenism, and as she sat down in the lonely little Rest House, she made up her mind not to move a step further until she had come to grips with the chiefs. Knowing that the Government would not object, she took possession of the building. It had a doorway but no door; the windows were holes in the wall high up under the eaves; the floor was of mud, and there was no furniture of any kind. But these things were of no consequence to the gipsy-missionary. She slept on a camp-bed borrowed from Miss Peacock, the girls lay on the mud floor among the lizards, and some pots and pans were obtained from the people until she could procure her own from Ikpe. The commissariat department was run on the simplest scale. A tin of fat, some salt and pepper, tea, and sugar, and roasted plantain for bread, formed the principal constituents of the frugal meals. Their clothes were taken off piece by piece as each could be spared, and washed in a pail from the little prison yard. "Ma's" calico gown went through the process in the forenoon, was dried on the fence in the hot sun, and donned in the afternoon, in order, as she humorously put it, to be ready for "visitors and tea." In her eyes it was a sort of glorified picnic. She did not pity the girls; she thought such an experience was better for them as African citizens and missionaries than a secondary education.

From this high centre as from a fort, she began to bombard the towns in the neighbourhood. Next day she summoned some disciples from a place called Ndot, and service was held in the yard. Then the lads pushed her chair out to Ibam, two miles distant, where she met the headman and his followers. These were an arrogant, powerful sept—not Ibibios—who had been allies of the slavers of Aros, and were disliked and suspected by all. She told them that she wanted the question of Gospel entrance settled. They looked at her indulgently. "We have no objection to you coming, Ma," said the chief.

"And the saving of twins, and the right of twin-mothers to live as women and not as unclean beasts in the bush?" she asked.

"No, no, we will not have it. Our town will spoil."

After much talk they said, "Go home, Ma, and we shall discuss it and see you again"—the native way of ending a matter.

Her next discussion was with the town of Odoro Ikpe itself. The old chief was urbane, and gave her every honour. Bringing out a plate with _3_s. upon it, he said, "Take that to buy food while staying here, as we have no market yet." She took the money, kissed it, put her hands on his head, and thanked him, calling him "father," but requested him to take it and buy chop for the children, and she would eat with him another day. The old man went away and returned with some yams, which he asked her to cook and eat. As they talked he gradually lost his fear, and then she asked him bluntly about his attitude to the Gospel. He and his big men told her frankly what their difficulties were, and these she demolished one by one. After two hours' fencing and arguing the tension gave way to a hearty laugh, and the old chief said, with a sweep of his hand toward the crowd:

"Well, Ma, there they are, take them and teach them what you like—and you, young men, go and build a house for book."

"No!" cried "Ma," "we don't begin or end either with a house. We begin and end with God in our hearts."

A young man came forward, and without removing a quaint hat he wore, said, "Ma, we can't take God's word if you bring twins and twin-mothers into our town."

It was out at last. Instead of arguing, "Ma" looked at him as witheringly as she could and replied; "I speak with men and people worthy of me, and not with a puny bush-boy such as you have shown by your manners you are."

Off came the hat, and then "Ma" spoke to him in such a way that the crowd were fain to cry:

"Ma, forgive! forgive! he does not know any better."

There was no more after that about twins, and when she left she felt that progress had been made.

Striking while the iron was hot she sent to Ikpe for school books, and going into the highways and byways, she began to coax the lads to come and learn. They stood aloof, half-afraid and half-scornful, and would not respond. Then she adopted a flank movement, and began to speak to them about the rubber and cocoa which the Government were planting in the district, and tried to awaken their interest and ambitions by telling them how the world was moving outside their home circle. Gradually the sullenness gave way, and they began to ask questions and to chat. She took the alphabet card, but they shied at the strange- looking thing, and would not speak. One little fellow who had been at Ikpe, and knew more than the others, began tremblingly, "A—B—," and she and Alice who was with her, joined in until one after another surrendered, and before long all were shouting the letters. By the end of the week the lads were coming every spare hour for lessons, and would scarcely give her time to eat.

The Ikpe disciples had ruefully watched this development, and at last went to her:

"Ma, we are glad you have got a footing out here, but are you forsaking us?"

Her heart ached at the words, and although now reduced to coming and going in her Cape cart, she determined to give them every alternate week when she was not at Use. Thus from now onwards she was keeping three centres going by her own efforts.

After a week at Ikpe in fulfilment of her promise, she returned to Odoro Ikpe to hold the first Sabbath service. A play was being enacted in the town, and scores of naked young men and women were dancing to the compelling throb of the drum. But some Ikpe and Ndot lads came to support the service, and their presence helped the local sympathisers to come forward. It was very simple; she said it would have seemed babyish to Europeans, but it was an epoch to the natives. Another meeting was held in the afternoon; and at night in the dark square, lit only by the light of the fires where the women were cooking their meal, she stood, and again proclaimed, with passionate earnestness, the love of God and the power of Christ to save and uplift. It was, no doubt, a day of small things, but she knew from long experience that small things were not to be despised.

A month later, when she was at Ikpe holding the services, she was astonished to see thirty of the Odoro Ikpe lads marching into church. They had grown so interested, that they had come the five miles to hear her speak. The Ikpe people at once rose and gave the strangers their seats, finding a place for themselves on the floor. It was pathetic to see their earnest faces and their ignorance as to what they should do during the service, which was more elaborate than they had been accustomed to. Having brought some food they cooked it at the house and remained all day.

On her return to Odoro Ikpe the chiefs appeared one morning, and asked her to come out at once and survey the land, and choose a site for a station. Her heart leapt at the significance of the request. She happened to be in her night attire, but as it might have been full Court dress for all they knew, she went and tramped over the land and chose what she believed would be the best situation in the Mission. It was on the brow of a hill overlooking a magnificent stretch of country, across which a cool breeze blew all the time. She immediately planned a house—one of six rooms—three living rooms above and stores and hall and girls' rooms below, with a roof of corrugated iron for security against wind and insects, and prepared to go down to Use to buy the material.

There was one town still holding out, Ibam (where she had been told to "go home and they would think about it"), and she prayed that it, too, might accept the new conditions. On the Sunday before she left for Use, while she was conducting service, six strange men came in and waited until all had gone. "We are from Ibam," they said. "Come at once, Ma, and we will build a place to worship God, and will hear and obey." She was so uplifted that she seemed to live on air for the next few days. The villagers of Ibam gave up their best yard to her, and, crowds came to the meetings.

All the citadels of heathenism in the district had now been stormed. Sitting one night on the floor of the Rest House, her aching back leaning against the mud wall, a candle, stuck in its own grease, giving her light, she wrote to her friends in Scotland, telling them that she was the happiest and most grateful woman in the world.

CHAPTER XVI
CLARION CALLS

The discovery of coal up in the interior at Udi brought a new interest into her life, for her far-seeing mind at once realised all the possibilities it contained. She believed it would revolutionise the conditions of West Africa. And when a railway was projected and begun from Port Harcourt, west of Calabar, to Udi, and there was talk of an extension to Itu, she sought to make her friends at home grasp the full significance of the development. That railway would become the highway to the interior, and Calabar would cease to be so important a port. Great stretches of rich oil-palm country would be opened up and exploited. She urged the need for more men and women to work amongst the rank heathenism that would soon collect and fester in the new industrial and commercial centres. Up there also was the menace of Mohammedanism. "Shall the Cross or the Crescent be first?" she cried. "We need men and women, oh, we need them!"

She had been saddened by the closing of stations for furloughs, and the apathy of the Church at home.

We are lower in numbers in Calabar than ever—fewer, if you except the artisans in the Institute, than in the old days before the doors were opened! Surely there is something very far wrong with our Church, the largest in Scotland. Where are the men? Are there no heroes in the making among us? No hearts beating high with the enthusiasm of the Gospel? Men smile nowadays at the old-fashioned idea of sin and hell and broken law and a perishing world, but these made men, men of purpose, of power and achievement, and self-denying devotion to the highest ideals earth has known. We have really no workers to meet all this opened country, and our Church, to be honest, should stand back and give it to some one else. But oh! I cannot think of that. Not that, Lord! For how could we meet the Goldies, the Edgerleys, the Waddells, the Andersons? How can our Church look at Christ who has given us the privilege of making Calabar history, and say to Him, "Take it back. Give It to another?"

She had been deeply interested In the great World's Missionary Conference in Edinburgh in 1910, and had contrasted it with State diplomacy and dreadnoughts, but was disappointed that so little practical result had followed. "After all," she said, "it is not committees and organisations from without that is to bring the revival, and to send the Gospel to the heathen at home and abroad, but the living spirit of God working from within the heart."

All this made her more than ever convinced of the value of her own policy. She believed in the roughest methods for a raw country like Nigeria. Too much civilisation and concentration was bad, both for the work and the natives. There should be, she thought, an office of itinerating or travelling missionary permanently attached to the Mission. It would have its drawbacks, as, she recognised, all pioneer work had, but it would also pay well. She was not sure whether the missionaries did right in remaining closely to their stations, and believed that short regular expeditions into the interior would not only keep them in better health, but give them a closer knowledge of the people. Not much teaching could be given in this way, but their confidence would be won, and the way would be prepared for further advance. Her hope lay in women workers; they made better pioneers than men, and as they were under no suspicion of being connected with the Government, their presence was unobjectionable to the natives. They could move into new spheres and do the spade-work; enter the homes, win a hearing, guide the people in quiet ways, and live a simple and natural life amongst them. When confidence had been secured, men missionaries could enter and train and develop, and build up congregations in the ordinary manner.

Even then she did not see why elaborate churches should be erected. She was always so afraid to put anything forward save Christ, that she was quite satisfied with her little "mud kirks." The raw heathen knew nothing of the Church as white people understood it. To give them a costly building was to give them a foreign thing in which they would worship a foreign God. To let them worship in an environment of their own setting meant, she believed, a more real apprehension of spiritual truth. The money they were trained to give, she would spend, not on buildings so much as on pioneer work among the tribes.

So, too, with the Mission houses. She thought these should be as simple as possible, and semi-native in style; such, she believed, to be the driest and most healthy. In any case disease could come into a house costing £200, as into one costing £20, and "there was such a thing as God's providence." Still, she recognised the importance of preserving the health of newcomers, and admitted that her ideas might not apply to them. "It would be wrong," she said, "to insist on mud-huts for a nervous or æsthetic person."

It was much the same feeling that ran through her objection to the natives suddenly transforming themselves into Europeans. Her views in this respect differed a good deal from those of her co-workers. One Sunday, after a special service, a number of women who had arrayed themselves in cheap European finery, boots and stockings and all, called upon her. She sat on a chair, her back to them, and merely threw them an occasional word with an angry jerk of her head. They were very upset, and at last one of them ventured to ask what was the matter. "Matter!" she exclaimed, and then spoke to them in a way which brought them all back in the afternoon clothed more appropriately.

On all these questions she thought simply and naturally, and not in terms of scientific theory and over-elaborated system. She believed that the world was burdened and paralysed by conventional methods. But she did not undervalue the æsthetic side of existence. "So many think that we missionaries live a sort of glorified glamour of a life, and have no right to think of any of the little refinements and elegancies which rest and sooth tired and overstrained nerves—certainly coarseness and ugliness do not help the Christian life, and ugly things are not as a rule cheaper than beautiful ones." Her conviction was that a woman worth her salt could make any kind of house beautiful. At the same time she believed—and proved it in her own life—that the spirit- filled woman was to a great extent independent of all accessories.

What always vexed her was to think of thousands of girls at home living a purposeless life, spending their time in fashionable wintering- places, and undergoing the strenuous toil of conventional amusement. "Why," she asked, "could they not come out here and stay a month or six months doing light work, helping with the children, cheering the staff? What a wealth of interest it would introduce into their lives!" She declared it would be better than stoning windows, for she had no patience with the policy of the women who sought in blind destruction the solution of political and social evils. "I'm for votes for women, but I would prove my right to it by keeping law and helping others to keep it. God-like motherhood is the finest sphere for women, and the way to the redemption of the world."

Many a clarion call she sent to her sisters across the waters:

"Don't grow up a nervous old maid! Gird yourself for the battle outside somewhere, and keep your heart young. Give up your whole being to create music everywhere, in the light places and in the dark places, and your life will make melody. I'm a witness to the perfect joy and satisfaction of a single life—with a tail of human tag-rag hanging on. It is rare! It is as exhilarating as an aeroplane or a dirigible or whatever they are that are always trying to get up and are always coming down!... Mine has been such a joyous service," she wrote again. "God has been good to me, letting me serve Him in this humble way. I cannot thank Him enough for the honour He conferred upon me when He sent me to the Dark Continent."

Over and over again she put this idea of foreign service before her friends at home. Some were afraid of a rush of cranks who would not obey rules and so forth. She laughed the idea to scorn. "I wish I could believe in a crush—but there are sensible men and women enough in the Church who would be as law-abiding here as at home."

CHAPTER XVII
LOVE-LETTEBS

During the course of her career Miss Slessor wrote numberless letters, many of them productions of six, ten, twelve, and fourteen pages, closely penned in spidery writing, which she called her "hieroglyphic style." She had the gift, which more women than men possess, of expressing her ideas on paper in as affluent and graceful a way as in conversation. Her letters indeed were long monologues, the spontaneous outpouring of an active and clever mind. She sat down and talked vivaciously of everything about her, not of public affairs, because she knew people at home would not understand about these, but of her children, the natives, her journeys, her ailments, the services, the palavers, all as simply and naturally and as fully as if she were addressing an interested listener. But it was essential that her correspondent should be in sympathy with her. She could never write a formal letter; she could not even compose a business letter in the ordinary way. Neither could she write to order, nor give an official report of her work. The prospect of appearing in print paralysed her. It was always the heart and not the mind of her correspondent that she addressed. What appeared from time to time in the *Record* and in the *Women's Missionary Magazine*, were mainly extracts from private letters, and they derived all their charm and colour from the fact that they were meant for friends who loved and understood her. In the same way she would be chilled by receiving a coldly expressed letter. "I wish you hadn't said *Dear Madam*," she told a lady at home. "I'm just an insignificant, wee, auld wifey that you would never address in that way if you knew me. I'll put the *Madam* aside, and drag up my chair close to you and the girls you write for, and we'll have a chat by the fireside."

She could not help writing; it was the main outlet for her loving nature, so much repressed in the loneliness of the bush. Had she not possessed so big and so ardent a heart, she would have written less. Into her letters she poured all the wealth of her affection; they were in the real sense love-letters; and her magic gift of sympathy made them always prized by the recipients. She had no home people of her own, and she pressed her nearest friends to make her "one of the family." "If," she would say, "you would let me share in any disappointments or troubles, I would feel more worthy of your love—I will tell you some of mine as a counter-irritant!" Many followed her behest with good result. "I'm cross this morning," wrote a young missionary at the beginning of a long letter, "and I know it is all my own fault, but I am sure that writing to you will put me in a better temper. When things go wrong, there is nothing like a talk with you.... Now I must stop, the letter has worked the cure." Her letters of counsel to her colleagues when they were in difficulties with their work were helpful and inspiring to the highest degree. On occasions of trial or sorrow she always knew the right word to say. How delicately, for instance, would she try to take the edge off the grief of bereaved friends by describing the arrival of the spirit in heaven, and the glad welcome that would be got there from those who had gone before. "Heaven is just a meeting and a homing of our real selves. God will never make us into new personalities. Everlasting life—take that word *life* and turn it over and over and press it and try to measure it, and see what it will yield. It is a magnificent idea which comprises everything that heart can yearn after." On another occasion she wrote, "I do not like that petition in the Prayer Book, *From sudden death, good Lord deliver us.* I never could pray it. It is surely far better to see Him at once without pain of parting or physical debility. Why should we not be like the apostle in his confident outburst of praise and assurance, 'For I am persuaded...'?" Again: "Don't talk about the cold hand of death—it is the hand of Christ."

It was not surprising that her correspondence became greater at last than she could manage. The pile of unanswered communications was like a millstone round her neck, and in these latter days she began to violate an old rule and snatch time from the hours of night. Headings such as "10 P.M.," "Midnight," "8.45 A.M.," became frequent, yet she would give love's full measure to every correspondent, and there was seldom sign of undue strain. "If my pen is in a hurry," she would say, "my heart is not." When she was ill and unable to write, she would simply lie in bed and speak to her Father about it all.

There was a number of friends to whom she wrote regularly, and whose relations to her may be judged from the manner in which they began their letters. "My lady of Grace," "My beloved missionary," "Dearest sister," were some of the phrases used. But her nature demanded at least one confidante to whom she could lay bare her inmost thoughts. She needed a safety-valve, a city of refuge, a heart and mind with whom there would be no reservations, and Providence provided her with a kind of confessor from whom she obtained all the understanding and sympathy and love she craved for. This was Miss Adam, who, while occasionally differing from her in minor matters of policy, never, during the fifteen years of their friendship, once failed her. What she was to the lonely missionary no one can know.

Mary said she knew without being told what was in her heart, and "how sweet," she added, "it is to be understood and have love reading between the lines." Month by month she sent to Bowden the intimate story of her doings, her troubles, hopes, and fears, and joys, and received in return wise and tender counsel and encouragement and practical help. She kept the letters under her pillow and read and reread them.

Never self-centred or self-sufficient, she depended upon the letters that came from home to a greater extent than many of her friends suspected. She needed the inflow of love into her own life, and she valued the letters that brought her cheer and stimulus and inspiration. Once she was travelling on foot, and had four miles of hill-road to go, and was feeling very weary and depressed at the magnitude of the work and her own weakness, when a letter was handed to her. It was the only one by that mail, but it was enough. She sat down, and in the quiet of the bush she opened it, and as she read all the tiredness fled, the heat was forgotten, the road was easy, and she went blithely up the hill.

Outside the circle of her friends many people wrote to her from Scotland, and some from England, Canada, and America. Boys and girls whom she had never seen sent her letters telling her of their cats and dogs, of football, and lessons and school. With her replies sometimes went a snake skin, a brass tray, a miniature paddle, or other curio. But it was the letter, rather than the gift, that was enjoyed. As one girl wrote; "You are away out helping the poor black kiddies and people, and just as busy doing good as possible, and yet you've time to send a letter home to a little Scottish girl, a letter fragrant with everything lovely and good, that makes one try harder than ever to do right, and that fills one's heart with beautiful helpful thoughts."

To her own bairns, wherever they were, she wrote letters full of household news and gentle advice. To Dan at the Institute she wrote regularly—very pleased she was when she heard he had been at lectures on bacteria and understood them!—and when Alice and Maggie were inmates of the Edgerley Memorial School she kept in the closest touch with them. Here is a specimen of her letters, written chiefly in Efik, and addressed apparently to Alice:

MY PRECIOUS CHILDREN—I am thinking a lot about you, for you will soon be losing our dear Miss Young; and while I am sorry for myself I am sorrier for you and Calabar. How are you all? and have you been good? and are you all trying to serve and please Jesus your Lord? Whitie has gone to sleep. She has been making sand and yönö-ing my bedroom, the bit that you did not finish. Janie has yönö-d the high bits, so Whitie is very tired.

Janie has gone to stay all night with the twin-mother and her baby in the town where Effiom used to live long ago. One baby was dead, but she is keeping the other, and the chief says, "Ma, you are our mother, but what you have done will be the death of us." But I tell them just to die.

The mother almost died. One child was born dead, and Janie and I stayed all night there. Mary is at Ikot Ekpene. We saw her as we passed in the motor. The whole town came to-day and put splendid beams in the verandah both in front and behind, swept all behind, and put on a corrugated iron roof, did the porch and various other things, and the safe.

Good-bye. Are you well? We are well, through God's goodness. Are you coming soon for holidays? My heart is hungry to see you and to touch your hands. Greetings to Ma Fuller. Greet Ma Wilkie and Mr. Wilkie for me. Greet each other. All we greet you. With much love to Maggie, Dan, Asuquö,—I am, in all my prayers, your mother, M. Slessor.

The girls and Dan also wrote regularly to her in Efik—such letters as this:

I am pleased to send this little letter to you. Are you well? I am fairly well through the goodness of God. Why have you delayed to send us a letter? Perhaps you are too busy to write, but we are coming home in a fortnight. If you hear we are on the way come quickly out when you hear the voices of the people from the beach, because you know it will be us. Greet Whitie, Janie, Annie and all, and accept greeting from your loving child MAGGIE.

After her death there was found at Use a bundle of papers, evidently much treasured, labelled "My children's letters."

CHAPTER XVIII
A LONELY FIGURE

She returned to Use, but only remained long enough to arrange for the material for the house at Odoro Ikpe. Of the special difficulties that would beset her on this occasion, she was quite aware. The timber supply on the ground was scarce, transport would be expensive, there was no local skilled labour, and she was unable to work with her own hands, while it was not easy to procure carriers and other work-people, since the Government, with the consent of the chiefs, were taking batches of men from each village for the coalfields and railway, a measure she approved, as it prevented the worst elements in the community drifting there. But nothing ever discouraged her, and she returned at the end of April and embarked once more, and for the last time, on building operations.

Friends kept tempting her to come to Scotland. Her friend Miss Young was now Mrs. Arnot, wife of the Rev. David Arnot, M.A., Blairgowrie, and from her came a pressing invitation to make her home at the manse. "I will meet you at Liverpool," Mrs. Arnot wrote, "and bring you straight here, where you will rest and be nursed back to health again." It was proposed that Alice should come with her, and be left at Blairgowrie while Mary visited her friends. She was delighted, and wrote gaily that when she did come she "would not be a week-end visitor or a tea visitor, but a barnacle. It is, however, all too alluring. One only thing can overtop it, and that is duty as put into my hands by my King." Then she paints a picture of the piles of timber and corrugated iron about her for the building of a house, "for the happy and privileged man or woman who shall take up the work of salvage," and of Ikpe waiting patiently, and the towns surrendering on all sides, and adds, "Put yourself in my place, and with an accession of strength given since I camped up here, how could you do other than I have done? I verily thought to be with the Macgregors, but this came and the strength has come with it, and there must be no more moving till the house is up, when I hope and pray some one will come to it. What a glorious privilege it all is! I can't think why God has so highly honoured and trusted me."

She entered on a period of toil and tribulation which proved to be one of the most trying and exacting in her life. The house itself was a simple matter. Large posts were inserted in the ground, and split bamboos were placed between; cross pieces were tied on with strips of the oil-palm tree, and then clay was prepared and pounded in. But fifty men and lads were employed, and she had never handled so lazy, so greedy, so inefficient a gang. Compelled to supervise them constantly, she often had to sit in the fierce sunshine for eight hours at a time; then with face unwashed and morning wrapper still on she would go and conduct school. If she went to Ikpe for a day, all the work done required to be gone over again. Sometimes she lost all patience, and resorted to a little "muscular Christianity," which caused huge amusement, but always had the desired effect. But she was very philosophical over it. "It is all part of the heathen character, and, as Mrs. Anderson used to say, 'Well, Daddy, if they were Christians there would have been no need for you and me here.'" Jean often became very wroth, and demanded of the people if "Ma" was not to obtain time to eat, and if they wanted to kill her?

Annie and her husband had been placed at Nkanga, and Jean now managed the household affairs. The faithful girl had her own difficulties in the way of catering, for on account of the isolation money frequently ran done, and she could not obtain the commonest necessities to feed her "Ma." An empty purse always worried Mary, but it was a special trial to her independent and sensitive spirit at this period, for she was in debt to the skilled carpenter who had been engaged, and to the labourers, and was compelled to undergo the humiliation of borrowing. On one occasion she obtained a loan of 5s. from one of her rare visitors, a Government doctor, a Scot and a Presbyterian, who was investigating tropical diseases, and who, finding her in the Rest House, had contentedly settled down with his microscopes in the Court House shed. After working all day in the bush he spent many evenings with her, and she was much impressed by his upright character, and his kindness and courtesy to the natives, and said matters would be very different in Africa if all civil and military men were of the same stamp. The only other two visitors she had at this time were Mr. Bowes, the printer at Duke Town, and Mr. Hart, the accountant, the latter bringing her all the money she needed.

By the end of July the house was roughly built, and she was able to mount up to the top rooms by means of a "hen" ladder, and there on the loose, unsteady boards she sat tending her last motherless baby, and feeling uplifted into a new and restful atmosphere. A pathetic picture she made, sitting gazing over the wide African plain. She had never been more isolated, never felt more alone.

> So lonely 'twas, that God Himself
> Scarce seemed there to be.

She was without assistance, her body was broken and pitifully weak, and yet with dauntless spirit and quenchless faith she looked hopefully to the future, when those infant stations about her would be occupied by consecrated men and women.

CHAPTER XIX
WHEN THE GREAT WAR CAME

Into the African bush, the home of many things that white men cannot understand, there was stealing a troubled sense of mystery. The air was electric with expectation and alarm. Impalpable influences seemed fighting the feeble old woman on the lonely hill-top. She was worried by transport difficulties. What the causes were she did not know, but the material did not come, and as she was paying the carpenter a high wage she was compelled to dismiss him. What work there was to do she attempted to accomplish with her own thin, worn hands.

In the early days of August the natives began to whisper to each other strange stories about fighting going on in the big white world beyond the seas. News came from Calabar that the European firms had ceased to buy produce: canoes which went down river for rice and kerosene, returned again with their cargoes of nuts and oil. She wondered what was happening. Then excited natives came to her in a panic, with tales of a mad Europe and of Britain fighting Germany. She pooh-poohed the rumours and outwardly appeared calm and unafraid in order to reassure them, but the silence and the suspense were unbearable. On the 13th she received letters and heard of the outbreak of the war. All the possibilities involved in that tremendous event came crowding upon her mind, the immense suffering and sorrow, and, not least to her, the peril to Calabar. Nigeria was conterminous with the Cameroons, and she knew the Germans well enough to anticipate trouble. The cost of articles, too, she realised, would go up, and as she had little food in the house she at once sent to the market for supplies. Already prices were doubled. Her kerosene oil gave out, and she had to resort to lighted firewood to read at prayers.

She went on bravely with the routine duties of the station—Dan, who was now with her, helping in the school—but she longed impatiently for news, "Oh, for a telegram," she would cry, "even a boy bawling in the street!" The officer at Ikot Ekpene, knowing her anxiety, sent over the latest intelligence, but she half suspected that he kept back the worst. The worst came in her first war mail which arrived when she was sitting superintending operations at the house. She read why Britain had entered the conflict and exclaimed, "Thank God! our nation is not the aggressor." Then came the story of the invasion of Belgium and the reverses of the Allies. Shocked and sad she essayed to rise, but was unable to move. The girls ran to her aid and lifted her up, but she could not stand. Exerting her will-power and praying for strength she directed the girls to carry her over to the Rest House and put her to bed. Ague came on, and in half an hour she was in a raging fever which lasted, with scarcely an interval, for a fortnight. She struggled on amidst increasing difficulties and worries, the horrors of the war with her night and day. Her old enemy, diarrhoea, returned, and she steadily weakened and seemed entering the valley of the shadow. She did not fear death, but the thought of passing away alone in the bush troubled her, for her skull might be seized and be worshipped as a powerful juju by the people.

At last she lay in a stupor as if beyond help. It was a scene which suggested the final act in Dr. Livingstone's life. The girls were crying. The church lads stood alarmed and awed. Then they raised her in her camp-bed and marched with her the five miles to Ikpe. Next morning they lifted the bed into a canoe and placed her under a tarpaulin and paddled her down the Creek. They landed at Okopedi beach, where she lay in the roadway in the moonlight, scarcely breathing. The agent of a trading-house brought restoratives and sent for Dr. Wood, then at Itu, who accompanied her to Use and waited the night as he feared she would not recover. All through the hours her mind was occupied with the war and the soldiers in the trenches.

Next day she was a little better, but would not hear of going to Itu to be cared for there. To her Use was home where the children could minister to her, but realising her lack of strength she sent a message to Miss Peacock asking her to come over. Miss Peacock said to her fellow-worker, "Ma must be very ill before she would send for any one," and she cycled to Use at once. Mary confided to her that it might be the end, and "Oh," she exclaimed, "if only the war were over and my children safe in the Kingdom, how gladly would I go!" She called the bairns to her and told them what to do in the event of her death. Like all natives in the presence of serious illness they were greatly upset and wept bitterly, but as the disorder passed they began to think that she would get better, and went about their duties, Jean to her marketing, and Alice to the care of the house, with Whitie to help, while Maggie looked after the baby.

The shadow of the war continued to darken her heart. She agonised for the cause which her native land had taken up, and many a cry went up to God on its behalf in the hour of trial. Miss Peacock remained several nights, and returned to Ikotobong with a strong presentiment that "Ma" was not to be long with them, and she and Miss Couper arranged to keep in touch with her as closely as possible.

As she plodded on towards strength and as better news arrived about the war situation she began to be more like herself and take up her old duties. For a time she lay in the verandah on a deck chair; and then went to the church, conducted the Sunday services, but was obliged to sit all the time and lean her body against the communion-table. Yet in the midst of her weakness and suffering she had always a bright laugh and a word of encouragement for others. Reluctantly she came to the conclusion that nothing would heal her but a voyage home and as she was longing for a few more hours—it was not years now—of work she made up her mind to face it, and to include in her furlough a visit to the graves of her mother and sister at Exeter. The difficulty of the east wind in Scotland was overcome by a proposal from Mrs. Arnot, who in the mystery of things, had suddenly been bereft of her husband, that she would take a small house where they could live together in quiet. "I shall meet you," that lady wrote, "and make a home for you and care for you if God puts it into your heart to come." The wonderful kindness of the offer brought tears to her eyes and she consented with a great content. Her plan was to return to Odoro Ikpe, complete the house, and leave for Scotland early in the spring; and she asked Miss Adam to send her a hat and boots and other articles which civilisation demanded. Her only regret was at leaving her people and specially those at Ikpe. "It is ten years since I first took them on, and they have never got a teacher yet. It is bitterly hard!" Miss Peacock and Miss Couper noticed, however, that the old recuperative power which had always surprised them was gone, and one day she said that she had been overhauling her desk and tearing up letters in case anything should happen.

The tragedy of the war came home personally to her. Two of her official friends, Commander G. Gray and Lieutenant H. A. Child, C.M.G., were serving in the Navy and were both drowned by the capsizing of a whaler when crossing the bar at the entrance to the Nyong River. "They were my oldest and most intimate friends here, capable, sane Empire-builders," and she sorrowed for them with a great sorrow. Sometimes her old fighting spirit was roused by the news of the deeds of the enemy. "Oh if I were thirty years younger, and if I were a man! ... We must not have peace until Germany licks the dust and is undeceived and stricken once for all." Her comments brought out the fact that she had followed European events very closely during the past thirty years, whilst her letters to her faint-hearted friends in Scotland showed her usual insight:

God does not mean you and me to carry the burden, and German soldiers are flesh and blood and must give out by-and-by, and they cannot create new armies, and with long-drawn out lines of battle on East and West they can't send an army that could invade Britain. They could harass, that's all, and our women are not Belgians; they would fight even German soldiers. Yes! they would stand up to William the Execrated. Moreover, Zeppelins can do a lot of hurt, but they can't take London; and Ostend and Antwerp are no nearer Britain for any kind of air attack than Berlin is, and above all our perspective is doubtless better than yours—any one can see that to try and take towns and to fight in streets filled with civilians has not a pennyworth of military value. It is a sheer waste of energy and life which should have been utilised on the armies and strongholds of a country. Brussels, Bruges, Antwerp, even Paris, had they got it, would be a mere blare of trumpets, a flash in the pan, a spectacular show, and if they took Edinburgh or London or Aberdeen, it would be the same, they would still have to reckon with a nation or nations. It has all been a mistake for their own downfall, and they will clear out of Belgium poorer than they entered it. Haven't the East Indians done nobly? Bravo our Allies!

She had now fallen into calmer mood. "Miss Slessor," she would say severely to herself, "why do you worry? Is God not fit to take care of His own universe and purpose? We are not guilty of any aggression or lust of conquest, and we can trust Him to bring us through. He is not to be turned aside from the working out of His purpose by any War Lord." She always fell back on the thought, "The Lord reigneth" as on a soft pillow and rested there. Writing one morning at 6 o'clock she described the beauty of the dawn and the earth refreshed and cooled and the hope and the mystery of a new day opening out, and contrasted it with the darkness and cold and fog experienced by the army and navy. "God is always in the world," she said; "the sunshine will break out and light will triumph." And she did not ignore the deeper issues, "May our nation be sent from its pleasures to its knees, and the Church be awed and brought back to Him."

On Christmas Day a service was held at which she intimated the opening of the subscription list for the Prince of Wales' Fund. She did not like to speak of war among Christian nations to natives; but it was current history, and she made the best explanation she could, though she was glad to turn their thoughts to the day of National Intercession on the following Sabbath. Dan acted as interpreter in the evening to Mr. Hart, who gave an address.

To a friend she wrote:

There will be few merry Christmasses in Europe this year. But, thank God, there will be a more profound sense of all Christ came to be and do for mankind, and a closer union and communion between Him and His people, through the sadness and insufficiency of earthly good. He will Himself draw near, and will fill empty chairs in lonely homes and hearts, and make His people—aye—and thousands who have not sought Him in prosperity—to know that here and now He is the Resurrection and the Life, that he that believeth in Him shall never die.

On New Year's Day Miss Peacock and Miss Couper went to spend the afternoon with her, and the former writes:

According to old-time customs I had made her her favourite plum-pudding and sent it over with a message that we meant to come to tea on New Year's Day. On our arrival the tea-table was set, and the plum-pudding with a rose out of the garden stuck on the top was on the table. Miss Slessor was as happy as a girl, and said she had to exercise self- control to keep from tasting the pudding before we arrived. And we had a merry meal. Then, when we left, she had to escort us to the end of the road. A new tenderness seemed to have come into her life, and with regard to those with whom she differed, she seemed to go out of her way to say the kindest things possible. She spoke to me of something she had written which she had torn up and said, "I wonder I could have been so hard." It was not difficult to see the last touches of the Master's hand to the life He had been moulding for so many years.

CHAPTER XX
THE TIME OF THE SINGING OF BIRDS

At the turn of the year her thoughts were again with her mother who had passed away then, twenty-nine years before. She was feeling very weak, but read and wrote as usual. Her last letter to Miss Adam told, amongst other things, of the previous day's service and how Annie's little girl would run about the church and point to her and call to her—"I can't say 'Don't bring her' for there should be room enough for the babies in our Father's house." Her closing words to her old friend were, "God be with you till we meet again." Even in her feeble state she was always thinking of others. David had taken his wife to Lagos, and her vivid imagination conjured up all the dangers of the voyage, and she was anxious for their safety. In the same letter in which she speaks of them, written on the 5th, she pours out sympathy and comfort to a lady friend in Edinburgh whose two sons had joined the Forces.

My heart bleeds for you, my dear, dear friend, but God's love gave the mother heart its love and its yearning over its treasures, so He will know how to honour and care for the mother, and how to comfort her and keep her treasures for her. Just keep hold on Him, dear one, and put your boys into His hand, as you did when they were babies. He is able to keep them safe in the most difficult and dangerous situations. I am constantly praying with you, and with others of my friends, who, just as you, are giving up their dearest and most precious at the call of Duty. God can enrich them and you and all the anxious and exposed ones even through the terrible fires. In God's governance not one precious thing can ever be lost.

On Friday the 8th she sat on a deck-chair in the little garden outside the door enjoying the sunshine, for the harmattan wind was cold, and writing some letters. The last she penned was to Mrs. Arnot, in which she said she was better though "a wee shade weaker than usual." It was never finished, and was found, later, on her pad. The final words were: "I can't say definitely whether I shall yet come in March—if I be spared till then …"

In the afternoon there was a recurrence of fever. Alice tended her unceasingly, seldom leaving her bedside, and stretching herself, when in need of rest, on a mat beside the bed. She was a great comfort to Mary. On Sunday spirit again dominated body; she struggled up, went over to the church, and conducted service. Next day she was suffering acutely from diarrhoea and vomiting, and one of the girls went to Ikotobong and summoned Miss Peacock, who immediately cycled over.

"I got a messenger," says Miss Peacock, "and sent him to Itu stating the symptoms, and asking Dr. Robertson to come and see her. All the afternoon the vomiting and diarrhoea continued until Dr. Robertson arrived. He had secured some ice at one of the factories, and gave her some medicine, and both the diarrhoea and vomiting were stopped. All the afternoon there had been a great restlessness and weariness, and unless to ask for something she seldom spoke. Her mails were brought into the room by one of the girls, but she took no notice of them. She was moved from her bed on to her chair, and back again several times, but did not seem to be able to rest anywhere; then she would give a great cry of weariness as if she were wearied unto death.

"As the evening wore on she became quieter, but had a great thirst, and begged that a little bit of the ice might be put into her mouth. She had a very quiet night, without any recurrence of the former symptoms, and I thought she was somewhat better, until the morning revealed how exhausted she was. The old restlessness began again, and I got a lad from the school to take a message over to Itu to Dr. Robertson. My report was that Miss Slessor had had a quiet night, but was suffering from extreme exhaustion. The doctor sent over some medicine with instructions, and she seemed again to be able to lie quietly. Once when I was attending to her she said, 'Ma, it's no use,' and again she prayed, 'O *Abasi, sana mi yok*' ('O God release me'). As I fed her with milk or chicken soup, she would sometimes sign to me, or just say 'Ma.' A lonely feeling came into my heart, and as I had to send a message to Ikotobong, I asked Miss Couper to cycle over in the afternoon. She stayed all the afternoon, and when she left Miss Slessor was still quiet, and her pulse was fairly good. This was the 12th.

"The girls—Janie, Annie, Maggie, Alice, and Whitie—were all with me, and we made our arrangements for the night-watch. It was not a grand room with costly furnishings; the walls were of reddish-brown mud, very roughly built; the floor was of cement, with a rug here and there, and the roof corrugated iron. Besides the bed, washhand-stand, and a chair or two, there was a chest of drawers which had belonged to her mother, and in which was found all that was needed for the last service. Her greatness was never in her surroundings, for she paid little attention to these, but in the hidden life which we caught glimpses of now and then when she forgot herself and revealed what was in her mind with regard to the things that count.

"As the hours wore on, several times she signed to us to turn her, and we noticed that her breathing was becoming more difficult. It was a very dark night, and the natives were sound asleep in their houses, but I sent off two of the girls to rouse two men to go to Itu; and we waited anxiously the coming of the doctor. A strange uneasiness seemed to come upon us. All the girls were round the bedside, and now and then one or two would begin to weep. The clock had been forgotten, and we did not know the time. A cock crew, and one of the girls said, 'Day must be dawning,' but when I drew aside the curtain there was nothing but pitch darkness. It was not nearly daybreak, and we felt that the death-angel was drawing very near. Several times a change passed over the dear face, and the girls burst out into wild weeping; they knew only too well the sign of the dread visitor. They wished to rush away, but I told them they must stay, and together we watched until at 3.30 God took her to Himself. There was no great struggle at the end; just a gradual diminishing of the forces of nature, and Ma Akamba, 'The Great Mother,' entered into the presence of the King."

And so the long life of toil was over. "The time of the singing of birds," she used to say, "is where Christ is." For her, now, the winter was past, the rain was over and gone, the time of the singing of birds had come....

When the girls realised that she was gone, they gave way to their grief, and lamented their position in the world. "My mother is dead—my mother is dead—we shall be counted as slaves now that our mother is dead." The sound of the weeping reached the town and roused the inhabitants from their slumbers. Men and women came to the house and mingled their tears with those of the household. They sat about on the steps, went into the bedroom and gazed sorrowfully on the white still face of her whom they regarded as a mother and friend. As the news was passed on, people came from Itu and the district round, to see in death her who had been *Eka kpukpru owo*, "Everybody's Mother."

As soon as Mr. Wilkie received the telegram announcing the end, he obtained a launch and sent it up with the Rev. W. M. Christie, B.A., who, Mr. Macgregor being at home, was in charge of the Institute. While it was on the way an English and an Efik service were being held at Itu. The launch arrived at 5.30 P.M., the coffin was placed on board, and the return voyage begun. It was midnight ere Duke Town was reached, and the body rested at Government Beach until dawn. There the mourners gathered. Government officials, merchants, and missionaries, were all there. The boys of the Institute were drawn up on the beach, policemen were posted in the streets, and the pupils of Duke Town school continued the line to the cemetery. All flags flew at half-mast, and the town was hushed and still. Great crowds watched the procession, which moved along in silence. The coffin was draped with the Union Jack, and was carried shoulder high by the boat boys, who wore black singlets and mourning loin-cloths, but no caps.

At the cemetery on Mission Hill stood a throng of natives. Old Mammy Fuller who had loved Mary so much, sat alone at the top of the grave. When the procession was approaching she heard some women beginning to wail, and at once rose. "*Kutua oh, kutua oh,*" she said. "Do not cry, do not cry. Praise God from whom all blessings flow. Ma was a great blessing."

A short and simple service was conducted by Mr. Wilkie and Mr. Rankin, and some of the native members led the singing of "*When the day of toil is done,*" and "*Asleep in Jesus.*" The coffin was lowered by eight of the teachers of Duke Town School, and lilies and other flowers were thrown upon it. Mammy Fuller uttered a grateful sigh. "Safe," she murmured. One or two women wept quietly, but otherwise there was absolute silence, and those who know the natives will understand the restraint which they imposed upon themselves. Upon the grave were placed crosses of purple bougainvillea and white and pink frangipanni, and in the earth was planted a slip from the rose bush at Use, that it might grow and be symbolic of the fragrance and purity and beauty of her life.

"Ma," said Mammy Fuller to Mrs. Wilkie when all was over, "I don't know when I enjoyed anything so much; I have been just near heaven all the time."

CHAPTER XXI
TRIBUTE AND TREASURE

Many tributes were paid to the dead pioneer. As soon as Sir Frederick Lugard, the Governor-General of Nigeria, heard of the event he telegraphed to Mr. Wilkie: "It is with the deepest regret that I learn of the death of Miss Slessor. Her death is a great loss to Nigeria." And later came the formal black-bordered notice in the Government *Gazette*:—

It is with the deepest regret that His Excellency the Governor-General has to announce the death at Itu, on 18th January, of Miss Mary Mitchell Slessor, Honorary Associate of the Order of the Hospital of St. John of Jerusalem in England.

For thirty-nine years, with brief and infrequent visits to England, Miss Slessor has laboured among the people of the Eastern Provinces in the south of Nigeria.

By her enthusiasm, self-sacrifice, and greatness of character she has earned the devotion of thousands of the natives among whom she worked, and the love and esteem of all Europeans, irrespective of class or creed, with whom she came in contact.

She has died, as she herself wished, on the scene of her labours, but her memory will live long in the hearts of her friends, Native and European, in Nigeria.

Testimony regarding her qualities and work was given in Scotland by the Mission Committees of the United Free Church, by officials, missionaries, and others who knew her, and by the Press, whilst from many parts of the world came notices of her career which indicated how widely known she had been. The appreciation which would perhaps have pleased her most was a poem written by a Scottish girl, fifteen years of age, with whom she had carried on a charming correspondence— Christine G. M. Orr, daughter of Sheriff Orr, Edinburgh. She would, doubtless, have had it included in any notice of her work, and here, therefore, it is given:

THE LAMENT OF HER AFRICAN CHILDREN

She who loved us, she who sought us
Through the wild untrodden bushlands,
Brought us healing, brought us comfort,
Brought the sunlight to our darkness,
She has gone—the dear white Mother—
Gone into the great Hereafter.

Never more on rapid waters
Shall she dip her flashing paddle,
Nor again the dry leaves rustle
'Neath her footstep in the forest,
Never more shall we behold her
Eager, dauntless on her journeyings.

Now the children miss their teacher,
And the women mourn their helper;
And the sick, the weak, the outcast
Long that she once more might touch them,
Long to hear her speaking comfort,
Long to feel her strong hand soothing.

Much in loneliness and danger,
Fevered oft, beset with trouble,
Still she strove for us, her children;
Taught us of the great good Spirit,
He who dwells beyond the sunrise;
Showed to us the love He bears us,
By her own dear loving-kindness;
Told us not to fear the spirits,
Evil spirits in the shadows,
For our Father-God is watching,
Watching through the cloudless daytime,
Watching at the silent midnight,
So that nothing harms His people;
Taught us how to love each other,
How to care for little children
With a tenderness we knew not,
How, with courtesy and honour,
To respect the gentle women,
Nor despise them for their weakness,
But, as wives and mothers, love them.

Thus she taught, and thus she laboured;
Living, spent herself to help us,
Dying, found her rest among us.
Let the dry, harsh winds blow softer
And the river's song fall lower,
While the forest sways and murmurs
In the mystery of evening,
And the lonely bush lies silent,
Silent with a mighty sorrow.

Oh! our mother—she who loved us,
She who lost herself in service,
She who lightened all our darkness,
She has left us, and we mourn her
With a lonely, aching sorrow.
May the great good Spirit hear us,
Hear us in our grief and save us,
Compass us with His protection
Till, through suffering and shadow,
We with weary feet have journeyed
And again our mother greets us
In the Land beyond the sunrise.

Both the Calabar Council and the Women's Foreign Mission Committee in Scotland felt that the most fitting memorial to her would be the continuation of her work, and arrangements were accordingly made for the appointment and supervision of teachers and evangelists at Use, Ikpe, and Odoro Ikpe, and for the care of the children. It was also decided to realise her settlement scheme and call it "The Mary Slessor Home for Women and Girls," with a memorial missionary in charge, and later an appeal for a capital sum of £5000 for the purpose was issued. It would have pleased Mary to know that the lady chosen for the position of memorial missionary was her old colleague Mrs. Arnot. She had worked hard and waited long for the accomplishment of this idea, and she may yet, from above, see of the travail of her soul and be satisfied....

By and by her more special possessions were collected and sent home. If she had been an ordinary woman one might have expected to see a collection of the things that a lady likes to gather about her; the dainty trinkets and souvenirs, the jewellery and knicknacks that have pleasant associations connected with them. When the little box arrived it was filled less with these than with pathos and tears. It held merely a few much-faded articles, one or two Bibles, a hymn-book (the gift of some twin-mother at home), an old-fashioned scent-bottle, a pebble brooch, hair bracelet, two old lockets, and her mother's ring— all these were evidently relics of the early days—a compass, and a fountain pen.

But there also came a large packet of letters, those received during her last years, which revealed where her treasures on earth were stored—in a multitude of hearts whose love she had won. They were from men in Nigeria—Government officials, missionaries, and merchants— from men and women in many lands, from the mothers and sisters of the "boys" to whom she had been kind, from Church officials, from children —all overflowing with affection and admiration and love. She had often called herself a "rich woman." One learned from these letters the reason why.

CHAPTER XXII
SEEN AND UNSEEN

Miss Slessor had a sure consciousness of her limitations, and knew she was nothing but a forerunner, who opened up the way and made it possible for others to come in and take up the work on normal lines. Both in the sphere of mission exploration and in the region of ideas she possessed the qualities of the pioneer,—imagination, daring, patience,—and like all idealists she met with opposition. It was not, however, the broad policy she originated that was criticised, so much as matters of detail, and no doubt there was sometimes justification for this. She admitted that she had no gifts as an organiser, and when she engaged in constructive work it was because there was no one else to do it.

What she accomplished, therefore, cannot be measured only by the visible results of her own handiwork. The Hope Waddell Institute was the outcome of her suggestions, and from it has gone out a host of lads to teach in schools throughout the country, and to influence the lives of thousands of others. She laid the foundations of civilised order in Okoyong, upon which regular church and school life has now been successfully built. When she unlocked the Enyong Creek, some were amused at the little kirks and huts she constructed in the bush, and asked what they were worth—just a few posts plastered with mud, and a sheet or two of corrugated iron. But they represented a spiritual force and influence far beyond their material value. They were erected with her life-blood, they embodied her love for her Master and for the people, they were outposts, the first dim lights in the darkness of a dark land, they stood for Christ Himself and His Cross. And to-day there exist throughout the district nearly fifty churches and schools in which the work is being carried on carefully and methodically by trained minds. The membership numbers nearly 1500, and there is a large body of candidates and enquirers and over 2000 scholars. The remarkable progress being made in self-support may be gathered from the following figures taken from the accounts of the five Creek congregations for 1914:

```
              Members Income Cash in bank
Itu . . . . 109 £113 9 4 £97 13 6
Okpo . . . . 101 76 7 7 62 16 8
Asang . . . . 428 184 17 10 865 13 6
Obufa Obio (Chief
   Onoyom) . . . 118 118 16 10 736 19 4
Ntan Obu . . . 111 83 11 9 204 1 2
```

All these churches and others that she began are spreading the Gospel not only by direct effort, but also by means of their members as they trade up and down the country.

One cannot estimate the value of her general influence on the natives; it extended over an area of more than 2000 square miles, from all parts of which they came to seek her help and advice, whilst her fame reached even to Northern Nigeria, where she was spoken of as the "good White Ma who lived alone." To West Africans, a woman is simply a chattel to be used for pleasure and gain, but she gave them a new conception of womanhood, and gained their reverence and confidence and obedience. Although she came to upset all their ideas and customs, which represented home and habit and life itself to them, they loved her and would not let the wind blow on her. She thus made it easy for other women agents to live and work amongst them; probably there is no similar mission field where these can dwell in such freedom and safety. And through her womanhood she gave them some idea of the power and beauty of the religion which could make that womanhood possible. Her influence will not cease, for in the African bush, where there are no daily newspapers to crowd out events impressions, and tradition is tenacious, she will be remembered in hut and harem and by forest camp fire, and each generation will hand down to the next the story of the Great White Mother who lived and toiled for their good.

Upon the Mission staff her example acted like a tonic. Her tireless energy, her courage, her enthusiasm, were infectious and stimulating, to the highest degree, and stirred many to action. Such an inspiring force is a valuable asset in a tropical land, where everything tends to languor and inertia. And in Scotland her influence was also very great. Round her name and work gathered a romance which deepened and widened interest in the missionary enterprise of the Church. Her career demonstrates how important is the personal touch and tie in sustaining and increasing the attraction of the work abroad. By the spell of her personality she was able to draw support not only from large numbers of people within her own Church, but from many outside who had little thought or for missions. It was because she not a mere name on a list, but a warm, living, inspiring, human presence. For while she was great as a pioneer and worker, she was equally great as a woman.

CHAPTER XXIII
THE ALABASTER BOX

But the interest in Nigeria on the part of the home people as a whole was never enough for Miss Slessor. It was largely an interest in herself and her work, and she wanted rather the larger vision which would realise the possibilities of that great field, and endeavour to conquer it for the Master. The general indifference on the subject was a deep disappointment to her. But it had always been so.

The story of Calabar is one of the most thrilling in the history of missions, yet through it also there runs an undercurrent of tragedy— the tragedy of unseized opportunities and unfulfilled hopes. As one reads, he can fancy that he is standing by a forest at night listening to the sound that the wind brings of a strange conflict between a few brave spirits, and legions of wild and evil forces, with incessant cries for help. From the first days of the Mission, urgent appeals for more workers have constantly been made; there is scarcely a year that the men and women on the spot have not pressed its urgent needs upon the home Church, but never once has there been an adequate response. To-day, as always, the staff is pitifully small. To minister to the needs of the many millions within the area assigned to the Church, there are only eighteen European missionaries, three medical missionaries, and thirteen women agents, apart from the wives of the married missionaries. In Duke Town and Okoyong, on the Cross River and the Enyong Creek, and far up at Uburu, the city of the salt lakes, all the stations are undermanned, and the medical men are overwhelmed by the thousands of patients who flock to them to be healed.

What Mary Slessor did, other women are doing in the same spirit of selflessness and courage, but with the same sense of powerlessness to overtake what is required. The number of these women agents does not appreciably increase, for, while fresh appointments are continuously being made, there are usually more changes amongst them than amongst the men missionaries, on account of resignations from ill-health or marriage. Yet in Nigeria women have unlimited opportunities for the employment of their special gifts.

The remarkable feature of the situation is that the Mission is face to face with an open door. It is not a question of sitting down in the midst of a religiously difficult and even hostile community as in India or China, and waiting patiently for admission to the hearts of the people, but of entering in and taking possession. The natives everywhere are clamouring for teachers and missionaries, education, enlightenment, and they are clamouring in vain. The peril is that under the new conditions governing the country, they will be lost to the Christian Church. With freer intercommunication, Islam is spreading south. All Mohammedans are missionaries, and their religion has peculiar attractions for the natives. Already they are trading in the principal towns, and in Arochuku a Mullah is sitting, smiling and expectant, and ingratiating himself with the people. Here the position should be strengthened; it is, as Miss Slessor knew, the master-key to the Ibo territory, for if the Aros are Christianised, they will carry the evangel with them over a wide tract of country.

Miss Slessor's life shadowed by the consciousness of how little had been done, as well as by the immensity of what was still to do. Making every allowance for the initial difficulties that had to be overcome, and the long process of preparing the soil, the net result of seventy years' effort seemed to her inadequate. There is only a Christian community of 10,800, and a communion-roll of 3412, and the districts contiguous to the coast have alone been occupied, whilst no real impression has been made on the interior. Over the vast, sun-smitten land she wept, as her Master wept over the great city of old, and she did what she could—no woman could have done more—to redeem its people, and sought, year in, year out, to make the Church rise to the height of its wonderful opportunity—in vain.

She knew, however, that the presentation of startling facts and figures alone would never rouse it to action; these might touch the conscience for a moment, but the only thing that would awaken interest and keep it active and militant would be a revival of love for Christ in the hearts of the people; and it was for this she prayed and agonised most of all. For with it would come a more sympathetic imagination, a warmer faith, greater courage to go forward and do the seemingly impossible and foolish thing. It would, she knew, change the aims and ideals of her sisters, so many of them moving in a narrow world of self, and thrill them with a desire to take part in the saving and uplifting of the world. There would be no need then to make appeals, for volunteers would come forward in abundance for the hardest posts, and consecrated workers would fill up the ranks in Nigeria and in all the Mission Fields of the Church.

She knew, because it was so in her case. Love for Christ made her a missionary. Like that other Mary who was with Him on earth, her love constrained her to offer Him her best, and very gladly she took the alabaster box of her life and broke it and gave the precious ointment of her service to Him and His cause.

Many influences move men and women to beautiful and gallant deeds, but what Mary Slessor was, and what she did, affords one more proof that the greatest of these is Love.